a virgin's guide to everything

a virgin's guide to everything

from sushi to sample sales—
a novice's handbook to / doing it right

LAUREN McCUTCHEON

5 SPOT ●●●●●

WARNER BOOKS

New York   Boston

Lyrics from "What Do You Hear in These Sounds" by Dar Williams, © 1997 Burning Field Music. Reprinted with permission.

Illustrations © 2005 by joyCards, Inc.

5 Spot
Warner Books
Time Warner Book Group
1271 Avenue of the Americas, New York, NY 10020
Visit our Web site at www.twbookmark.com.

5 Spot and the 5 Spot logo are trademarks of Time Warner Book Group Inc.

Printed in the United States of America

First Edition: December 2005
10 9 8 7 6 5 4 3 2 1

Library of Congress Cataloging-in-Publication Data

McCutcheon, Lauren.
    A Virgin's guide to everything : from sushi to sample sales—a novice's handbook
to doing it right / Lauren McCutcheon.—1st ed.
        p.   cm.
    ISBN 0-446-69573-4
    1. Life skills—United States.   I. Title.
  HQ2039.U6M33 2005
  646.7—dc22
2005019062

Book design and text composition by Stratford Publishing Services

To my mother, who, like me, is a virgin

ACKNOWLEDGMENTS

This book would never have gotten close to begun—and nowhere near done—had it not been for the great virgins who went before me. Most gracious thanks to thinker-uppers Veronica Chambers and Angela Kyle, the original Go-to Girls: two women who take chances, talk sense, and, as Mariah would say, make it happen. Big props to Amy Einhorn, the brains behind this book-writing business, and to Jim Schiff, the brains behind Amy's brains. Agent extraordinaire Christy Fletcher earns major praise for her stylish book-shopping-around skills.

How could a fancy lady get by without a pal like Chris Meck, major author photographer, coolest mom-friend, and baker of cupcakes, the staff of life? How could a hapless writer do anything at all without crafty counselor and fellow vegetarian-ham-addict Rachel Hezlep? Where would a youngest daughter be without a mother who mails Rice Krispies treats to her and leaves her three-minute-long voice mails, two big sisters named Debbie and Betsy who always let her steal the spotlight, and a dad whose gray-blue eyes will forever smile at her?

Thanks to Tim for the Ben & Jerry's; to Carter for the seasons in the SATC; to Sally, for entering my life and getting her furry head stuck in boxes of Puffs at just the right moments. To my friend groups—knitters, rockers, yoginis, writers, publicists, ornithologists, college chums, cafe owners, karaoke masters and cocktail buyers—you are nothing less than stars for preserving my sanity in a jar, keeping it safe and warm during the January and February of my first-time-author discontent.

But really, truly, this book belongs to my Go-to Girls, women who turned a nifty idea into a seriously fun resource. But the Go-tos on these pages aren't the only ones who own *A Virgin's Guide*. The following ladies, whose contributions appear between the lines, deserve my deepest thanks, super-sized:

Dany Levy, DailyCandy diva and the girl I want to be
Stephanie Elizondo Griest, author and around-the-world girl
Real Simple editor and baby-shower-er Riza Cruz
Memphis music diva Andria Lisle
Sundance-goers Kate Wingard and Erin McCarthy
Burning Woman Leslie Pritchett
Glamorous techie and Splendora creator Gina Pell
Top shopper Jane Shepherdson
Blog-woman and marathoner Meg Hourihan
Fearlessly wired Rebecca Hurd
Smartphone goddess Rose Rodd
Kim Arbuckle, digital camera addict

Madison Avenue money whiz Linda Schoenthaler
Chicago Shop mom Kate Prange
L.A. puppy lover Hannah Brand
Cowgirl Creamery's Lenny Rice
Intrepid traveler Pam Villacorta
Solo voyager Mary-Jo Lipman
Job-pert Tyya Turner
Sexy author Wendy Straker
Amazing racer Cynthia Palormo
Styling photographer Kate Schelter
P.R. divas Maggie Gallant and Christina Skogly
Workout guru Tenley
Yoga practitioners Ellen Greenberg and Miko Doi-Smith

CONTENTS

FOREWORD

I always wanted to be a Hepburn. It never really mattered which one. Glamorous like Audrey. Sporty like Kate. Breakfasting at Tiffany's, like Audrey. Woman of the Year, like Kate. Instead, I ended up as the world's oldest virgin. My sex life aside, it seemed like I was the only girl in town who had never had a bikini wax, gone out for sushi, started a stock portfolio, or been to the opera.

Because I'm the oldest child in my family, I've always turned to books for big sister advice. When I was in high school, I read books about how to pick a college, study for the S.A.T.s, write a killer essay. When I graduated from college, I read a book about how to format my résumé, write a formal business letter, kick butt in a job interview. But where was the book about all the little things that add up to make the big thing that is actually your life?

Case in point, I was too embarrassed to consult my girlfriends the first time I went for a facial. So I let some Swedish chick named Helga "purify" my pores with a *gigantic* needle. Suffice it to say I screamed—I was bleeding from the face after all!—and I was too scared to visit a spa again for a very long time. My friends say that they can no longer see the scars, but I see them to this day. If I'd had this book, of course, that wouldn't have happened. After my facial fiasco, I got better at asking for advice. After a business meeting with a writer named Tracie Howard, to which she came looking like Kate Spade's hipper, better-dressed sister, I called to ask her for some fashion tips. She not only came to my house and helped me to pare down my wardrobe over champagne and chocolate, she drove me to my very first fashion outlet. (At the time, I didn't have a car—or a clue.)

My friend Cassandra helped me buy my first business suit, and guided me through my first visit to a sushi bar. My friend Shandana took me to my first wine tasting. My friend Caroline was there for me when (in the interest of safety and sanity) I answered my first personal using a fake name, then halfway through the date answered my cell phone with my real name—"Hello, this is Veronica!"—only to have the guy walk out in a huff because I'd lied to him about something as basic as my name. Throughout all of these events, a pattern began to emerge: I realized that it wasn't so bad being a virgin at so many grown-up things, as long as I had my Go-to Girls to turn to for advice, comfort, and laughs.

I called one of my best friends, Angela Kyle, and asked her if she would be interested in working with me on a book called *A Virgin's Guide to Everything*. I've known Angela for more than ten years, and it's only because I know her so well, that I can admit to her what a goober I am about fashion, food, friendship, high culture, and society in general. Angela is what my grandfather would have called "a long, cool drink of water." She is tall, she is model thin, she divides her time between Los Angeles and London because, well, she's fabulous, and that's what fabulous people do. To my surprise, despite the fact that on the surface she is the picture of perfection, Angela was happy to explore this virgin territory with me. She had, after all, taken me to my first strip club and had been the purveyor of my first Krispy Kreme donut. She's a Go-to Girl extraordinaire.

Next up, I called my good friend, Lauren McCutcheon. Lauren is a writer in Philadelphia, and she is one of the funniest girls I know. We had shared a few virgin experiences: Lauren had been in yoga class with me when I attempted my first headstand (and failed, miserably, the pain—I can still feel it now). Lauren was also the first girl to tell me that cute, lacy things aside, nothing beats a well-made, expensive French bra that you will have forever. I wasn't totally useless in this friendship. I invited Lauren to join me at Rancho La Puerta, her first destination spa. And because I had always loved the way she slings ink, I thought Lauren would make the perfect writer for this book. (I was in Los Angeles, writing a lot of bad jokes as a newbie writer on a television show.)

So Lauren became a virgin author, I became a virgin sitcom writer, and as I write this, Angela is dotting the *i*'s and crossing the *t*'s to launch our new production company, Interesting Women, making us virgin entrepreneurs.

We—Angela, Lauren, and I—wanted drawings of us, and girls like us, working their way through all these mucky first time experiences. I thought immediately of my friend Joy Chen, who owns the coolest design studio and card shop in Princeton. Joy helped me design my first Christmas card and created a handmade book that my husband gave me on my wedding day (which still makes me break into tears every time I see it). Joy's illustrations brought the whole virgin package together.

But enough about us, let's talk about you. As your own personal Go-to Girl, let me tell you this: You are the star of your own life. You don't need a fairy godmother (or a Prince Charming) to wear outrageous lingerie, to power lunch your way to the top of the corporate ladder, to throw the kind of parties that people never, ever forget. And if, like me, you don't have sisters—then consider yourself adopted. Get thee to the *Virgin's Guide* Web site, sista (www.virginsguide.com) and hop onto our message boards. There, you can buy cool Virgin swag with our trademark cherry logo. The book is grand: I suggest you keep one copy by your bedside and one copy to read underneath your desk at work, but on our Web site, you'll meet other virgins, who will only be too happy to answer all the questions we couldn't cram between these two covers. Believe it or not, we need *you* to be a Go-to Girl as well. So write to us, e-mail us, tell us where we can get cute Chloe dresses at ridiculously low prices and whether or not any of those cellulite creams actually work. And if you can tell me how to walk in four-inch heels without twisting my ankle, or teach me how to drive a stick shift, I'd be eternally grateful. Because everybody's a virgin—at something.

—Veronica Chambers

P.S.—I am still too chicken to get a bikini wax. Or an eyebrow wax. Or to go anywhere near anything involving wax. Except for car wax. And that's only because I've got a Mini Cooper that I love like some people love their pets. Speaking of which, if you're at all interested in *Virgin's Guide to Cool Cars and Other Modes of Transport,* send me an e-mail at veronica @virginsguide.com. I'll see what I can do.

INTRODUCTION

There I was, alone in a small room, looking into a mirror. I bit at my bottom lip and stared at the reflection of a twenty-something woman wearing a pair of jeans and a lacy black push-up bra. It was a sad sight: Not only was I a virgin, I looked like one too.

Half of me said: Go for it. Leave the room. Change your life forever. But the other, wimpier part hesitated. Is it wrong? Will I have regrets? What would Mom think if she found out?

A voice came through the latched door: "You doing OK in there?"

I wiped my hands on my jeans, took a deep breath, and replied with a quivering, "Um. Yes?"

In what felt like a flash, my camisole slid back over my head, my lungs took a last hit of air, and my body turned away from the mirror. I flung open the door. Digging into my purse, I yanked out a credit card, approached the sales clerk behind the counter, and asked, "Is it OK if I wear the bra home?"

First times can be nerve-wracking—even little, everyday firsts, like purchasing your first sexy bra. Every day, we women enter some kind of virgin territory. We nosh our first sushi. We strike up our first online romance. We crawl up onto a massage table or throw a dinner party for the first time. There are firsts we know we oughta do, like go to the gynecologist, volunteer for a good cause, and save up for retirement. There are firsts we dream of doing, like signing up for surfing lessons, dining at a four-star restaurant, and escaping to a foreign country.

But where to start? Wouldn't it be great if we could wiggle our noses, *Bewitched* style, and conjure a cool, older sister who'd offer advice without judgment? Wouldn't it be nice to have known not to pile that spicy tuna roll with a teaspoon of wasabi, not to go on a marathon date with a guy you just met on Match.com? Wouldn't it be awesome to understand that going to a gyno can be wholly liberating, or to be able to pack light for a trip to Paris?

A Virgin's Guide is custom made for everyone who's said "I want to do that," but wimped out at the last minute. It's for those of us who've considered the out-there possibility of camping or asking for a raise but never felt prepared enough to follow through. It's for those of us who know there's no guarantee that we'll get it perfect on our first try but believe it sure would be nice to come pretty close.

We—meaning the author and the sisterhood of expert Go-to Girls she suckered into helping with this project—picked out some of the most fun, and useful, firsts we could think of, and left the big milestones—first marriage, first job, first child—to the jillions of other advice givers.

From time to time, we'll warn you of "virgin's downfalls," the bumps and potholes that can prevent your first time from being all we crack it up to be. (If you must know, the original virgin's downfall was a tiki bar cocktail that once caused the author to get lost in her own neighborhood.) And, because not all of us get it right the first time, we present "born-again virgins," tales of brave maidens who aren't about to let an initial fumble keep them from their *Guide*-given right to unlimited do-overs.

So, welcome to *A Virgin's Guide to Everything.* On your way in, please heed the invisible sign over our imaginary door that reads: We're All Virgins (at Something).

a virgin's guide to everything

1

ENTERTAINING

Hosting a first shindig is a big step in a virgin's life—even if that shindig is holing up on a Tuesday night with takeout. A virgin's willingness to entertain reveals she inhabits a reasonably presentable living space, one with a refrigerator, possibly a freezer, a table, one or more chairs, and cabinets and drawers holding dishes, glasses, and utensils, mismatched though they may be.

But more than that, tossing out an invite and seeing who shows up indicates a virgin's going places. She's not daunted by the size of her studio apartment or her meager MP3 collection. Her main concern isn't the thread count of her duvet cover—or the fact that she's still shopping for curtains. It shows she values good friends, times, food, and drink above all else. (After all, she's going to be vacuuming and shoving stuff in the closet before they come over.)

Furthermore, our little girl—all grown up—has come to the place in her life where she's prepared to spend the equivalent of a month of mani-pedis on simply playing host, with her only guaranteed, immediate rewards being a few hours of prep time followed by a few more hours of cleanup, possibly while hungover.

COCKTAIL PARTY

I like to have a martini
Two at the very most—
After three I'm under the table,
After four, I'm under my host
—DOROTHY PARKER

A cocktail party. How hard can that be? Drinks. Music. More drinks. Kind of like a kegger, but with refined shaken-or-stirred libations instead of beer from a tube.

Oh yes, and a few other things. Like nicer clothes. And more polite conversation. And clever garnishes for each drink. And food you spear with a toothpick instead of grab with your hands. And glasses instead of Solo cups. And fancy napkins ... But no keg stands. Definitely none of those. More like pure, completely adulterated party-scene-in-*Breakfast-at Tiffany's*-style fun.

GO-TO GIRL*

Sarah Gray Miller

Founding Editor,
Budget Living Magazine

Sarah Gray—the double first name reveals her Mississippi roots—is the ultimate cocktail party hostess. She says her talent comes naturally. "I'm Southern. We take babies to cocktail parties down there." Her fondness for bourbon (when it's not Woodford Reserve, she's fine with Jim Beam), her ability to remain lucid after polishing off a six-pack, her categorical rejection of the chocolatini, and her conviction that an apartment is not an abode without a fully stocked liquor cabinet are impressive, but her real party-throwing skills reside in her creativity. She's a whiz at thinking up clever party themes, and always looks out for inexpensive favors—like a New Year's Eve piñata to stuff with hangover remedies or embossed matchbooks that double as Prohibition-theme party invitations. Sarah Gray measures a soiree's success by how long guests want to stay and is always prepared to let friends spend the night. Her cocktail party mantra: "The worst, worst thing is if the hostess isn't having a good time."

*Go-to Girl: A bonafide, flesh-and-blood-big-sister type who's been here, done this, and lives solely to tell (you) about it.

What You'll Need

Budget. How much you can spend determines what kind of party it's gonna be. Expect to lay out $100 to $200 for fifteen to twenty guests. Got a bit more dough to drop? Hire a bartender. Says Sarah Gray, "A lot of colleges and universities have bartending schools where you can hire a college student who's learning to be a mixologist" for a low, low price. Or, call a local bartending school.

Theme. Doesn't have to be huge, but does set a tone. Stir some summer into a frosty February by cranking up the heat, blending up frozen margaritas, and playing Jimmy Buffett. Celebrate the 100th-something birthday of Cary Grant—January 18—with martinis, pink champagne, a mini film festival and black-tie-only rules (we stole this idea from some virginal boyfriends). Hurricane headed your way? Batten down the hatches and mix up some dark 'n' stormies, or match a grown-up drink to an immature theme: piña coladas and a piñata. Prosecco and a bubble machine.

Invitations. Invite twenty to thirty friends. "You can count on 30 percent of the people not showing up. And any less than fifteen people, and you don't really have a cocktail party on your hands." Sarah Gray prefers the mailed invite to the Evite, so save a few bucks by sending out postcards instead of envelopes. (Now there's something you can do with those leftover postcards from Las Vegas and Dollywood: Throw a casino party hoedown!)

Decorations. Log on to www.ustoy.com or www.orientaltrading.com for "hilarious little anythings in bulk. Rather than splurging on crème de cassis for the bar, spend your money on those little details that are going to make people remember the party." Cheap stuff we love: blow-up tiki bars, glow-in-the-dark necklaces, plastic grass hula skirts, Mardi Gras beads, feather eye masks.

While you're installing your fabulous cheap disco ball and glitter streamers, be sure to put away anything that would make you very sad if it were harmed when your best friend inevitably busts out with her MC Hammer.

Drinks. A premixed signature drink cuts down on costs—and relieves the host of bartending duties. Stick to vodka for the main bevvie. "Because not everyone is crazy for bourbon or scotch," says Sarah Gray. Count on eight ounces of hard liquor per guest—more if your buds are serious boozehounds.

Stock up on beer and wine. "There's nothing I hate more when I go to a cocktail party than when they do the signature cocktail thing and nothing else." Serve beer in a galvanized tub filled with ice, or in an ice-filled bathtub (a little frat-y, but it'll do in a pinch). Look for second label wines (less expensive vintages made by high-end producers, like Hawk Crest Margaritas by Stag's Leap). If you're running low on liquor funds, skimp on wine. "I never expect it, but most people do bring a bottle of wine . . . I always seem to wake up the next morning with seven or eight bottles of great wine."

Food. Low-maintenance only. Save the soufflé, the gougères, the fondue for a dinner party. If it can be poured into a bowl and eaten with toothpicks or fingers, it's appropriate for a cocktail crowd.

> Finger food we love to nosh:
> Mini egg rolls from Trader Joe's
> Hummus and pita chips
> Cheese plate with cornichons, hot mustard, and sliced baguette bread
> Blue cheese–stuffed olives
> Spanish nuts
> Nonna's Cucina tortilla chips, homemade salsa, and guacamole (keep the guac fresh by burying the avocado pit in the bottom of the bowl)
> Terra Chips
> Homemade sweets: bar cookies are infinitely faster than drop cookies: Ghirardelli box-mix brownies, mini chocoalate chips, lemon squares, raspberry oatmeal bars
> Imported sweets: mini cannoli from an Italian bakery, sweet bean pies from a Chinese pastry shop, mini cream puffs, eclairs, and bite-size fruit tarts from a French or French-Vietnamese patisserie

Glasses. Stock up on less expensive glass vessels at Ikea, Kmart, etc. "You don't wanna break out the Baccarat at a rowdy party. But I don't believe in the plastic stuff either," says Sarah Gray. If you're using Popov or another, um, un-costly liquor as the base for your signature drink, consider transferring it into a comely decanting vessel.

Music. Burn a few CDs. Start with getting-in-the-mood music (Nicola Conte, Bebel Gilberto). End with impossible-not-to-dance-to tunes (Out-Kast, Scissor Sisters, Lauryn Hill, vintage Prince, way vintage Jackson 5). "I always keep one or two CDs that are retro or dance music. Normally I kick them in once the party starts to get out of control—in a good way." Stash your CD collection to prevent you or anyone else from playing part-time DJ.

Activities. Have parlor games standing by, ready in case there's ice to be broken. "There's nothing like a round of celebrity," says Sarah Gray. Charades, Pictionary, Name That Tune, Twister, even drinking games in-evitably fizzle out in the first fifteen minutes, which means people are more interested in each other.

Sarah Gray also likes to turn her bedroom into a photo booth, with a digital camera, props, and a printing station.

Wing women. "Make sure there are one or two people at your party who are close enough friends to you that they can help you out—with beer runs, etc. You certainly don't want to have a cocktail party of thirty people you've just met."

Arm your steadfast assistant social directors with information about guests—"Oh, you're Tony, the Tony who's just returned from Turkey"— as well as any household details that might pop up while you're busy put-ting your right hand on red and left foot on green—"Oh, don't worry about the toilet, it overflows all the time."

BORN-AGAIN VIRGIN

Pauletta Party Girl had her Gimlet Gauntlet planned down to the very last lime slice. She'd dusted every bunny from underneath her dining room table. She'd received RSVPs from a savory blend of friends and associates. She poured herself a juicy libation and pushed play on her get-the-party-started mixed CD at T minus ten seconds. Guests arrived, appropriately attired, in a steady stream. The mini quiches, lamb kebabs, and chocolate soufflés were a huge hit. Pauletta made sure the buffet was never empty. When the beer supply wound down to four, Pauletta called in reinforcements from the grocer who delivers. Glasses emptied. Pauletta refilled them. She also fluffed pillows, changed CDs, recycled empties, relit candles, turned the living room into a dance floor. Before she knew it, her well-applied Benefit High Beam shimmer turned into a full-fledged, foggy-day sweat. And it was 1:00 a.m. And guests headed to the door. They had a great time. Pauletta, however, didn't. Because she failed to party at her own party, Pauletta is a born-again virgin. Still, she's a game gal, that P.P.G., and got right back in the saddle for the next month's Mojito Meltdown. This time, she relaxed, laughing in the face of spills, dancing atop her own coffee table, and generally proving Sade wrong: A second time can be as good as a first—even better.

The Big Night

Pre-party duty: Have your first drink. Start to sip (gently) the moment the party is supposed to begin. Most guests will arrive twenty minutes after the SET start time.

Party duties: Have fun. Refill, restock, casually, remembering you set the tone for everyone else. Translation: Flitter, float, and be the first to disco. Deal with the spilt red wine tomorrow. Don't get sloshed.

Post-party duty: Take it easy. This means if a guest or two ought to spend the night, let them spend the night. Put them to bed with a pillow, a glass of water, a couple of tablets of pain prevention, and a trash can lined with a plastic bag. Allow them to take you to breakfast the next morning, and to help with the cleanup. It's the least you can do.

PROPER MEAL FOR ONE

> When I'm home alone, I will open up a bottle of wine, set a place mat down, and have a civilized dinner. Just because I'm alone, it doesn't mean that I have to eat like an animal.
> —CLAUDINE PÉPIN

In the beginning, there was the boob—that, and/or the bottle. We cried, and the nipple delivered. Next, we slurped up jarfuls of pureed vegetables and fruits. Then came the boxed food phase, when we put our baby chompers to work, first with Cheerios, eventually moving on to Crunch 'n' Munch. Big kid food led to cafeteria grub.

Now, graced with a fridge of our own, we grown-up eaters face a whole new challenge: feeding ourselves.

To some of us, this chore comes easily. Like to you, for example, who, at this very moment are pondering: sauvignon blanc or chardonnay for tonight's roast capon and rosemary potatoes followed by apple tart à la mode? Others of us, however—ahem, you, on the floor, munching pretzel logs dipped in peanut butter, slugging down flat Diet Coke with Lime and watching *Judge Judy* reruns—could use a little help.

Here's the secret to a successful meal for one: It's not what you eat; it's how you eat.

No time to puree your bisque or brûler your crème? Oodles of Noodles can be as much a meal as a Julia Child–like feast *pour une.* That's not to say there isn't room to improve from the ramen realm. It's just that we all gotta start somewhere.

Step away from the sink. Get up off the floor. Cordon off any sleeping area. If your first real meal on your own isn't occasion enough to use your dining table (or, at the very least, a TV tray) for its intended purpose, then nothing is.

Phase One: Table for One and Takeout

Clear the dining surface of all junk mail, laptops, pets, bank statements, stamp collections, cosmetic brushes, etc. Do this completely. Bring out a partial (place mat) or full (tablecloth) covering. Place the covering on the table surface. If desired, add freshly cut flowers and/or one or more unscented candles.

Spelunk your kitchen drawers and cabinets for one each: clean napkin, fork, knife, spoon, full-size plate, small plate, or bowl—because a meal always tastes better on real plates—water glass, wineglass. Lay them out neatly. Fill the water glass. Fill the wineglass (or at least open the bottle).

Now you're looking good. Depart your nifty new dining arrangement to retrieve a pizza and a salad from your neighborhood Italian take-out joint. Return home.

On a non-dining surface, open the take-out bag. Transfer the salad to the small plate or bowl. From box of pizza, extract one slice. Bring the salad and slice to the table setting. Sit. Eat.

While chewing and swallowing, you will be tempted to turn on the tube, catch up on bills, read a book, call your mom. Don't do it. You may, however, play the music of your choice.

Congratulations: You just completed your first meal for one.

Phase Two: Making Dinner

Don't panic. Campbell's finest tomato bisque and a grilled cheese sandwich count. But hardcore DIY counts for more.

The trick here is timing. Do you work late or go to the gym right after the office? Then prepare in advance meals you can reheat: lasagna, roast chicken, veggie burgers, anything ending with "Parmesan" — or anything made in a Crock-Pot.

The stove life of lots of foods — starches like pasta and rice, fish, fowl, and meats, steamed veggies — has a small window of pleasant edibility. Serve yourself the hot food when it's ready, even if this means shifting the first course to second place. Salad after a meal is actually a nice switch — and good for your digestion. (At least that's what the French say.)

Our favorite cookbooks for meals for one.

Bowl Food — The New Comfort Food for People on the Move: soups, salads, stir-fries, curries, pasta — this book offers up simple but hearty recipes for one-dish meals

Girl Food, Cathy Guisewite and Barbara Albright: one of our favorite comic book heroines serves up quick-and-easy recipes with a liberal dash of her deadpan wit

How to Eat: The Pleasures and Principles of Good Food, Nigella Lawson: the uber-domestic goddess breaks down the basics in fun recipes that are dee-lish and easy to execute

Joy of Cooking, any edition: supplies basic techniques for when so-called simple recipes turn complicated

The Girl Can't Cook, by Cinda Chavich: a no-fail guide around the kitchen with recipes organized into "sustenance, decadence, and observance."

GO-TO GIRL

Claudine Pépin

Chef, Author,
and Intrepid Solo Diner

In college, Claudine had a minor revelation: "Why should I wait to have company to eat off a plate?" Of course, to the daughter of a world-famous chef and a mom who insists on using the good silver for every meal, this revelation came somewhat naturally. What came a little less naturally were culinary skills. Her favorite tale of cooking floppery: "I was in my second year at college and invited my father over for dinner. One of my father's favorite meals is roasted chicken, a good green salad, and roasted potatoes. So, I went to a fancy food store in Boston, bought a hen, green salad, and potatoes. I started cooking too early. He arrived late. As it turns out, a hen is meant for soup. The thing was like eating a piece of shoe leather. I looked at him with big, second-year-of-college eyes and asked him how it was. He looked at me and asked, 'As a father or as a chef? . . . As a father, it was delicious.'" Then she learned quickly. She and Papa Jacques racked up on-air hours taping the show *Cooking with Claudine.* In front of a live TV audience, Claudine picked up the finer points of shopping to supping. Claudine Pépin is our cook-for-yourself Go-to Girl.

Kitchen Essentials, According to Claudine

Knives: four of them. "A small knife, a paring knife, a large knife, and a good bread knife. Only four, because you can use only one knife at a time. And you need them to be sharp. Buy knives that are easy to sharpen. I like Lamson Sharp because I have small hands. If you cook twice a month, get them sharpened once every eight months. When you feel like you can't easily slice through a tomato, get your knife sharpened."

Oil. "If you don't cook a lot at home, it's very important to keep oil in the refrigerator. Oil can go rancid quickly, especially sesame oil." After time in the fridge, "it might look like it's congealed. Just take it out, and in twenty minutes it will be fine."

Salt 'n' pepper. "Go for kosher salt over iodized salt. If you look at iodized salt under a microscope, you see the shape of it is round, which means it falls off food. Kosher salt is jagged, like broken glass. You use less of it and you get more flavor. It sticks to your food properly."

Don't bother with pre-ground pepper. It's like using old fresh herbs. Or, think of Folgers or Maxwell House and really nice freshly ground coffee. That's the difference between pre-ground and freshly ground pepper. Pre-ground pepper has a really bland taste. Freshly ground pepper is nutty and spicy . . . Invest in a good Peugot pepper mill."

Pans. "I'm a fan of really good, no-stick pans. People buy a whole set of pots and pans. You don't need them. Remember the thin, dinged-up pots and pans you used in college? You felt like you could burn water in them. You want a piece of metal that's thick." Think Le Creuset. Think All-Clad.

Whisk. "You need one whisk."

Wooden spoon with a straight edge. "If you make a sauce, you can scrape the bottom of the pot with the edge."

A rubber spatula. "One that is heat resistant."

A slotted spoon. "You'd be surprised how much you use a slotted spoon."

A really thin spatula. "One that's made of flexible, thin metal. You can't get big spatulas under what you need to get out."

Pastry scraper. "This is my favorite kitchen utensil—and I don't make pastry. I use it all the time. When you cut a bunch of onions, use it to push the onions into a bowl or pan. It's like a big hand."

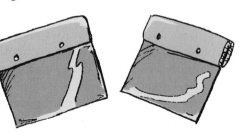

To Recap: The Top Ten Most Beautiful Things about Eating Alone

- You're always on time to dinner.
- You're always impressed by your own cooking.
- No permission required for seconds.
- You don't have to finish your vegetables.
- Spilling is OK.
- Burping, too.
- Farting is permitted, but discouraged.
- Talking with your mouth full is a nonissue.
- No need to share.
- No need to finish your spinach in order to have dessert rights.

ROMANTIC DINNER FOR TWO

Find me a man who's interesting enough
to have dinner with and I'll be happy.
—Lauren Bacall

It isn't just the seventy-five minutes you wait to be seated at that chic new bistro across town. It isn't just the wobbly table, wedged between an espresso station and a swinging kitchen door. Nor is it merely the noise level that incites a polite shouting contest between you and your date, or the server that scoffs at your choice of wine—and then spills it onto your suede skirt—or the bill that exceeds your monthly rent check. It is all of these combined—and, perhaps, one of those handy, courage-bolstering espressos—that leads you to do the unthinkable.

"How about I fix you dinner next week . . . at my place?" you ask.

The question hangs in the air, suspended in a cartoon bubble. Its presence is shocking. Suddenly, you're back in junior high health class, raising your hand and asking, "What's a testie?" You recognize the voice as yours, but the idea itself surely came from a nether region of your unconscious.

But there it is. Floating up there, above your head. Across the table, a face smiles, a head nods. Your offer has been accepted.

So this is how it's gonna be. You. Your significant other (or as significant an other as a former stranger can be after four dates). A rendezvous for next Saturday night. At your apartment. With food you've promised to make yourself. Oh man.

The upside: no restaurant-related inconveniences. The downside: little previous experience cooking for yourself, let alone for someone you find irresistibly cute, highly intelligent, and sweaty-palm inducing.

Wipe off those hands. Pick up your favorite cookbook. You can do this. You've got a whole week.

P.S. Words to the wise. Remember to ask ahead of time your date's likes, dislikes, allergies, intolerances, etc. Anaphylactic shock is such a date dampener. Stick to three courses: starter, main, and dessert. And make these courses light. "If you're thinking of—let's face it—trying to get busy afterward, you don't want to be full of heavy food. After a heavy meal, you're not feeling sexy," says our next Go-to Girl . . .

GO-TO GIRL

Thia Boggs
Caterer, Event Planner,
Culinary Program Coordinator
for Macy's Union Square in San Francisco

Quality-over-quantity girl Thia began her culinary career assembling pear slices into the shape of a bunny, as per the instructions of *Betty Crocker's Cookbook for Boys and Girls*. Nowadays, she books top chefs for appearances in the test kitchen at San Francisco's Macy's Union Square—a job for which, on occasion, she spends weekends baking hundreds of Nigella Lawson's mini chocolate cheesecakes. Thia's our number one for the classic lines: "If something occurs to you and you're like, that's not the way they do it in the books, well then screw it. Do it your way." And, "There's nothing sexier than confidence."

The Mantra According to Thia: "You are the greatest dish in your whole dinner."

The Meaning of the Mantra: "You don't have to make the meal the star: You're the star."

The Meaning of the Meaning: This time, "It's not all about the food. If you're going to have an eight-person dinner party, it's about the food. In this scenario, it's about you eating with someone. Whatever you do, don't make yourself feel more self-conscious."

The Application of the Meaning of the Meaning: The first production of dinner at your place emphasizes tangible inedibles as much as edibles. In other words, the scene, costumes, and rapport are just as important as the meal itself. This should be good news for less-experienced home chefs.

Rethunk Rules of Dinner for Two

Lighting before flowers. Fluorescent overheads render a room about as seductive as an office cubicle. A decent dimmer or a ten-pack of votives makes a much better investment than a bouquet of exotic blooms.

The lighting is a must, but if you're flush enough to afford both, buy one kind and color of mildly scented to unscented flowers—chrysanthemums, zinnias, white crocus. Float blossoms in a bowl or make sure the centerpiece is below eye level. Keep a few empty vases in reserve in case your date brings you an arrangement.

Clothes before food. If it's T minus sixty minutes and you're still in sweats, crank up a smooth soundtrack and get thyself to wardrobe.

Your date will be fine if hanging out in the kitchen while you mix the salad dressing. Your date will be less fine hanging out in the kitchen/at the table/on the couch while you dress. The food can wait. Your adorable outfit cannot.

Make space stove-side for your special guest to hang out while the sauce simmers. "It's totally cute to watch somebody cooking," says Thia. Possible jobs to delegate: the selection of mood music (from your carefully and recently edited music assemblage, minus the Ricky Martin/ Savage Garden/ RuPaul). The mixing and pouring of cocktails. The complimenting of your obvious and numerous culinary skills.

Pre-cleaning before post-cleaning. Tidy up the homestead ahead of time. But when dinner's done, forget about the mess.

Behold the lesson Thia learned from her dear grandma, who imparted these grandmotherly words: "Screw that. Put away the food that you don't want to spoil, but NEVER CLEAN UP THE SAME NIGHT."

If your date wants to play dishwasher, fine. But if your loveseat compels the two of you to employ it for its intended purpose, soak the Fiestaware in the sink and get down to some old-fashioned postprandial necking.

Starter

Think spicy or extremely fresh, to wake up the appetite. Try a simple salad of tomatoes, basil, and fresh mozzarella drizzled with olive oil and balsamic vinegar. Spring rolls with peanut sauce. Bruschetta brushed with pesto. Cantaloupe wrapped in prosciutto. Baked goat cheese with dandelion greens. If you're feeling daring: raw oysters, the original aphrodisiac. Things that add panache to Boston bibb lettuce or mesclun: crumbled blue cheese, smoked trout, grilled pears, spiced pecans, golden and red beets, roasted garlic, heirloom tomatoes, pine nuts.

Main Course

Go with what you know. Think of where you grew up. Of your ancestry. Of your year abroad. "Don't try to cook food that isn't you," says Thia. Plus, a recipe with a story attached to it "takes the pressure off because you're not trying to be fancy or perfect; you're really making something from the heart."

Come from a home where Mom and Pop considered the stack of take-out menus their own personal *Joy of Cooking*? No problem. Simple yet impressive:

- Pasta (seasonal). Butternut squash ravioli in fall. Pesto farfalle in summer. Creamy, Parmesan-topped gratin in winter. Classic primavera in spring. "The Italians understood this so well: total *cucina amore.*"
- Grilling. (Let your guest show his skills.) Tuna steaks briefly marinated in soy sauce and O.J. Petite filet mignon. Shish kebabs. Or, because you can't beat 'em, burgers and dogs.
- Roasting. Capon or Guinea hen, those little flavorful birds that one-up chicken any day. Pot roast (it worked for Grandma when she was wooing Grampa). Roasting requires a little more time, but you get to pay less attention.

Dessert

Anything that doesn't require your extended presence in the kitchen. Ice cream with fresh fruit. Ice cream with a quick and easy strawberry lavender sauce. Brownie sundaes. Cookies you baked yesterday and nuke for ten seconds tonight. Thia's into the s'more thing. A few graham crackers, a few marshmallows, a chocolate bar, and a heat source make the meal's end interactive. (Extra note to self: Eating with hands is the ultimate leveler—half child-like, half très adult!)

It's No Sin to Order In

Just couldn't get your act together in time? Good old-fashioned takeout will rescue you. Feel free to amp it up with a few of your own creations. Order fried chicken from that great little soul food restaurant down the block. Pair it with sweet tea, homemade mac and cheddar, and Grandma's Coca-Cola cake.

Pick up some steaming pho from your favorite Vietnamese. Add fruity rum drinks. Follow with warm rice pudding with coconut milk.

Or, prepare your own savory starter and main course, and purchase the strawberry shortcake from a qualified professional.

POTLUCK

You can't forget the Jell-O salad. You watched it wiggle, saw it jiggle, that mass of grass-green goo magically holding aloft a variety of canned fruits and miniature snacks. Each pretzel, each mini marshmallow was evenly distributed in midair. Or mid gelatin. There it was. In your fridge. At the church picnic. At your family reunion. At any gathering that required each participant to bring a covered dish.

The thing is, there's nothing wrong with the potluck concept. Even a 1979-style potluck, complete with meats served directly from the Crock-Pots that cooked them. A potluck virgin ought not to allow her painful Jell-O salad memories to come between her and the luck of the pot.

GO-TO GIRL

Mindy Fox   Cookbook Writer
                                                and Potluck Mobilizer

Smart girl, that Mindy. She moved to NYC not knowing a soul, gathered up women she met through culinary publishing, and started an eating

(continued)

GO-TO GIRL (*continued*)

club. These days, Mindy and ten friends assemble a few times a year at the home of the pal with the largest dining room table for a potluck dinner. Each pal brings a dish. There doesn't need to be an occasion, but there usually is. "There's always something to celebrate, and we make somebody the guest of honor," says Mindy. A new job here, the passing of Julia Child there, a yen for crawfish etouffée: Any reason to get the gals together. The collaborative effort, all-homemade meal is "an old-fashioned kind of thing. It's from before the time when you could buy a roast chicken at a gourmet food store. It's from a time when people cooked . . . And it's a really nice way to build your community."

The Potluck Players

The organizer. Must be adept at delegation. Must be willing to send and to answer multiple e-mails. Must be unafraid to ban store-bought dishes.

The host. Must be the owner of a kitchen with a real stove and a genuine full-size oven. Must have room to store items in a genuine full-size refrigerator. Must also own a dedicated dining area (be that a large table with an adequate number of chairs or a room with enough seating or carpet space to accommodate guests). Must possess ample supply of cleaning items as well as emergency condiments, serving dishes, flatware, glasses, Tupperware or the equivalent.

The cooks. Must know how to prepare one decent dish. In the absence of such knowledge, must be willing to master one decent dish through practice—by testing it out on willing tasters in the days before the potluck. Must be able to transport the dish to the host's home without ruining it. Must arrive on time or early to help the host set up for the meal. Responsibilities may also include staying late to assist with cleanup.

The non-cooks. Must check with the organizer, cooks, and host to arrange libations commensurate with the meal. Must chill white wine, beer, champagne, or bottled water beforehand. Must assume the role of dishwasher, dish dryer, or leftover packer-upper.

The Potluck Rules

- Pick a theme (to avoid culinary clashes). Indian food. Diner food. Southern food. French food. Senegalese food. Says Mindy, "You wouldn't want to have one person making barbecue chicken and another person making a soufflé."
- Gather a reasonably sized group. Any less than five isn't a party. Any more than fifteen is too much of a party.

- Distribute food responsibilities evenly. At the minimum: two hors d'oeuvres, one salad, one main course, one dessert, one beverage delivery for five people. Translation on this last one: a bottle of wine and a liter of water for every two dinner guests.
- Enlist help. Anyone who'll need to use the oven or stove should arrive early. Non-cooks who brought the beverages shouldn't shirk dish-doing duties after the dessert plates are cleared.

Potluck Tips

- BYO recipes. Ask each cook to bring copies of her dish's recipe, one for each eater. As the host, you'll supply a hole punch and affixing devices (string, clips, etc.). Assemble a casual cookbook.
- Plan to serve hot and cold foods, to avoid crowding on the stove and in the oven.
- Salad maker: Prepare dressing(s) ahead of time, reserve in bottle(s) then toss on site, at last minute.
- The more people you invite, the more food you'll have. No need to overfeed.

DINNER PARTY

It might as well be the impossible dream. The idea that you, of your own free will, would invite more than three friends to your home to serve them a sit-down, multicourse dinner that you make yourself. The concept seems much more fantasy than reality.

But something is calling you to do it. That something might be your grandmother's French country dinnerware. Or the shame you feel from years of reading a decade's worth of gourmet magazines and never testing out a single recipe.

Maybe you've mastered a vinaigrette. Or inherited a shiny set of All-Clad. Or want to show off your new digs. Could be payback time for all those times you've mooched squares from settled-down pals. Of course, it's also possible that you harbor a secret desire to be Martha. Or that you're nuts. After all, you've just started feeding yourself. What would possess you to think you're equipped for feeding others is, well, anybody's guess.

The thing is: If you pull off the dinner party, you automatically enter the sacred realm of the platinum virgin goddess.

Here's how to get there.

What You'll Need

- A kitchen
- A table big enough to seat all your guests, and chairs for them to sit in
- Some idea of a menu
- Calm in the face of culinary stress
- Pots, pans, casserole dishes, linens, and the serving items (plates, flatware, glasses, etc.) from "Proper Meal for One" (see page 9)

GO-TO GIRL

Jennifer Arronson

Mystery Guest and
Mostess Hostess

"No one wants to spend the whole party in the kitchen," says entertaining expert Jennifer. This Manhattan-based editor works for the one of the premier homemaking magazines in America—modest Jennifer would rather not name drop—but she completely appreciates the plight of the first timer. Her advice for pulling off a first dinner party: "Try not to be too ambitious at first. Start with dishes you know are tried and true. This is not the time to experiment. Try out dishes at home before attempting them on guests. Don't make your guests guinea pigs."

Jennifer's Rules for Making a Guest List

- "Invite two couples who don't know each other but that you've been wanting to introduce."
- "Try to avoid the odd man out. If you're inviting a large group, be sure to include more than one person who doesn't know anyone."
- "Try not to play matchmaker at a dinner party. If you must, invite the people you want to set up to a larger party so that if they're not interested they won't have to spend the whole party trying to make small talk."

- "Make a list around something to celebrate. Invite a group that will appreciate someone's recent accomplishment, trip, or announcement."
- "Enlist a friend who's done this before, who won't mind making an emergency run to the grocery, who is glad to lend a gravy boat, will be kitchen backup—and will ensure you'll have a glass of wine by your side at all times."

How to Plan a Menu

Part one: culinary reconnaissance. Start by scoping out farmers' markets to find out what's in season. Stumbling upon a crate of fresh white asparagus / baby lettuces / Honeycrisp apples will inspire you to plan around what's freshest.

Part two: victim reconnaissance. Feel out your guests for possible likes, dislikes, allergies, etc. You likely know those of your pals already. But you may not know those of your pals' wives, hubbies, and dates.

Part three: Girl Scouts are prepared. Replenish staples—olive oil, butter, kosher salt, black peppercorns—days in advance. Lighten your last-minute load.

Part four: strategic planning. Plan a few dishes you can cook a day or two ahead. Not everything, but most things. "Try not to choose recipes that depend on perfect timing," says Jennifer. Restaurant tricks to remember: Risotto and pasta can both be cooked partway and finished off without much fuss. Braising doesn't require as much finesse as roasting and usually improves the meat the longer it cooks. For roast poultry, leave the bird in the fridge, uncovered, on a baking rack twenty-four hours before you roast it (the skin will be extra crispy). Grilling or searing are both last-minute methods that don't take too long, but do require an expert touch. Veggies get blanched first (cooked to brightness, immediately chilled in ice water bath), then reheated in sauté pan with olive oil.

Part four: the budget. Balance out special indulgences—caviar, oysters, French champagne—with economical fare. Tougher, inexpensive cuts of meats—pork shoulder, oxtails, short ribs, chicken thighs—can be delicious when slow cooked.

Shopping/Preparing

"I make four stops: the farmers' market, the regular market, either the fish store or meat market, and the liquor store. Be sure to make a thorough list so you don't have to run out again." (Of course, you will have to run out again. The day of your dinner party, start an hour early just in case.)

Advanced prep. "If you've chosen your dishes wisely, you can prepare almost everything ahead of time. A dish of braised short ribs can be made the day before, then reheated right before guests arrive. Mashed potatoes can be made ahead of time, then reheated in a pot with extra milk or cream stirred in to bring back creaminess. A shellfish stew can be made up until the point of adding in the shellfish at the last minute."

Other things to do ahead: Baking (desserts), making the salad dressing, washing (and drying!) salad ingredients.

"Make sure to have plenty of alcohol. Try not to rely on guests to bring wine—it may not be appropriate for the meal you're serving. Have a plan for what kinds of drinks you will serve."

Shopping the day of. Pick up perishable vegetables, fruit, seafood, plus flowers and bread. Reminder: Buying produce at the last minute is not always the smartest move; for example, mangoes, pears, avocados, tomatoes, and bananas often need time to ripen.

How to Set a Table

"Keep it low. Large flower arrangements or tall candles make conversation difficult. Stick with low votives, flowers, and fruit on the table top," says Jennifer.

"Get inspired by a theme. For a party with French bistro food, you might want to set your table as they do in cafés in France, with paper over white linens and short juice-type glasses for wineglasses, white napkins, silver salt and pepper shakers, small flower vases." Or use a bright cotton shawl as a table runner for an Indian feast, Chinese lanterns overhead for a Mandarin meal, a vase of American flags for a Fourth of July dinner.

"Limit colors. Try not to overwhelm your table with too many colors. Sticking with white china and a few bold colors will make your food look its best."

How to Set a House

Clean and straighten any areas where people will be. For example, the bedroom (coats may be thrown on the bed, people will peek in the bedroom whether you know it or not). In the bathroom remove all lingerie from the shower head, toss the towels in the hamper, break out the guest towels, and light a candle or two.

Good places to stash junk—*classic:* under the bed and in the closet; *risky:* behind the shower curtain; *foolproof:* in the car.

Pulling It Off

The classic delay. Cocktails (see signature cocktail ideas in "Cocktail Party," page 2) or wine and cheese (see "Wine Tasting" and "Cheese & Chocolate Encounters," page 124) in living room. Favorite sources for at-home mixologists: www.exhale.com and www.drinknation.com.

Keeping it cool. "Make sure to toss salads at the last minute to avoid sogginess."

Keeping it hot. "Keep food that was cooked in the oven in a low (200°–250°F) oven, covered, until ready to serve (unless it is something that will dry out or overcook). Keep food at a low simmer or in a low oven—each course will not take long to reheat if it's already on its way to warm." Blanching veggies or a quick greens steam happens just before serving. Store serving dishes in a warm place.

THE HOLIDAY MEAL

The Upside

You know when it's coming. You have access to unlimited decorations, recipe ideas from a barrage of months-ahead press coverage. You often have a whole day off to get ready, a day when relatives and friends are available to help out.

The Downside

Those relatives and friends may well spend that day watching a series of televised professional sporting events, frustrating you no end

(continued)

THE HOLIDAY MEAL *(continued)*

as you attempt to perform culinary feats that include removing bags of organs from large birds and re-creating Grandma's collards and/or Bubbi's brisket.

Depends what traditions guests have.

Your Family

You already know that you must make a perfect chess pie or extra crispy latkes. You also know everyone will be eternally grateful if you can improve on Mom's cloyingly sweet ham or skip the fruitless fruitcake.

Your Pals

Ask for input—and consider a potluck so that everyone can bring her favorite dish. (See "Potluck," page 22.)

Someone Else's Family: Laid-back Version

Get a general feel for what they'd like to have, then do your own thing. Ask for help freely. Don't expect to get it. Don't worry if you're running late or you burned the bread pudding. Prepare plenty of pre-meal munchies.

Someone Else's Family: Uptight Version

Enlist advance assistance from a ranking member on the family board of directors. Go to this person with all pertinent questions, including requests for recipes and nontraditional recipe approval. Cover your tracks and you won't feel so stressed when something goes wrong. Do not—we repeat—do not attempt to reinvent or to reproduce a holiday meal if you have not attended the same meal with the uptight family.

Lower-Pressure Suggestions

The holiday brunch: less pressure at the last minute. Baked goods you can bake or order in advance. Coffee before and during the meal puts everyone in a good mood, as do mimosas and Bloody Marys. Fresh fruit. Scrambled eggs or egg casserole. Salmon, onion, capers, lox, and bagels. Chocolate croissants and coffee cake. You're done—even with the dishes—before nightfall.

2

HEALTH & FITNESS

We admit it: We're addicted to *Self* magazine. Month after month, cover to cover, reading each issue feels like eating a salad, taking a brisk walk, and having a heart-to-heart. Every thirty days, we get a new chance at our New Year's resolution—and if we break it, a new edition's on its way in a few weeks.

It's possible our addiction to *Self* is the reason this chapter's the longest in the book. But what were we gonna do, write a book about living the good life without including exploits taken from fun-filled visits to the docs we rely on most from our teens through our thirties: the gyno, dermo, and therapist? No way. Nor could we resist debunking the Hans-and-Franz myth of the personal trainer, or the Dharma-and-Greg-driven idea of what yoga is all about. Toss in a sweet Swedish rubdown, and dreams of all-inclusive destination spas, and what do you get? Several pages that are entirely self-centered.

GYNECOLOGIST

Wear socks.

Nobody ever tells you that one, essential piece of information required for your first trip to the gyno. They tell you—and we'll tell you—a lot of other, bigger advice. But the socks thing. That part inevitably seems to slip everyone's mind.

Socks are way important.

You're lying on an examination table, wearing nothing but a thin paper sheet and a very non–Diane von Furstenberg wrap garment. Your butt has dutifully scooted down to the end of the table. Your legs are bent and akimbo, heels placed in stirrups. You are one nervous nudie—most obviously because you're currently exposing body parts that haven't been scrutinized in this sort of fluorescent lighting since the brilliant day you made your debut into the world.

So there you are, in your full glory. You try to make polite conversation with your doctor and a nurse or two while a large metal object invades your insides. Despite all these attention stealers, all you can think is, man, my feet are freezing.

To their credit, an increasing number of gynecologists swaddle their tables' stirrups in custom-made felt booties (which, more often than not, coordinate with the wrap garment). It's a really nice gesture. But the booties don't keep your toes or the tops of your feet toasty. And they have a tendency to disappear from examination rooms in the same fashion that socks disappear during the laundry. (Somewhere out there a nurse is walking a Great Dane bedecked in really nice felt footwear.) The moral of this story: Bring socks.

Girl, You'll Be a Woman, Soon

We are, quite obviously, getting ahead of ourselves here. You may be wondering if you need to make your maiden voyage to the gyno at all.

Honeys, if Aunt Dot's making her monthly visits, you do. If you've done the dirty, you do. If you're planning to run the bases, thinking of bearing young, experiencing any abnormal pain, discharge, bleeding, itching, or lumpiness, you do.

How often? Usually once a year. That's it. Unless you need a new prescription, or have a new concern that can wait however long it takes to get an appointment.

Get Set

How to find a good doc. Ask your friends. Ask your primary care physician. Ask your sisters. Ask your health insurance provider.

(Important thing to remember: If someone else pays for your health insurance—if you're in school, this is very likely—that person will receive an invoice detailing the services you receive at the doctor, services that could include pregnancy testing, STD testing, birth control, other details you might not want to discuss with Dad or Mom. If you want to keep this part of your health private, look for a Planned Parenthood or a free clinic.)

It's perfectly fine if you don't want to go to your mama's ob-gyn. It's also fine to request a woman.

Docs who share a large practice will likely be able to see you sooner and more often. Popular single or small-office docs are typically harder to book, but they will know you each time you return.

When to schedule your appointment. Best timing is one week after your period, when your insides are relaxed and your boobs aren't bloated. Most gyns won't see a patient during her period. Most prefer not to see a patient the week before.

Before you go. Make a list of questions you'd like to ask the doctor.

The day of. Bathe. Shave. Don't douche. Pack socks.

In the Office

Most doctors' offices ask you to arrive early so that you can enjoy some paperwork. Pick up your clipboard and stash your creativity and modesty under your chair. There's nobody gonna share your answers with the rest of the class. If you check yes in the "Do you think you could be pregnant" box, you'll be treated to a little plastic cup and shown to the loo. You get to give a golden sample.

Next: Your name is called. You follow a person wearing a scrub top covered in cartoon characters to a little room, where you do a pediatrician-style pantomime. You're weighed. You get your blood pressure taken. You tell the first day of your last period. Or you guess it. No sweat.

Hop On Up

Ha. Then you see the outfit you'll have to put on. At least you get to don it in private. The thin cottonesque dress ties in front. The paper sheet serves as your no-thread-count leg blanket. So take off your pretty clothes. Leave your socks on. And hop up onto that table, Girlie!

There's a knock on the door. No need to get up to answer it. A frightened "Come in" will do.

This, dear patient, is your doctor. If this doctor's a he, he's bound to bring a female assistant along. If your doc's a woman, she may bring one along, too. Either way, you have the right to ask for a sidekick to come in who will look at you sympathetically, hold your hand, or tell you jokes while the deal goes down.

If your doc would like to bring anyone else—a doctor in training, the cast of *Grey's Anatomy*—you have the right to say no way.

Your Pelvis, Elvis?

The next universal law of the examination: You never can slide your booty too close to the edge of the table. Your doc will ask you to do it once, twice, three times, lady.

Be prepared for four quick things to occur during this less-than-discreet stage. Feel free to request a play-by-play from your doctor.

Probe. A silvery or plastic-y speculum—the down-there equivalent of a tongue depressor—is inserted into your vagina, so that the doc can

WHEN BAD THINGS HAPPEN TO GOOD PARTS

Yeast infection: The unjust reward for working out a lot, this gooey itchy annoyance is easily remedied with over-the-counter nighttime medications. More serious or frequently occurring cases require a doctor's visit and prescription help.

Papilloma virus or HPV: We'll be blunt. Genital warts. As gross as they sound, they're really common. Ten to 20 percent of sexually active Americans have 'em. And they're no big deal to care for, if caught in time. If they're not, they can creep inside you (sorry, but it's true) and cause cervical cancer. If caught in time they can be removed with a quick and painless surgical procedure called a loop.

Anemia: Lack of iron in your blood, which causes dizziness that worsens when your period arrives. Protect yourself against this by eating three squares. Chicken, fish, meat, eggs, green leafy veggies, nuts, peas, beans, and whole grains are good sources of iron.

Ovarian cysts: A veritable cornucopia of unpleasantness, these fluid-y sacs mostly are caused by ovulation gone wrong or hormones gone wild. Though they're normally mild and temporary in young women, they can do serious harm. See your gyno.

Urinary tract infections: Lucky us! Half of all women are treated to UTIs at least once in their lives. Caused by bacteria, causing pain

(continued)

WHEN BAD THINGS HAPPEN TO GOOD PARTS *(continued)*

while peeing worsened by the urge to pee at all times, these nasty little infections are easily treated with antibiotics. Common causes: sex, sex with more than one partner, and postponing tinkling. Common preventions: good hygiene, cotton panties, hydration, vitamin C, cranberry juice.

Trichomonas: Known as "Trick" to its pals, this common STD comes from a germy protozoan that causes—if you're eating, read this later—a yellow-green or gray bubbly discharge, itching or burning, pain in the lower abdomen, and/or pain while peeing. Cured with pills. Men have fewer symptoms, but they have to be treated because they're carriers, too.

Bacterial vaginosis ("B.V."—don't you love these cute nicknames?): a mysterious, yeast-infection-esque disease with various and serious reproductive repercussions. The basic trouble? Too many germs in there, which can be aggravated by douching, because douching kills naturally germ-fighting bacteria. Solution: pills.

And guess what? There's more! Much more! Like herpes! And crabs! Gonorrhea and chlamydia! We're gonna spare you the gory details, but know that most every STD can be treated—and benefits from early diagnosis.

get up close but not personal with your cervix. You may feel a little cramping.

Pap test. Into the tunnel of the speculum goes a long cotton swab. Swish! This, my delicate dears, is for your fast, but not so furious Pap smear, the lab test that will reveal the state of your uterine cells.

This test comes back in usually three to four weeks. (Notification may come in the mail, or by phone, or, you might have to call in to the office or to an automated service.) The varying results:

Normal: satisfactory, with no signs of cancer.
Unsatisfactory: inconclusive, you gotta go back for a redo.
Inflammation: irritation found, possibly from an infection or an STD.
Atypical: with mildly abnormal cell changes. You may need another visit, or your doc might just want to keep an eye on them at your next annual visit.
Abnormal cell changes: which may indicate HPV (see page 41 for our witty description of genital warts) or precancerous changes in the cells. You're headed back.

Palpation. Two gloved fingers feel around for your uterus, fallopian tubes, and ovaries to check that everything's where it's supposed to be. Feels weird. Doesn't hurt.

Boob check. Know how the dental hygienist asks if you floss daily, and, even if you do, you feel like she doesn't believe you, because everyone else fibs at that point of the trip to the dentist? Your gyno is going to ask if you've been doing your monthly breast exams to check for lumps or discharge. No matter if you say yes or no, she's gonna do what you're supposed to do, basically medically feel you up and around. Then she's gonna remind you that every month, the week after your period, you're supposed to do what she just did (more on this in "You're Such a Boob," opposite.)

Put Your Clothes On

And pull that list of questions from your boat tote. During this first visit—and, if you request, on following ones—you get an exclusive invitation to chitchat with your doc in her digs. She'll tell you what she saw, she'll make recommendations, and—here it comes—she'll ask if you have questions. Don't be bashful. Fire away. She's heard it all before.

Parting Gifts

Your reward for playing in this medical ritual? Promotional goodies—yours for the asking.

Condoms
Birth control pill samples
Pain relievers
Tampons
Booklets

Charts on how to conduct a breast self-exam, and check or care for HPV, herpes, crabs, you name it.

You're Such a Boob

You've worn the pink ribbon. You've raced for the cure. But when that post-period time of the month comes around, you can never seem to find fifteen minutes for your breast self-exam. You should. And here's the person to tell you why.

GO-TO GIRL

Dr. Shenin Sachedina   A Surgeon with Something to Get Off Her Chest

Breast-wise, Shenin has seen it all. After all, this doc founded the Central Florida Breast Center, a place where women go for boob jobs that have nothing at all to do with the ladies of *Baywatch*. Why should young women—even teenagers—concern themselves with more than their bra size? "We're seeing breast cancer in younger and younger women," she says. Nonetheless, the standard age for a first mammogram is between thirty-five and forty. So why should we young ones take heed? "In this younger age group, the breast tissue is very dense." Translation: They may be perfectly perky, but their insides are harder to diagnose.

The Monthly Self-exam

Lying down or standing up. In front of a mirror or in the shower. This simple self-check takes all of fifteen minutes and could save your life. Remind yourself how at www.breastcancer.org or www.komen.org.

What if I find a lump?

If it's during or before your period, wait until your cycle's done. "Lumps that go away with your menstrual cycle are usually not a problem. It's the lumps that are persistent that have to be checked," says Dr. S.

What if the lump overstays its welcome?

See a doc who'll pay attention. "One of the biggest pitfalls is that patients are told, 'You're too young to have breast cancer.'"

Play it safe; seek out a center that specializes in mammograms. "Make sure the center is staffed by dedicated mammographers [not just general radiologists] and that it's accredited by the American College of Radiology and the MQSA, Mammography Quality Standards Act. It should be a facility that does a lot of mammography—not an X-ray facility that does a little bit of everything."

If your five-minute-or-less, pretty much pain-free mammogram is inconclusive, you'll be treated to a luxurious ultrasound, and, possibly, later on, to a needle biopsy.

Take heart. "Just because a woman has a lump doesn't mean she needs surgery."

THERAPIST

When I talk about therapy, I know what people think
That it only makes you selfish and in love with your shrink
But oh how I loved everybody else
When I finally got to talk so much about myself
—DAR WILLIAMS, "WHAT DO YOU HEAR IN THESE SOUNDS"

No way. You don't need therapy. Not you. Nope. You are a thoroughly together and completely at-peace-variety person. You don't work at a job you hate, date a guy you argue with, fume during family reunions, shirk social responsibilities, or lose sleep from worry.

To summarize: There is absolutely nothing you'd like to change about your life. Well, good for you. But just for the record, we think you're a big, fashion-conscious fibber.

Because everyone—even the well-adjusted kids from *Free to Be You and Me!*—can use professional noggin clean out. We may not qualify as mentally ill, but we all have a l'il something-something we'd like in or out of our heads and lives.

Want examples? You don't believe the compliments others give you. You hurt others despite your nice intentions. Or, you're so nice to everyone that you attract meanie friends. You talk too much about yourself—or you can't seem to speak up. Your parents/sister/brother drive you crazy. You just got dumped. You just got married. You cry at commercials involving puppies (OK fine, we all do that and know it's 100 percent sensible). There's something you're doing—or not doing—and you just don't know why.

Psychotherapy doesn't have to be for a blatant, diagnosable disorder (although if you suspect there's a disorderly issue at issue, then get thee to a therapist, right away). It's usually for that little daily itch that you just can't scratch. It is not—as people who need more therapy than mostly stable girls like you and us will ever require say—reserved for crazies (that way of thinking is SO two decades ago).

Plus, in its own way, psychotherapy is totally chic. (Come on now, all the celebs do it . . . Even Tony Soprano.)

Move it along, princesses. Y'all are late for the Therapy Ball.

Psychotherapy Is . . .

In short, you and a professional sitting in a room and talking for forty-five minutes to one hour. No lattes. No MTV. Possibly a little small talk. Usually a box of tissues. You do most of the talking. The therapist asks most of the questions. The therapist is your guide, the person who facilitates your own catharsis—think Robin Williams in *Good Will Hunting*. The idea is, if you draw your own conclusions, you create your own change.

Psychotherapists Are . .

Take your pick.

Psychiatrists ($200/hour). Because they went to medical school, these mental health pros can prescribe pills. Their residency was head-related but did not necessarily involve human subjects or talk therapy. On the whole, psychiatrists work with patients with biologically based disorders that require hands-on, medicated, physical care, which include chemical depression, ADD, schizophrenia, and bipolar disorder. Still, some do specialize in traditional, one-on-one talk therapy. They just get to charge more for it.

Psychologists ($75–$150/hour). Since anyone with a BS in psych can call himself a psychologist, we'll be precise. We're talking about doctorate-holding psychologists, ones who spent an average of seven postcollege years studying and training to earn a PhD tacked behind their names. Many are schooled in or ascribe to one or more theoretical orientations: Freud-based psychoanalysis and cognitive therapies concentrate on beliefs; humanistic psychology focuses on a patient's emotional state. Most use a combination of orientations to treat a patient. Psychologists don't prescribe medication. They heal by getting their patients to talk — often at length — asking questions along the way, and encouraging their patients to find their own solutions to deep problems. If necessary, they'll refer you to a psychiatrist.

Licensed clinical social workers ($50–$125/hour). Also talk therapists, these counselors most often hold master's degrees in social work, usually with an emphasis on psychotherapy, often with in-the-field work.

LCSWs frequently work in hospitals, medical clinics, and churches. Many specialize in specific areas, such as eating disorders, disease, and grief. Good to go to if you want a particular problem dealt with in few sessions.

Finding a Therapist

As always, word of mouth is the best bet. Avoid going to a psychotherapist who is a friend. Consider, however, going to a friend's psychotherapist—if it worked for your bud, it just might work for you.

Your primary care physician. Can't hurt to try here. At the very least, your doc may be able to pick out someone who accepts your insurance.

Your college/university clinic. Lucky you if mental health is included as part of your tuition package. Take advantage.

Anyone you trust who knows a slew of people. Especially pals or associates in the helping professions, like members of clergy or hairstylists. (Come on, you know the salon is THE place to get the best referrals.)

Professional associations. The American Psychological Association: www.apa.org. The American Psychiatric Association: www.psych.org. The National Association of Social Workers: www.naswdc.org. All offer references.

Your insurance provider. If you happen to be signed up for primo coverage, this might be the way to go. If not, see "A Boring Word on Insurance," page 53.

Next. Call 'em up. Any psychotherapist worth the degrees hanging on her wall will do you the honor of a five-minute, between-session callback. Which will give you just enough time to ask:

- Are you accepting new patients? (If not, can she offer you another name, based on the rest of your questions and requirements?)
- Are you licensed?
- How long have you been practicing?
- Do you treat many patients like me?
- What is your theoretical orientation? (Just write it down. You can Google her answer later for a definition.)
- How can I pay? (Some offices require payment or copayment upfront. Others bill insurers.)
- Do you accept my insurance? (A "yes" answer is an extra reason to go. A "no" should not keep you from going for a first session. It just might be worth it, and you can most likely deduct the cost of your sessions as a medical expense from your taxes.)

If the person on the other end of the line is abrupt or otherwise off-putting, don't bother scheduling a first session. The most important quality you'll need is measured compassion, some sense of connection. If you don't have that kind of trust, that comfort level, you're not gonna wanna tell her your stories and secrets anyway.

And now, a word from our sweetly singing/songwriting sister.

GO-TO GIRL

Dar Williams   Singer-Songwriter and Eloquent
                                    Advocate of Psychotherapy

Dar is the kind of gal who knows just what to sing. And to say. She musically muses about how sessions with her therapist changed—and saved—her life in her song "What Do You Hear in These Sounds?" Dar was a mere college girl when she sampled her first few counseling sessions. She went three times before quitting. Then she got dumped. And depressed. And went back. This time, she "got it. It was like a personality lab . . . [My therapist] was opening up a lid on my life." Those first few sessions, "felt hard, but in a New England spring kind of way," she says. "Things were emerging."

A BORING WORD ON INSURANCE

It's hard enough getting an HMO or one of its nonglamorous medical-coverage cousins to cover your annual checkups. Getting one to foot your mental health bills can be a double-wide pain in the derrière, regardless of the ga-jillions of studies that prove a happy person is a healthy person. You've gotta be really, really, hammer-out-the-details when it comes to getting an insurer to pay up. Even then, it's not over. Your treatment may show up in future records—or even in HIPPA-unprotected files in your company's HR department. For a best, updated list of questions to ask about benefits, choice, limits to numbers of visits, confidentiality and such, go to the Web site of the American Psychological Association's Help Center: www.apahelpcenter.org.

Your First Time

So. You've talked on the phone. You've established whether, when, and how you're paying for this session. You arrive. On time. For real. This is not a spinning class, where you can sneak in unnoticed and hop on a bike in the back. For this, and all future sessions, your therapist—or potential therapist—will set aside an exact block of time for your session. If you're late, you're still going to end at the same time—and you'll still pay the same amount.

You'll likely be in session for forty-five minutes to an hour. Little tip: Skip the mascara, just in case things get teary. Don't be bothered if your therapist looks at her watch. She wasn't born with a built-in timer.

Dar says the first thing to look for in a new therapist is "warmth. Even in very soft-spoken, reserved people, you can still kind of sense that they care about what they're doing." Remember: You're here to feel safe and comfortable. Don't sign up for sessions with someone you just click with.

The second essential element of those initial sessions is, as Dar puts it, "a bell of recognition . . . I've been to three different therapists. Every one of them has one thing in common: They said something insightful in the first session that made me want to come back." Listen for the ding-a-ling. Feel for the rush. You might require Puffs. You might burst out laughing. Not sure if your bell's been rung? Test out how you feel on the way home. If your heart is somehow lighter, if you feel like your session flew by, if you're singing "What Do You Hear in These Sounds" to yourself, then you're on your way, baby!

Remember, whatever you say in session is confidential, between you and your therapist alone.

The Next Sessions

There'll be ups (laughter). There'll be downs (tears). Can we think of one more cliché? Sure we can. How about this one: Therapy isn't always easy.

You'll want to quit. But trust us on this one: Don't. It's when you're most resistant that you're closest to a breakthrough. Feel yourself getting PO'd at your own, personal Dr. Phil? Can't remember what brought you to his show in the first place? These are likely signs that you're struggling against your own progress. Try to stick around. Work through it.

Overall, psychotherapy should feel intriguing, like you're getting a new window into your own life. You should go away with tidbits of insight that feel obvious and ring true. You should notice small changes in your day-to-day life: You watch yourself get angry with your dad, and you express it calmly. You notice when you need more attention, and you ask for it.

It Should Go Without Saying

If your therapist makes sexual advances, quit—and report the unethical doc to a licensing board. If your therapist makes you feel unsafe at all, take off. If Frasier is acting bored or mean or stops paying attention, tell him so. If he betrays the confidentiality of your sessions, quit—and report him to a licensing board.

Do You Tell?

We've found for the very most part, the people who care about you are happy to know that you're doing something to benefit your overall well-being. Still, not everyone appreciates the clearheaded benefits—or the celebrity-based chicness—of psychotherapy. You know you're brave and wise for going. Your boss, however, still refers to therapists as "head-shrinkers." There's no shame in keeping your therapy status on the down-low. But there are extra gold-star points for owning up to your mentally healthy practices. Talk about it, and you'll be doing your part to erase society's last traces of its anti-therapy stigma. Remember, as Dar says, "Therapy is such a non-thing once you do it."

When It's Time to Move On

Here's the thing. Some people stick with their therapists for life. Others like to shake things up a bit, to move on after a year—or even sooner, after a single problem feels resolved.

It takes time to tell a life story—and even more time to let it come out truthfully. Patience is essential. But so is honesty. Feel like you've hit a wall? Speak up. Either there's something in that wall that you're gonna need to dig out, or it's time to move to another place, maybe even another therapist, who can take you in a new direction.

As Dar—and her therapist—say, "We can only go as fast as our emotions let us."

DERMATOLOGIST

Beauty, to me, is about being comfortable in your own skin.
That, or a kick-ass red lipstick.
—GWYNETH PALTROW

The memory is as fresh as yesterday, but it's almost too painful to recall: that fateful junior high morn you awoke, padded to the bathroom, brushed your teeth, looked up at yourself in the mirror . . . and gasped.

Overnight, a crimson mound had sprouted from the tip of your nose, a bright, unwelcome red carnation constellation. It shone. It throbbed. It might have been as small as a pencil's eraser, but it made you feel as sore as the pre-foggy-Christmas-Eve-Rudolph.

Ever since that day, you've been engaged in a touchy-feely war with your skin. Sure, there are days of détente, stretches when fair weather, menstrual conditions, and stress levels magically align to provide the dermatological equivalent of good hair days. On those days, you rejoice. This is it, you think. My skin has finally surrendered. I have won. I have outgrown the breakout.

But then the bump returns. Maybe on your chin. Maybe on your cheek. Maybe beneath your nostril. Hopefully behind your bangs. But it's back, as glaring and mean-spirited as ever.

You'd like to regard this series of eruptions as continued signs of your youthfulness. But until the day society considers zits to be beauty marks, you'll continue to struggle to prevent, destroy, and forever banish them.

Back in the eighth grade, your only weapons were Clearasil Cleanser, a cotton ball, and cover-up. Today, however, you have Dr. Dina Anderson. Wanna know why we picked her to represent? Because when we asked her, "Is it OK to go to the dermo for just one pimple?" she said, "Absolutely."

GO-TO GIRL

Dr. Dina Anderson

Dina's a Manhattan superfly dermo whom we'd swap places with in an instant. World-renowned—she lectures on cosmetic dermatology all over the globe, and even helped introduce Botox to India—she's not above taking time for a patient needing quick zit removal. Most of Dina's patients are women in their twenties and thirties, just the sorts who appreciate that she pipes ambient indie rock through her fun and funky office, a homey Upper East Side brownstone she's decorated with art collected from her travels. In her spare time, Dina teaches at SUNY Downstate Medical Center and serves as dermo in residence at Completely Bare, a luxe Manhattan medispa where she's been lauded as a guru with the Botox, laser hair removal, microdermabrasion, and chemical peels. "I'm in a happy field," she says. "Visiting a dermatologist should be a fun experience."

VOCABULARY CHECK

Medispa: A spa with medical privileges. Often staffed by dermatologists and other medical professionals—but sometimes not—these centers start at your basic, deep-cleansing, one-hour facial and move on up to the latest in cosmetic procedures. The destination medispa is custom-made for the consumer who needs a little R&R with her nips and tucks, peels and pedicures.

Botox: Trademark name for botulinum toxin, an enzyme formerly used to correct muscle twitching and now injected to diminish crow's feet, scowl lines, and worry wrinkles. Results last up to four months. Cost: $250–$500 for each area injected.

Microdermabrasion: A little like that St. Ives apricot scrub, except in this case, crystals and sometimes diamond dust do air-powered exfoliating. Smooths out the appearance of wrinkles. Common in day spas with a medical bent, also available in cosmetic dermatologist's offices. Feels like pleasant scratching. Results last three to six weeks. Cost: $100–$300 per session.

Chemical peel: Aka chemexfoliation, a process that involves application of an often alpha hydroxy–based chemical solution that, in less than a minute, removes dead or damaged skin cells and promotes growth of new skin. Often used to repair sun damage and

(continued)

VOCABULARY CHECK (*continued*)

pill-caused splotching. Can be dangerous if the peel peels too deeply into the skin. Results last a week to a month. Cost: $100–$300 per session.

Laser treatments: High-tech light machines that work lickety-split to treat breakouts, target old scars, and shut down oil glands. Different kinds of light and wavelengths offer different effects and results. (Blue/clear light blasts bacteria and brings down inflammation. Intense Pulse Light—IPL—works on acne, brown spots, rosacea, and hair removal.) Results are virtually permanent. Cost: $250–$850.

Reasons to Go Dermo

The reasons to book a visit to the skin doctor may be as beauty based as frequent hair breakage—or as medically concerning as a misshapen mole. A rule of thumb for what's covered by insurance and what isn't:

Covered. Any medical condition causing pain or concern of future harm: a mole that looks suspicious or bleeds; severe burns, including the sun-induced variety; a toenail-crumbling foot fungus; a rash caused by anything from allergic reactions to poison ivy.

Not covered. Treatment for pigmentation issues, especially common on darker-skinned women and women on the pill; hair removal; chemical peels; microdermabrasion; acne, even the cystic, scarring kind; Botox.

Detecting a Dermo

"Most of the time, the best way is to ask your friends for a reference," says Dina. "It's just a good way to find out. A lot of patients will be in a certain health plan, so it's also important to find a doctor in your network." Check with your health care provider to find out if you need a referral to have your visit approved for coverage.

Dermo Tabs

Most practices—but not all—charge an initial consultation fee that costs more than any following visit fees. Expect to spend $100–$300 for a first time—again, covered or partially covered if your dermatological concern is not of, as Dina says, the "I don't like this and I want it off" variety. Follow-up visits usually fall in the $75–$175 range. Expect to pay additional fees for additional procedures.

Dermo Details

You arrive. You sign in. You fill out some general paperwork. "Expect to wait, but not more than twenty minutes," says Dina. Once you're in the examination room, you strip down to your skivvies and put on your typical couture medical gown—no matter whether you're in for something on your face or an initial visit, they do an overall body check.

The doctor comes in. She'll look over your chart. She'll ask you what medications you're taking. She'll look you over, attend to your itchy rashes, burns, and nail fungus. She might even write you a prescription.

You'll spend ten to fifteen minutes talking. This is the time to bring up your cosmetic concerns. Maybe irregular periods are causing cystic acne. Maybe your autoclave sterilizer-less nail salon is causing your nail beds to yellow and crumble. Your diet or hair processing could be the reason you're losing your locks. Maybe you're interested in cosmetic procedures. Maybe you want to know if it's OK to go for aromatherapy facials at your favorite salon (it is).

She'll do a body check for aberrant moles, morphed, raised freckles that have asymmetry, irregular borders, color variations, and diameters bigger than a pencil top. She'll draw a nifty little constellation-looking mole map (your moles are the stars, your bod is the galaxy). She'll biopsy anything suspicious: a tiny shot to numb the skin, a swift slice, a possible stitch, a careful application of goo and a Band-Aid. In less than five minutes, you're done and outta there.

Dina's Peeves

Sun. "My patients' number one problem is the sun," she says. "People continue to go in the sun, even if they have a family history of skin cancer . . . Melanoma is the number one killer of women ages twenty to twenty-nine. It's very important to avoid the sun and to get your moles checked—even under your feet and on your scalp."

Picking. "My number two problem is people who pick at their face a lot. For young women, this is a big thing. Picking at pimples leaves scars, especially if you have fair skin." If you insist on picking, make sure that the pimple's grown a head, that your face and hands are as clean as whistles, and that you don't push. "I hate to say this, but if you must, you can make a little knick in it." Also: Older skin heals much more slowly than young skin. Think before you squeeze.

High-tech skin care without proper supervision. "I don't think salons or spas should be operating high-powered machines without extensive training or authority. Some states have very gray laws about this. In New York, there has to be an MD in charge, but he can be in another city." The danger of getting a peel from a poor practitioner: "I've seen so many cases of scarring, blistering, and permanent pigmentation scars from hair removal and chemical peels that go too deep." Instead, seek out a medical office or medispa where doctors and nurses perform these procedures.

Dina's Free Advice

Diet. "I recommend that teenagers drink organic milk, because a lot of regular milk has hormones in it."

"I do believe antioxidants help." Antioxidant-rich foods: wild blueberries, red beans, raspberries, strawberries, pecans, sweet cherries, black plums, artichokes, cranberries. "Patients who have rosacea should avoid spicy food, alcohol, and caffeine."

Daily Skin care. Are the caviar creams and platinum body butters worth their price tags? "No. A lot of that stuff is marketing. Cetaphil cleanser, Aveeno, even Neutrogena products, like their powder with SPF30, are popular with my patients." Although frequent breakouts and other common concerns require special products.

"You do need to keep your face out of the sun and wear sunscreen. Smoking and drinking cause constriction of your blood vessels, and all kinds of bad things."

MASSAGE

This book is a book of firsts. Many of these firsts are important steps in a woman's life. Many are just fun things to do. But not one single one—except, perhaps, chocolate—compares to this, your first massage.

Because when it comes to stripping down, crawling up on a padded table, shimmying under that white sheet, and resigning your aching muscles to a pair of strong, supple hands, a girl's first time is indeed a very beautiful thing.

Ask any deflowered massage recipient about the first time she was touched by an angelic massage therapist. She'll be able to recite the exact hour, spa's address, name of the Enya album that was wafting through the stereo system, and how afterward she was in such a supremely relaxed state that she required assistance locating not only her credit card but also her car keys, car, and hands and feet to operate the vehicle.

Massage regulars have a certain expression for this state of dreamy, weightless, limpless, relaxation, but because it sounds a whole lot seamier than it is, we'll just let you find out for yourself. On the street, this state can be confused with being under the influence of a mild sedative, a bottle of champagne, or a quarter ounce of Humboldt County's finest. But it's not. It's pure bliss—and it should be preserved as long as possible, even if that means going home, lying on the floor to admire the ceiling for hours on end, or swinging by the park, removing your shoes, and dancing barefoot on the grass.

But we've gotten ahead of ourselves. Because to those of us who don't regularly disrobe for strangers—and who especially don't disrobe and then submit to a full-body touching by a stranger—a first massage can be an intimidating prospect.

Let us console you with this fabulous truth: Unlike Roquefort cheese or top-shelf martinis, a good massage takes little to no time to develop a taste for. It's just a matter of getting over that first hurdle: nudity.

Which really isn't a hurdle. Because if you don't want to be nude, you don't have to, thanks to:

Chair Massage

You: Fully clothed, sit in a kind of reverse chair, where the chair back is in the front and you are leaning into it.

Therapist: Works on your back, shoulders, and neck, usually for about ten or fifteen minutes, or by the minute.

Shiatsu

You: Fully, loosely clothed, lie on a mat on the floor.

Therapist: Manipulates your arms, legs, and back while encouraging deep breathing.

Thai Massage

You: Fully clothed, sit on a flat surface.

Therapist: Helps you into yoga-like poses and makes adjustments.

These are all great places to start—or to stay. But it must be said that there is something wholly liberating about a traditional massage that requires the massaged to get totally—or at least mostly—naked.

An Argument for Naked

One of the first things a person learns at massage school is draping. Draping is the art of arranging sheets and towels, of turning away or holding up a sheet when someone is turning over, and of generally keeping undercover body parts that are illegal for an adult to display at most American beaches. (In other words, whether you're facing up or down, a sheet hides your stuff.)

And, just in case we need to clarify things a little more: Like it or not (and we kind of like it), you are topless. So the real question is: Undies or not? Massage recipients disagree on the answer. But any good massage therapist will tell you, bottoms on or off are both acceptable. (Trust us: They've seen it all.)

KINDS OF MASSAGE (AKA "BODYWORK")

Aromatherapy: An essential-oil-based rubdown that might include your choice of lavender or chamomile for soothing and calming, rose for confidence, peppermint for energy and mental clarity.

Reiki: Japanese for "universal life energy," a soft-touch session that aims to channel healing energy to the recipient. Feel free to keep your clothes on for this one.

Swedish: What we think of when we think massage: sweeping strokes and gentle kneading to work out tension, increase circulation, and promote relaxation.

Deep tissue: Swedish but stronger, where strong thumbs or hard elbows seriously knead knots and tight places. Virgins beware: This can hurt.

Hot stone: Where smooth and warm basalt stones first rest on your back, relaxing its muscles, then are used for the massage itself.

Targeted (hands and feet): An extended version of the quick rubdown your hands and legs get during manis and pedis, a great quickie service if you don't have time for the whole deal.

Reflexology: In a nutshell: Each l'il spot on the foot represents an organ. When the therapist moves a piggy, she's really soothing your kidneys. China, Egypt, and India have been doing this fancy footwork for pretty much ever.

Myofascial: A therapeutic version of the deep tissue massage. This bodywork involves stretching, movement, and controlled breathing in order to increase blood and oxygen flow to impaired muscles by detaching the fascia (thin transparent connective tissue) from the underlying muscle tissue. (Didn't think we would get all medical on you, did you?)

Rolfing: A technique that involves extreme manipulation of the joints with a stated goal of structurally reorganizing the body. Ouch. For the masochist in you, this—also known as "structural integration"—has a near-cult following of practitioners and advocates.

Bottoms On: The Pros

You're guaranteed your privacy. This can make you more relaxed, especially if your massage therapist doesn't have body parts in common with you.

The elastic waistband of your drawers is a good place to tuck in a sheet.

Bottoms On: The Cons

Restriction of blood flow, especially if your drawers are of the control persuasion.

Drawers on is a sign that you don't want a glutes rub. And we gotta say, if you sit, run, walk, drive, or ride a lot, you could use a little bum-steered attention.

Massage Clients' Bill of Rights

- You have the right to request a specific therapist.
- You have the right to request, more generally, a male or female therapist.
- You have the right to keep your drawers on (see above).
- You have the right to arrive very early to relax in the lounge with a book or a magazine and a cup of mint water.
- You have the right to make conversation or to request silence. (A simple "I've been yapping all day and am very much looking forward to this quiet time" at the start of the session should do the trick.)
- You have the right to ask about changing the atmosphere: Is the room close to a ringing phone or busy hallway? Are you too hot or too cold? Do you have a music preference? Request ambience adjustments at the start of the session, before you hop up on the table.
- During the massage, you have the right to say, "That area feels a little tender," "Can you go deeper?," and "Oooo, that's great."
- You have the right to ask that your head remain untouched by oils, oily hands, or hands at all.

Tipping

Just like at the brasserie or the beauty shop, you give your caretaker a gratuity that reflects an additional 15–20 percent of the service fee. This is true even if the therapist owns the place. We know, we know, it didn't used to be that way. But that's the etiquette now. We even checked with Peggy Post, Emily's great-granddaughter-in-law. (If the owner you're tipping doesn't follow tipping trends, she'll say so.)

Things We Love to Receive

Gift certificates for massages.

Things We Love to Give

Gift certificates for massages.

Women Who Need a Good Massage

- Your pregnant friend
- Your engaged friend
- Your stressed-out friend
- Your friend who has everything
- Your friend who has very little
- Your friend in graduate school

- Your friend in a new job
- Your boss
- Your co-worker
- Your subordinate
- Your mom, aunt, and sisters
- You, as often as possible

YOGA CLASS

Yoga is not a work out. It's a work in.
—JOAN WHITE, TEACHER OF ADVANCED IYENGAR

Yoga is a many-mysteried thing. To us regular-type, non-yoga practitioners, the central mystery may be: How does sitting cross-legged and chanting "om" explain the seven bodily wonders of the celebrity world? Namely:

Madonna's biceps
Sting's sexual stamina
Sarah Jessica Parker's post-baby six-pack
Kristen Davis's calves
Kate Hudson's ability to make Uggs look haute couture-esque
Everything about Christy Turlington

(OK, so that's six. But when you're in touch with your inner self, do numbers really matter?)

Put the mystery more succinctly, and it becomes: What is it about yoga?

Why has your gym converted an aerobics studio into a meditation room? Why are your spinning classmates trading in their cycling shoes for sticky mats? Here's why. According to the legions of deflowered, Prana-pants-wearing yogins, a good yoga class easily bests a run on the treadmill, a go around the circuit training course, and, according to a few, a romp in the sack.

We love yoga's quietness. Its slowness. Its ability to calm us down and wake us up. Its power to strengthen some muscles and relax others. Did you know that Karim Abdul-Jabbar practiced yoga through his entire basketball career—and never missed a game because of an injury? We knew! That is why Karim Abdul-Jabbar is the seventh wonder of the celebrity yoga world.

There's no denying that this world of hatha (movement) yoga has grown to confusing proportions. You got your vinyasa. You got your iyengar, your ashtanga, bikram, power yoga, gentle yoga, athletic, and flow.

Then, there are your instructors: friendly burners of incense, strict rule-player-byers, graceful ballerina types, rote drill sergeants, joke-cracking ektar players, stretchy showoffs, and, of course, the Yoga Instructor You Want to Follow Home Like a Puppy Dog, aka the Yoga Instructor Whose Life You Covet. So before you attempt the lotus pose, it's important to know which yoga is right for you.

Way Before You Go

Decide what you want from the class, based on who you are. Here's a yes/no quiz, with the answers right alongside of it, because who ever has the energy to turn a page upside down to look for answers?

Are you flexible?

Yes: Good for you. Go to a beginner's class.
No: Good for you. Go to a beginner's class.

Are you in shape?

Yes: Good for you. Go to a beginner's class.
No: Good for you. Go to a beginner's class.

Do you want to relax during class?

Yes: Avoid classes with "power" or "sports" in their descriptions. Avoid bikram or ashtanga. Hatha, vinyasa, and flow will work best.
No: See below.

Do you seek a sweat-drenched struggle to make it through the hour-and-a-half workout?

Yes: Try the power stuff. But be warned: This is where people get hurt most often (see below).

No: Look for classes whose descriptions include "gentle" or "basics."

Are you injured?

Yes: Be careful. Yoga may look easy, but it can do serious damage if taught by someone who pushes you too hard or who lacks extensive training. Iyengar classes have the most rigorous certification program for teachers and were developed specifically for students with physical issues or restrictions. Also, very important: Tell your teacher about your injury before class begins.

No: Good for you. But take it easy the first time anyway.

Do you like orderliness, and to know exactly what to expect?

Yes: You might be a candidate for ashtanga or bikram. The first is an unchanging series of challenging movements that flow from sun salutations to balancing poses. The second is the biggest brand of hot yoga, where instructors use scripted phrases to teach the same series of twenty-six poses in classrooms that are 105 degrees Farenheit. Of course, if you like orderliness but hate to sweat—and would rather not look at yourself in the mirror while twisted into pretzel-type shapes—this may not be the way to go.

No: Look for classes described as "vinyasa," "hatha," "flow," "kripalu," or "iyengar."

Do you crave philosophy with your class?

Yes or No: All schools of yogas have quiet instructors and Chatty Cathy instructors. Some may quote or read from the Yoga Sutras, a series of thousands of years–old Hindu texts laying out the many splendors of yoga. Other teachers like to read poetry. Still others take to quoting themselves. Or singing. You gotta try on before you buy in.

Are you deeply religious?

Yes: Fear not. No one is trying to convert you. Yoga as we know it is not a religion. It is a mind-body practice based on the idea that the more you stretch and strengthen your body, the more you stretch and strengthen your mind, the more patient you are with your body, the more patient you'll be with yourself and others, the nicer you are to yourself, the nicer you'll be.

No: Don't worry about it.

So, You've Picked Out a Class

Two to three hours before: Stop eating. Stop caffeinating. Juice is OK. Water is better. Lots of it, especially if you're going to a hot yoga class.

One to two hours before: Have you bathed today? Please do. Nobody appreciates a stinky yogini.

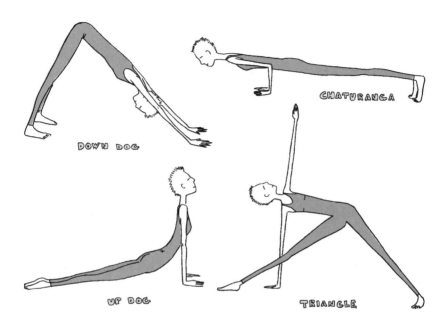

DOWN DOG

CHATURANGA

UP DOG

TRIANGLE

One hour before: Dress. Yoga pants are cute, but some instructors want to see your ankles and knees, so be prepared to pull them up. Shorts are fine—mandatory for heated-room yogas like bikram. Tank tops are better than T-shirts, but T-shirts are fine, too.

Five to fifteen minutes before: Arrive at class. Lateness is regarded by most instructors and students as a major interruption, especially when the late arrival coincides with the quiet sitting period at the start of class. If you must be late, enter once the class has started moving. And apologize after class. (But if you're more than fifteen minutes late, don't be surprised if you're asked to come back another time, on time.)

Essential to remember: Have an open mind and an empty belly.

Before Class

Take off your shoes. Take off your socks.

Grab a mat. If other students are sitting on blankets, grab a couple of those too. If other students have also taken objects including belts, Styrofoam blocks, or bolster pillows from the supply area, grab those too.

Have a seat in a simple cross-legged position.

Did you remember to tell the instructor that you have a bad back/ankle issues/a sore shoulder/a broken toe? Is this your first class ever? Quick. Tell the teach before she gets going.

During Class

Take your time. Most yoga classes last ninety minutes. There's no rush to get it right; you'll have plenty more chances.

Watch your breath. When you notice yourself holding your inhalations, grunting, panting, etc., take it down a few notches.

Can't do a pose? Go into child's pose (kneeling, with butt on heels and belly on thighs, arms outstretched: Think Muslim prayer position).

YOGA VOCABULARY

Hatha: Movement-related yoga, the most general term

Asana: A yoga pose

Vinyasa: Flow yoga, usually starring the classic sun salutation which is, in its most basic form, a toe-touch, pushup, moving into an upside-down V called downward-facing dog

Ashtanga: A series of poses that includes sun salutations and ends in balances

Bikram: Twenty-six patented, unchanging poses in front of a mirror and in a room heated to 105 degrees

Iyengar: A practice emphasizing precision of poses, often involves props (belts, blocks, rope walls, bolsters, folding chairs), ideal for anyone with an injury, or anyone not wanting to be injured

Power yoga: Challenging vinyasa, often in a hot room, yoga that emphasizes physical feats over form

Got your period? Good news: no headstands, handstands, shoulder stands, arm balances, or upside-down anything for you. Instead: down dog or child's pose.

After Class

Provided you haven't fallen into a deep dream state during final savasana (where you lie on your back with eyes closed and palms up), you turn to the right side, sit up (eyes still closed), go back to crossed legs, and thank your instructor by saying, "Namaste" (pronounced *na-ma-stay*). (Translation: "The divine light in me recognizes the divine light in you.") Or, if you're not in the Sanskrit mood, "Thank you." There's no right or wrong answer to how often you should go to yoga class. Instructors like to say that even a few minutes a day of quiet stretching is beneficial.

SPA TRIP

The Calgon just isn't doing it anymore. Nor is your biweekly mani-pedi. The last time you treated yourself to an hour aromatherapy massage, the lavender oil just began to take effect around minute 58. You've tried to break the evil spell of a stressful lifestyle. You've gone on long weekends, done the extended holiday weekend, taken impromptu days off, run to your folks' place for quality time wrestling the dog and snuggling under Grandma's crocheted blankets.

But somehow, no matter where you go, you always wind up rushing around, trying to cram in cocktails with Cousin Sue and football games with Dad, scheduling four museum visits on a Saturday, using your extra few hours to begin ambitious baking projects, and, when it all catches up with you, spending your next free Sunday sleeping until four in the afternoon, leaving you a mere six to seven hours to shower, dress, eat, and go back to sleep until you have to get up for work the next day.

What you need is a real getaway. To a place where the toughest choices that face you are morning hike or sunrise yoga? Whole grain pancakes or homemade granola? Hot stone massage or mud bath? A place where your greatest responsibility is dressing yourself in the morning—and that's an easy one, because your wardrobe options are limited to the contents of your suitcase or the fluffy white terry robe hanging in the closet.

This magical, mystical, healing place is a destination spa. You may have to travel a distance to get there. You may have to dip into your savings to swing it. But you're going. And that's that.

Who Goes to Spas

Mostly women. Women of all shapes and sizes and physical abilities. Stressed-out women. Leisurely women. Women who want to lose weight. Women who want to lose the daily grind. Women who want to be alone. Women who want to be together.

Once in a while, a man. (But chances are, a woman brought him there.)

How to Find Spas

Travel & Leisure. Condé Nast Traveler. www.spafinder.com. www.leadingspasoftheworld.com. *Life & Style, Star,* and *US Weekly* to check out where the celebs are getting scrubbed and rubbed and put to bed early. A relaxed-looking rich woman. Your yoga instructor. Your massage therapist.

How to Afford a Spa

Off-season. Work bonus. Birthday money. Frequent flyer miles. Bank robbery.

What to Pack

Yoga fashions. Hiking fashions. Tennis fashions. Gym fashions. One all-purpose wrap skirt or dress. Fun reading in the form of novels with pink covers, gossip mags. Inspiring reading in the form of poetry, or at least something ambitious with a cover large enough to hide aforementioned nonliterary items.

Chocolate. Champagne. Cigarettes (not necessarily to smoke: just to make you feel like a rebel).

Cash: $5, $10, and $20 bills for tips.

Whom to Take

A girlfriend you don't see often enough. A co-worker, but only if the two of you solemnly swear to ban all office talk. Your mom. Your grandmother. Your sister. Your sister-in-law. Your favorite aunt or cousin. Your college chums. Yourself.

GO-TO GIRL

Annika Jackson

General Manager of the
Generally Fabulous Mii amo Spa

This is one Go-to Girl to know. From the mystic setting of Sedona, Arizona, Annika runs one of the world's must luxe—luxe-est?—boutique spas. Mii amo's sixteen guest rooms, five theme itineraries, and endless treatment options are proof that a virgin gets what a virgin pays for. Why do seasoned spa-o-phites flock to this place? "Simply to have a luxury vacation, or because they want to start working with a personal trainer, or want to learn to cook with less salt, want to explore the spiritual nature of Sedona, or just de-stress by learning yoga and meditation," says our new best pal. Mii amo pampers its guests with cinnamon facials and floating-in-water massages, challenges them with cardio and chakra yoga, fills 'em with whole foods—but still has room for a relaxed policy on cocktail hour. "We're not a boot camp. If somebody wants to have a margarita at the pool, we allow it." See? We told you Annika was the Go-to to know.

How Most Spas Work

You book your reservation: Rates are static, no matter if you're booking online or over the phone.

You book your various spa treatments. At popular spots, appointments for massage, foot, face, and all other manner of bodily care book up long before guests arrive, and, at most places, cost extra. Reserve more treatments than you think you need. Most spas allow cancellations without penalty with twenty-four hours' notice but availability of appointments can be scarce. Once you're there, the sixty bucks you shell out for the Happy Hands and Feet Package will seem like small change.

You check in. You go to your room. You receive a schedule of activities, like at camp, except none is mandatory. These activities may include, but are not limited to, aerobics, water aerobics, stretch, strength training, classes targeted to bodily areas, yoga, Nia, Feldenkrais, golf, tennis, squash, meditation, pottery, nutrition, making dream catchers.

You eat in a common dining room, sometimes at an assigned table. You may sit alone. You may sit with strangers. These strangers may be great. These strangers may be nuts. It's the chance you take if you need a little conversation. Food is buffet style or served to the table. Dishes are often labeled for nutritional value, or calorie, fat, and carb content. Caffeine is often discouraged. Alcohol is rarely served.

Let's repeat this last one. Cocktail hour, wine with dinner, wine spritzers with lunch, brunchtime Bloody Marys are not part of most spa repertoires (Mii amo is the delightful exception.) Regard this fact as

SPAS WE LIKE

Bronze: Do-able Day Spas: You're not sleeping over and there's no fiber-rich meal plan, but you'll get some of the best pampering around ($200 for two to three hours of services). Belladonna Day Spa in New Orleans, Tru in San Francisco, Aqua in Santa Monica, Rescue Rittenhouse Spa Lounge in Philadelphia, Key Lime Pie in Atlanta, Bliss in New York City.

Silver: Great Getaways: You're splurging—but only a little—for the whole shebang ($300–$400-ish per day for à la carte or all-inclusive deals). Rancho La Puerta in Tecate, Mexico; Green Valley Spa in Las Vegas; Two Bunch Palms in Desert Hot Springs, California; New Age Health Spa in Neversink, New York.

Gold: Exceptional Escapes: Really, can one assign something as cold and as unfeeling as a monetary value to such well-deserved R&R? (All-inclusive packages range $400–$500 per day.) Mii amo in Sedona; Hilton Head Institute in Hilton Head; Lake Austin in Austin; Green Valley Spa in St. George, Utah; Sonnenalp Spa in Vail.

Platinum: Pampering at a Price: For those times when you really, truly need to be treated like a princess. (All-inclusive packages exceed $500 per day.) Miraval in Catalina, Arizona; The Golden Door in Escondido, California; Maya Tulum in Tulum, Mexico; SpaHalekulani at Halekulani in Honolulu.

something to embrace. You are at a spa, not at a resort or on a cruise. Enjoy the detox, with all the healthful buzz therein. And, when all else fails, break into your stash of smuggled champagne.

PERSONAL TRAINER

> *We're here to pump* [clap] *you up.*
> —SATURDAY NIGHT LIVE, HANS AND FRANZ

A personal assistant. A personal chef. A personal stylist, valet, or masseuse. Wouldn't it be nice? Doesn't it seem out of reach?

A personal trainer, however, is one of those luxuries that's not as extravagant as it sounds. Sure, paying someone to set weight machines and to count reps is somewhat superfluously indulgent. But at least it's superfluously indulgent in a thoroughly good-for-you way.

Sessions with a personal trainer won't be like saving last year's over-the-top bejeweled designer flip-flops, too ridiculous to wear but too expensive to give away. Nor will hiring a personal trainer cause regret akin to that resulting from a bad investment, a trip to a casino, an evening of $12 cosmopolitans, or a hot fudge sundae.

Hiring a personal trainer will, however, ensure that you go to the gym faithfully. It will teach you new ways to exercise. It will breathe new life into your same ol' fitness regime. It will teach you how to use new machines and unfamiliar devices. It will tone parts of your body you thought could never shape up—and transform other parts you didn't know existed.

Most important: A personal trainer will make workouts whiz by.

All Trainers

You want someone with a college degree in health and physical education, or exercise physiology. Not only that, you want someone with certification from the National Strength and Conditioning Association or the National Academy of Sports Medicine (which keep trainers up-to-date), plus liability insurance and certification in CPR and first aid.

Unlike chefs and artists, personal trainers can't pass muster by claiming to be "self-taught."

You want someone who's done this before. Best to seek out a trainer with at least two years of experience, more if you have an injury or less-than-average physical situation.

Not so sure? Ask for references.

An experiential bonus: if the trainer is or has been a competitive athlete. Athletes know firsthand that discipline and hard work are the keys to achieving fitness goals.

Beware . . .

The chatty trainer. Especially if you plan to use what you learn in a solo workout. (If you're talking about what happened last night on *The Daily*

Show, you won't remember how to position yourself on the ab buster when you come back to try it alone.)

The newbie trainer. Who might be enthusiastic, but might not understand how your old skiing injury affects your ability to do curls.

The pushy trainer. Who could harm your bod by exceeding its limits. Trainers should be protecting you from injury, not causing it. You ought to be sore the day after a session—but not the week after.

The celebrity trainer. Who can charge more for less just because he once handed Janet Jackson a towel.

The jaded trainer. Who gravitates toward the same machines for everybody on each workout.

The know-it-all trainer. Who thinks exercise is the end-all cure-all, has no sympathy for your inability to get rid of that freshman fifteen, doles out medical diagnoses, and recommends herbal supplements.

Gym Trainers

Most trainers work on the staff of health clubs. Maybe you've noticed one of them standing over a grunting man kneeling on the glute buster, as she counts to fifteen with a bemused look in her eye. She'd be a cool one to work out with.

Here's the deal with training in a gym. You must train with one of the trainers on staff. You may not bring in a trainer from elsewhere. Trainers from other places are not insured to train in your gym. Trainers from your gym are insured.

Likewise, a gym trainer can't bring in a non-gym member for training sessions. You have to be a member of the gym, too.

So, while you spin your feet on the elliptical trainer or lie back for a few bench presses, take note of the trainers working there. In other words: Spy. Is there one who looks serious? (Do you want someone serious?) Is there one who appears funny? (Do you want someone funny?)

The easiest route is to get a recommendation from an in-training friend. (This goes for private trainers, too.)

The one—surprising—thing to ignore is appearance. We know it sounds counterintuitive. But hear this. The extra-buff bodybuilder with perfect chocolate bar abs may provide great visual inspiration, but he doesn't necessarily know how to motivate you after a long day at the office. Look instead for experience. And that's in any trainer. Even in a . . .

Private Trainer

A private trainer could be a trainer who has his own workout studio, or a trainer who makes house calls. The latter, quite obviously, requires that you have the home gym. Make sure this person carries liability insurance.

HOW TO KEEP YOUR TRAINER HAPPY

Give twenty-four hours' notice before rescheduling—or expect to pay full price for a missed session.

Work out between sessions. Getting in regular DIY sessions with yourself benefits you because

- You'll learn how to manipulate machines, those giant blowup balls, and free weights on your own. This will come in handy for times when you can't be with your trainer.
- You'll be stretching your money: The more you become accustomed to machines, etc., the less time your trainer will have to spend on setup and instruction.
- But most of all: You'll reach your fitness goals faster. Especially if your goal is weight loss. A rule of thumb: Work out three times a week to maintain weight. Work out four or more times a week to lose it.

If you don't work out between sessions—and if you stick to poor eating habits—don't gripe that you're not seeing results. Complaints from clients looking for a quick and easy fix are a personal trainer's biggest pet peeve.

GO-TO GIRL

Dylan Lauren   Owner of Giant Candy Store,
                                    Daughter of Fashion Icon

When you're Dylan Lauren, you've got two times the reasons to work out. First, you're Ralph Lauren's daughter and, therefore, have a familial responsibility to look awesome in Dad's all-American couture. Second, you're the gummy-candy–addicted owner of Dylan's Candy Bar, a New York City sweets store that's basically the Wonka factory meets Barneys. A lifelong athlete, Dylan supplements her daily six-to-eight-mile runs with twice weekly sessions with trainer Tony Molina at his oh-so-clubby Evolution Studio. "Tony doesn't let me get away with things," says Dylan. He keeps her lunging, balancing on balls, and sticking to a healthful diet. Well, except for one, essential part of her daily routine. Dylan's mantra: "I believe you can eat candy and stay fit."

Paying for a Trainer

Rates are hourly and generally $30–$100 per one-hour session.

Discounts. Gym-based trainers charge a fixed rate. Self-employed trainers might hook you up if you prepay for several sessions.

Big budget. What you can get: house calls or private sessions, which may include nutritional counseling and, if you're really lucky, gossip about the day's session with various supermodels who love to brag about how they never work out.

Moderate budget. What you can get: a reliable coach with good reputation and solid client list, and proven track record.

Low budget. What you can get: a trainer who's willing to design a fitness program for you and check in on your progress each month.

A trainer who's willing to take on two clients at once. (The way this works best is if you and a buddy have similar workout goals and physical abilities. Plus, you and your pal can motivate each other between sessions.) Rates per hour are higher, but you're splitting costs.

3

SPIRITS & SUSTENANCE

Back in the day, it was an all-out battle: you versus Spinach, in a title match that lasted from main course through dessert. There you sat, bottom planted on chair, eyes affixed to a giant mound of steamed, buttered greens. Your mother cajoled. You refused. The mound grew chilly. You held strong. Your siblings snickered. Dad extracted a half gallon of chocolate marshmallow ice cream from the freezer. You clung to your fork, staging your own, personal protest against this—and, indeed, all vegetables. Sometimes, you won out. But more often than not, the spinach prevailed.

These days, you can't get enough of those leafy greens. You eat them tossed in bacony salads, tucked into ricotta-rich lasagna, filling layers of phyllo and feta: hot, cold, tepid, whatever. You savor every last, Popeye-fied bite.

Behold, hungry virgins, a greatest joy of growing a wee bit older: Your taste buds mellow—and you develop a palate. Suddenly, you find joy in Roquefort, bluefish, portobellos, pine nuts, and the official sprouts of Brussels. Your days of conscientious spinach objection are through. You bask in the glorious dawn of a new dining era. So, rise up! Rejoice! And, while you're at it: Eat, drink, and rejoin the eating race! The world is your oyster. Now's the time to figure out which fork to use to eat it.

FOUR-STAR RESTAURANT

> *Life itself is the proper binge.*
> —JULIA CHILD

Your favorite food is anything that can be described as finger. Your idea of a nice restaurant is one that serves its entire menu in colorful plastic baskets and employs name-tagged servers who call you "hon." You think all truffles are made of chocolate and sweetbreads involve cinnamon, sugar and dough. Your favorite meal: breakfast all day.

Bless you, my biscuit. You are a woman after our own, familiar food–comforted hearts. But as much as we know where you're coming from, as much as we share your love for plain dealing blue plate specials and the occasional TV dinner, we feel compelled to break this news: It's time to join the world of grown-up eaters. Time to trade in your frequent sandwich buyer card for a bona fide dinner reservation. It's time, fellow sister at the lunch counter, to dine fine . . . at a four star.

A four star, you say? Aren't those places staffed exclusively by thick-accented servers named Pierre-François and Claude-Thierry-Jacques who stare down their neat little mustaches at diners who order anything less than vintage Dom and beluga (as if you knew what exactly those things were, aside from prohibitively expensive)? Who in her right mind would pay more for a five-course meal than she'd pay for a car repair?

Dear. Darling. Adorable lover of waffles past midnight. Four-star restaurants are not just for preening gourmets and self-important

princesses. They're for me. They're for you. Most of all: They're totally fun—and completely unforgettable.

Fear not the Périgord truffle shavings, or the panoply of gleaming silver and crystal that borders your place setting. The cardinal trick to surviving—and thoroughly enjoying—a meal at Maisonette, The French Laundry, Charlie Trotter's, The Mansion at Turtle Creek (and a righteous handful of other elegant houses of delicious excess) is a lot like the trick to enjoying a massage (see page 64): The more you let yourself be taken care of, the more you'll savor it.

Behold, the four-star 411.

GO-TO GIRL

Gail Simmons   Merchandising Manager for
                                    Food & Wine Magazine

Blossoming food world citizen Gail went from writer to culinary student to Le Cirque chef to assistant to illustrious *Vogue* writer Jeffrey Steingarten to marketing guru at *Food & Wine.* If the restaurant's a big deal, she's been there. Nonetheless, her fondest dining out memory is of wearing red patent leather pumps when she was eight years old and—gasp—riding an elevator to a fancy meal with her family. Ah, "the pomp and circumstance of going to a place that required an elevator and party shoes!" she says. Her next big time out was an eight-course lunch chez Jean

Georges, where she remembers "being so drunk on the whole experience of the food and the wine and flow of the waiters and the head spinning-ness of it all." She was hooked. Her best advice for first timers: "If you're going to eat something adventurous, a four-star restaurant is the place to try it."

Before You Go

- Inquire about the dress code. Then stick to it. This is not the night to test the so-called go-everywhere-ability of your strategically holey $300 jeans.
- Skip the perfume. Taste is inexorably linked to smell. You wouldn't drink that bottle of Creed, so please don't wear it *à table*.
- Stock up on small bills. You'll need $2 per coat for the coat check, a few more if you're valet parking.
- Program the restaurant's phone number into your cell. Call ahead if you expect to be a minute over five minutes late (a-hem, if you're going to be six or more minutes late).
- Expect to spend at least three hours at dinner. At least. If you make post-meal plans, allow at least four hours.

YOUR RIGHTS
(as reinterpreted from the official taxicab
passenger's bill of rights)

- You have the right to ask questions.
- You have the right to request ice (tap) water.
- You have the right to drink bottled water, and once you've finished a bottle, to request ice water.
- You have the right to be on a budget. If the $200 Margaux recommended by the sommelier is out of your price range, ask, "Is there anything else you'd suggest?" If that hint goes unnoticed, simply state your budget. "I would like to stay under $70 a bottle" works well. (Go-to Gail reassures us, "A great restaurant won't have a bad bottle on the menu.")

Virgin's Downfalls (and Their Remedies)

We'd like to give you a play-by-play of what happens when a girl doesn't get it right the first time. No worries, though; she can always be born again. Take heed.

You're late. Fashionably late does not apply to restaurant reservations. If your table is booked for 8:30 and you're still debating little black dress versus saucy flamenco frock at 8:15, make a realistic estimate of your ETA, phone the restaurant, and be honest. You *will* lose your table if you're fifteen minutes late and haven't called and your name doesn't happen to be Gwyneth.

You don't like a dish. This is a tricky one. If you are sure and certain the contents of your plate don't match the description on the menu, you may use your best firm manners to hail a server, to explain the misunderstandings, to send it back and quickly to order a replacement. Warning: These actions are likely to disrupt the progress of service and may cause your fellow diners distress, because they'll feel bad eating in front of a foodless you. If you do return to sender, be sure to put the table at ease by politely insisting they dive in. On the other hand, if the unpleasurable dish facing you is one of multiple courses—and especially if you are not footing the bill—you might want to chalk this one up to a learning experience, and make a mental note for next time that as far as you're concerned, crispy organ duos are not going to be part of your dining future.

You need to spit out food. Emily Post is adamant on this count. Use your forefinger and thumb. Others say, remove the un-swallowable bit with the utensil that put it there in the first place. All agree: Bones, pits, etc. go on the edge of your plate. You may cover any offensive expectorants with food. Never spit because you simply don't like. Never ever spit into a napkin.

You spill. Please, no squealing. You're not the first—and won't be the last. Dab for a minimum time period. If you absolutely must, ask the server to meet you at the restroom door with a cup of club soda.

You drop your napkin, knife, roll. Leave it where it fell. Servers should notice and replace the fallen object. If they don't, ask for a new one. Say thank you.

Little Things That Mean a Lot

The bare hands. It's becoming increasingly permissible to eat with your fingers, especially when it comes to the case of the omnipresent four-star french fry. Silverware remains the preferred method, however. If in doubt, ask your table mates for permission to proceed flatware-free.

The thank you. These two words will get you further than duking the maître d' or donning your plunging-est neckline. The host pulls out your chair, you say "Thank you." The server clears your plate: "Thank you." A busboy refills your water: "Thank you."

BORN-AGAIN VIRGIN

Sally Special Order has *dîner'*d chez Jean Georges and supped in style at Seeger's. She can identify Mario Batali and Thomas Keller on sight. Trouble is, she's forever letting her dining quirks—including those pesky, trendy food-group-excluding diets—get in the way of Meal Appreciation 101. Sally requests bisque sans crème, main courses sans starch, foie gras sans fat. Her waistline looks great, but her behavior itself is a waste. Sal, doll, four stars don't do sauce on the side; chefs' creations are not yours to makeover. If you want to conserve calories, take small bites. Just for *ce soir, le restaurant* is in charge. Sally is a born-again virgin.

The reposing of the hand-beaded clutch. The lap is the preferred location. By your side on a banquette runs a close second. The floor is acceptable, but there it runs the risk of getting smashed, spilled on, or snatched (you'd be surprised how often this last one occurs in high end restaurants). Dangling it from the back of your chair is a no-no.

The beauty of the small bite. Once the food is on its way, airborne, on a direct flight to your lips, the special delivery must arrive in its entirety. There are no partial shipments. Finish the contents of your spoon/fork/spork in one bite.

The gratuity. Sure, you may never see these people again. Sure, you've already dropped a bundle just to get you to the table. But please, tip generously. (You should tip 20 percent on the pretax total. Figure out this number by moving the total's decimal point one place to the left and doubling that number.) If the wine steward has helped you make your selections, tip him 10 to15 percent on your wine tab. This is not the time or place to pinch pennies.

The Place Setting

1. This is your napkin, the friend who covers your lap from the moment the last person sits down at table—and not a moment before. It's the cloth that goes on your chair when you leave the table during the meal, and to the right of your plate when the meal ends.
2. These are your forks, knives, and spoons. Use the outside ones first—don't forget the little shellfish *fourchette* up top—and place the ones you've used from five to eleven o'clock when you've finished a course. No fretting if you use the wrong utensil: Your friendly server will make replacements as needed.
3. These are your glasses. Use them gingerly. Return them to their original locations after each use. Water is on lower left. Wines are on right.
4. These are your bread plate and butter knife. Break off your roll one bit at a time, and butter it just before you consume it.
5. These are the salt and pepper shakers. Use them only after you've tasted your food. As they are lonely apart, please pass them together, even if your companion asks for only one.
6. This is the person across from you. If you forget any of the previous rules, copy her.

WINE TASTING

*Wine is a little like love. When the right one
comes along, you know it.*
—Anonymous

Dear, sweet (and dry) wine, how do we love thee? We love that you elevate take-out pizza to a romantic dinner for two, that you see us through Saturday nights home alone with Buffy DVDs, that tied with a bow or placed in a canvas tote you make the quintessential hostess gift, that you vastly improve our ability to speak French and to dance like Ginger Rogers.

Three cheers to you, marvelously sophisticated libation made of smashed grapes! No matter if you're playful bubbly in a pink can or vintage Bordeaux in a dusty bottle—we, like Mark Darcy likes Bridget Jones, like you just the way you are. But let's face it: sometimes, just like Mr. Darcy doesn't *get* Bridge, we just don't *get* you.

Welcome to the deliciously educational world of wine tastings. Napa Valley harvest festivals, petite food-pairing seminars, local in-store uncorkings, extracurricular restaurant classes, and casual invites from pals who want to clean out cellars—these events offer the unique opportunity to drink and to learn in a succinct, simultaneous, and, it bears noting, stylish fashion.

The challenge: Such delightful ceremonies possess mysterious etiquette and an off-putting snobbery that inspires oenophiles (um, wine lovers) to utter phrases such as "I detect a hint of ripe blueberry, rustic oak overtones, and vestiges of nineteenth-century truffle hunts in Umbria," while all you can muster is "Tastes like Welch's."

The point of sampling a bunch of wines at once is to whittle out which ones you like. It's like going shoe shopping. You gotta take those babies for a spin around the store before you commit to wearing them to cocktails at eight or a jog at six (as if).

To taste wine is to make comparisons, to participate in an infinitely more elegant version of the Pepsi Challenge. And there's a way to do it right. Grab a glass. Fill the glass with a couple sips. Go from the lightest to darkest. (Champagnes and Proseccos first, then whites, rosés, reds, and desserts.) If you're at one of those wine festivals where every vineyard has a table, circle the room.

If you really want to learn something, two glasses are better than one. Trying French chardonnay alongside a California chard tells you what region you prefer. Comparing an Australian Syrah with an Australian merlot tells you what grape variety you like.

If at all possible, try to remember grapes and regions, not brands and years. If all else fails, take notes.

Countin' Down the Top Ten Varietals (*Varietal* = Grape Type)

Chardonnay. The One You Know: America's top-selling white gets its appeal from ice cream sundae, breakfast, and fruit flavors: vanilla, butterscotch, buttered toast, green apple, lemon, pineapple, tropical fruit. It's often described as creamy, lush, full-bodied, and is usually aged in oak. Great ones come from all over, especially California.

Chenin blanc. The Classic: Before California grew chard, California grew chenin blanc. This white wine has wide range, going from bone-dry to quite sweet, sparkling to smooth, usually floral, zesty, and honeyed. Best-known varietals come from France's Loire Valley and include Vouvray, Anjou, and Savennières. It's also known as "Steen" in South Africa. Try it when you're ready to graduate from chardonnay.

Riesling. The Food Lover's White: Grown in colder climes like Germany, Alsace, northern Austria, and upstate New York, this one—pronounced like Ms. Witherspoon's first name plus "ling"—is known for its high acidity, light body, and low alcohol. This trio of characteristics—especially the acid, which gets those saliva glands going—makes Riesling bring out the best in loads of foods.

Sauvignon blanc. Chardonnay's Skinny, Nature-Loving Sister: Graceful, thin, and herbal, this perfect-for-a-hot-summer-afternoon white is the opposite of a buxom, buttery chardonnay. World-class favorites include France's Sancerre and Pouilly-Fumé, which Californians call Fumé Blanc.

Sémillon. The White Glove White: This least-known of the top five whites is the purest of the crop. Often found in dry white Bordeaux and dry Australia blends such as Sauternes, it is a sweet and subtle New Year's Day libation that can hold up to both chocolate truffles and lush patés. Thirsty yet?

Merlot. The Chardonnay of Reds: If chard is pineapple upside-down cake, merlot is devil's food cake. Chocolate, cherry, mocha, black currant, and plums are the intended impressions of Bordeaux's leading grape. It's also been described as what happens after one consumes too much of that devil's food cake: fleshy, soft, and plump. All in all, merlot is a great place to start loving red.

Cabernet sauvignon. The Big Red: Cab is like a merlot, but more so. Take merlot's flavors, add some floral aromas plus the imprint of oak barrel aging, and you get a cab. The red with the greatest range, and often great aging potential, it is California's biggest wine crop. Cab is also grown well in Italy, France, Australia, and Washington state.

Pinot noir. The Go-Anywhere Red: Like merlot or cabernet sauvignon lite, pinots are often slimmer in body, silkier in texture, lighter in color:

earthy enough to stand up to red meats, but pliant enough to go with fowl and fish. Tannins—which come from grape skins—are less abundant here, too. Take them anywhere, and they'll have a good time.

Syrah. The Serious One: Despite a recent upsurge of inexpensive, extra-sweet Syrah (aka Shiraz) coming from Australia and California, this red varietal is classically peppery, spicy, smoky, even leathery. The most famous comes from Châteauneuf-du-Pape. Not related are Petite Syrah and Petite Shiraz, whose West Coast origins are obscure. Syrah goes best with dishes that require steak knives.

White zinfandel. The Much-Maligned Pink Drink: Served chilled and often from boxes, white zins get a bum rap among wine snobs because they're usually oversweet and mass produced from low-grade grapes. No wine snobs we: We say if you like it, drink it. You wouldn't be the first virgin to enter the wide world of wine through this rose-colored doorway.

The Virgin's Downfalls

Just getting drunk and making the standard fool of yourself is too easy in this case (see "Born-again Virgin," page 112.) There are subtler faux pas to avoid.

Virgin's downfall #1. That Pretty White Pantsuit: Wine stains. Badly. If powder puff blue and palest peach are in this season, wear black anyway.

ESSENTIAL WINE VOCABULARY

Dry/Bone-dry: Not sweet.

Off-dry: Sweet.

Drinkable: Good for drinking alone, not necessarily with food.

Crisp/Clean: Refers to acid content; usually means good with food.

Tannic: Refers to red wine only; means the wine dries out your mouth. Often confused with "dry."

Legs: The drips that form on the side of the glass.

Body: The texture of the wine—as in thick or thin, like half-and-half or skim.

Old World/New World: Old = Europe. New = Everybody else.

Corked: Happens to 10 percent of wood corked wines, means wine's gone bad, as indicated by strong mildew smell.

Virgin's downfall #2. Chanel No. 5, Aqua Net, or Designer Impostors: More than half of taste comes through the nose. Skip the perfumed products, or risk the wrath of self-important wine geeks.

Virgin's downfall #3. Smoking in the Wine Room: Expect to be kicked to the curb for this offense.

Virgin's downfall #4. Altoids, Aquafresh. Use of breath fresheners one to two hours before you taste will mess with your taste buds in the same way that brushing your teeth spoils your morning OJ. Avoid, too, strong flavors like chocolate or coffee.

Virgin's downfall #5. Not Eating Beforehand: Empty Stomach + Abundance of Vino = Embarassing Behavior à la Dino Latino (as in Dean Martin, Sinatra's pal). Have a sandwich.

Virgin's downfall #6. Smelling the Cork: Or worse, smelling the screw cap. Neither tells you a damn thing about the wine.

Virgin's downfall # 7. Judging By the First Sip: Obviously not a problem for most of us, but it bears noting that the first taste never tastes as good as the second.

GO-TO GIRL

Marnie Old   Sommelier to the Stars

Wine instructor Marnie has the teaching talent of your favorite professor, the taste buds of a pro—and the graceful glamour of a ballet dancer. One of the youngest women in the world to hold prestigious Master Sommelier credentials, Philadelphia's Marnie works for herself teaching four-star chefs, big-wheel execs, students at New York City's prestigious French Culinary Institute, and regular gals like us just what's so great about wine. Maybe it's her engaging brown eyes, maybe it's the way she jiggles her hips as she swishes a big mouthful of chardonnay, maybe it's her refreshingly anti-snob approach: Whatever Marnie's got, it works. Two minutes in her Wine 101 seminar, and suddenly you're not so scared by that dusty bottle of Bordeaux. Two hours later, you're psyched to order for the table the next time you're out for a fancy dinner. We love her motto: "If you put wine in your mouth, and it makes you smile, it's good for you."

The Moves

Impress your friends and nearby wine snobs with these easy actions:

The swirl. With the glass on the table, grasp the stem like it's a pencil and you're writing. Keep the glass on the table. Draw circles. (You know you've hit the big time when you can pull this one off with the glass in midair.)

The sniff. When trying a wine for the first time, bring the glass to your face. Stick your nose in the glass. Sniff hard, with your mouth closed, like you're vacuuming money through it. Put the glass down. Look at the

---

BORN-AGAIN VIRGIN

This is not Maddie Merlot's (as always, names have been changed to protect the not-so-innocent) first wine tasting. But it might as well be. Maddie, like many wide-eyed wine enthusiasts, attended an event like this one a couple of months ago. She came with her pal Viv Vouvray. Together, the drinking duo attacked the unlimited supply of adult-strength grape juice with pie-eating-contest gusto. Instead of savoring, they slurped. Instead of going easy, they went for broke. Before long, our ladies in wining were voguing behind the piano, belting show tunes, revealing tannin-stained teeth and black tongues to all before slogging home, where they ordered two large pizzas and passed out on top of the mozzarella. Needless to say, the only things our gals gleaned from their learning experience were nasty hangovers. Viv and Maddie are born-again virgins.

---

wine steward. Smile. Nod. If you're feeling especially bold, never even take a sip.

The sip and swish. Follow the sniff with a big gulp, enough to fill your mouth. Swish it around as if it were mouthwash. Swallow. Smile. Nod.

The lines. Useful phrases for when you're stumped.

"What a lovely finish." (Translation: nice aftertaste. Or lack of after-taste.) Replace "lovely" with "beautiful," "nice," or any other phrase you'd use to describe sublime spring weather.
"Beautifully balanced." (Translation: You like it.)
"Yum." (In a pinch, works very well.)

The fine art of spitting. Considered terribly uncouth in any other arena except the rodeo and the dugout, projectile expectoration is often the only way to protect oneself from passing out during an event that re-quires one to fill one's mouth with vast quantities of juice containing 5 to 14 percent alcohol. There's really no graceful way to do it. But to avoid major stainage, lean in and pretend you're at the sink and you just fin-ished gargling. Curl your tongue. Aim. Using minimal force, let gravity do its work. Pa-tooie! *Voilà!*

LOBSTER

> *A woman should never be seen eating or drinking, unless it be lobster salad and Champagne, the only true feminine & becoming viands.*
> —LORD BYRON

Remember that summer road trip your family took in Maine when you were ten? The one where you and your sister sat in the back of the station wagon, thighs fused to gold vinyl seats while you signaled out the window to passing cars that you were being held captive by strangers and to dial 911?

Then, when Mum and Pops pulled up to a tiny cabin belonging to some family from back home, people who purchased this second house far, far away precisely to escape mooching families like yours, Dad announced he was taking everybody to dinner? So it was back in the car for another endless drive to some ship-wheel-filled restaurant called the Seafood Shanty that overlooked a smallish body of water and resembled not a shack at all but instead a tacky yacht club?

Recall how it was kind of fun there until you realized that the greenish-black beings bobbing in the aquarium you were pressing your nose against were intended to be your dinner, not just low-maintenance pets like your goldfish at home, whom you started to worry about because he was in the care of the elderly next-door neighbor you called "Aunt" who possibly was feeding l'il Bubbles Hershey's kisses instead of fish food flakes?

Remember how by the time the plastic bib was knotted around your neck and a nutcracker joined your place setting and the brilliant red one-pound crustacean arrived, you were (1) practically in tears, (2) confused about how to tackle the ancient-looking and recently boiled to death creature in front of you and, (3) not hungry because you'd just noshed five rolls dipped in the ramekins of drawn butter intended for the lobster? Then, at the end of the night, your sister snapped off the long, skinny feeler things from the lobster carcass and suddenly you were happy because she showed you how you could break up the feelers into small beads and make a cool orange bracelet? Remember that?

That doesn't count as your first lobster.

Your first lobster is one you order of your own free will at a chic, one-word, white-tablecloth bistro or a bona fide New England lobster shack where you can wear flip-flops and a loose-fitting sundress and relax at a candlelit picnic table on a sunset-bathed deck and stare into someone special's eyes as you daintily grasp a claw and gingerly crack it open with that nutcracker. (After dinner, of course, you still snag the feeler things—which, by now, you know are called the feelers—to make another one of those bracelets.)

Other Lovely Forms of Lobster

The roll. A controversial sandwich that New Englanders like to dispute incessantly. Basically, there are two forms: plain lobster with butter on a roll, and fresh lobster salad on a roll. In our book, they're both wicked awesome.

The bisque. A rich concoction that combines multiple dairy products with mild seasonings, this is the crème de la crème of crustacean purees.

The pot pie. When baked gently, the lobster pie puts the shepherd's version to shame. Tastes like a November dinner in a bayside cottage in Nantucket.

The tail. Oft considered the finest part of the lobster, this fan-shaped section is curled when the lobster is fresh. A word to the wise virgin: Loads of lobster tails marketed in seafooderies come from the ten-legged spiny lobsters that dwell in warmer waters, and most have been frozen.

The lobster mashed potato. The lobster plays the part of a truffle here, adding depth of flavor and more than a little glamour to a regular old pile of spuds.

The lobster omelet, the lobster scrambled eggs. See above. Substitute "pile of spuds" with the word "brunch."

Lobster thermidor. Precooked lobster tails in a rich, mustardy béchamel sauce and stuffed back into the lobster shell. Easy to handle, because it's been pre-extracted. Not always easy to finish.

How to Eat Lobster

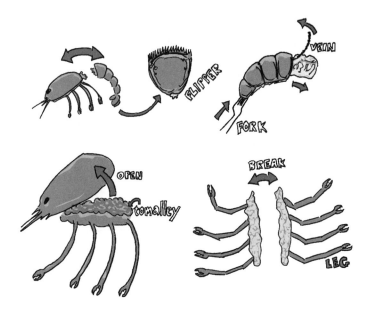

- Don a bib.
- Twist off the claws.
- Crack the claws and knuckles with a nutcracker. Remove the meat.
- Separate the tail from the body and break off the tail flippers. Remove the meat from the flippers.

- Insert a fork or, if you're lucky, a pointy-ended lobster pick and push the tail meat out in one piece. Remove and discard the black vein (blech) that runs the length of the tail meat.
- Separate the shell from the body from the underside by pulling them apart and discard the tomalley, the greenish liver part that's vaguely reminiscent of—oh, you don't want to think about this. (Double blech.) (Extra deflowering points for eating it, since, like so many swishy organs, the tomalley is considered a delicacy.)
- Open the underside of the body by cracking it apart in the middle, with the small walking legs on either side. Extract the meat from the leg joint and the legs themselves by biting down on the leg and squeezing the meat out with your teeth.
- Alternative to all of the above: Copy the person across the table.

Virgin's Downfall

See Daryl Hannah in *Splash*.

SUSHI

> *There are plenty more fish in the sea.*
> —YOUR FAVORITE AUNT

You and that Southern California Boy—SCB—who works in your office building have been stare-smile-and-look-down flirting in the elevator for three months. Now that it's another Monday morning after another weekend of bad dates, you're seriously motivated to make the first move. You hide behind the lobby ficus forest, wait for him to walk in, follow him, and act surprised to see him.

Ground Floor: Take a deep breath. Summon nerve.

Floor Two: Smile slyly (to mask the sheer fright you feel). Propose meeting somewhere other than between floors one and eight.

Floor Three: Listen to him reply "Love to."

Floor Four: Recover from the shock of his response.

Floor Five: Stammer "Friday evening?"

Floor Six: Hear him say "Sushi?"

Floor Seven: Exclaim "Great!" your voice squeaking to an off-the-charts soprano and your neck prickling with nerves.

Floor Eight: In a flash, he hands you his card, a happy look is exchanged, and you bolt through the closing doors. Your heart beats deep in your ears. You bolt to your desk, awaken your computer, pound out "sushi" on citysearch.com, book a two-top for 8:00 p.m.

It's set. In another twinkling of brilliance, you instantly plan your outfit for the night, along with an alternative route from the restaurant that will take you and your superstar corporate surfer past a jazz bar, dance club, and scenic lookout in the probable case you two, now quite possibly entering a Long-term Relationship, choose to hang out past green tea ice cream.

The only glitch? You don't know sashimi from salami. Not to worry. Sushi virgins exist even among the chicest of circles. You're not alone. But you ought to be prepared.

Sushi Mnemonics

How to remember the basics: *Some Rich Nerds Pay Slinky Strippers Most Righteously To Cha-cha*

Translation: Sushi = Rice; Nigiri = Pillows; Sashimi = Strips; Maki = Rolls; Temaki = Cones

Sushi Etiquette

- It's OK to forgo the chopsticks and eat with your fingers.
- At the bar, make eye contact with the chefs. Offer to buy them sake (they may not accept, but they'll appreciate the offer) and smile sweetly. Tip generously.
- Soy sauce is for flavoring the fish, not the rice. Lightly dip each piece rice side up, fish side down. Place it in your mouth the same way.
- Wasabi goes in the soy sauce—not smeared onto fish or rice like peanut butter on Wonder bread.
- Ginger is eaten between courses—not layered on top of fish à la a Dagwood sandwich.

ESSENTIAL SUSHI VOCABULARY

Sushi: Vinegared rice. (We know, we know, most of the world thinks sushi means raw fish. No reason to be like most of the world.)

Maki: Seaweed (nori) roll-ups of rice, fish, and/or vegetables, omelet, tofu, made into a tube called a roll and cut into four to eight pieces. Maki is what most people think of as sushi.

Soy sauce: A dark brown, thin, salty sauce made by fermenting soybeans and roasted wheat or barley. Common in most Asian cooking. In Japan, aka *tamari*.

Nigiri: A pair of rice pillows dabbed with wasabi and covered with raw fish.

Sashimi: Strips of raw fish served with crunchy daikon radish and, in nicer places, shiso, an aromatic herb in the basil and mint family.

Temaki: A cornucopia-style seaweed cone brimming with rice and fish. Meant for eating with fingers.

Wasabi: Japanese horseradish paste or shavings often mixed into soy sauce for extra spiciness. The green spicy stuff.

Gari: Pickled ginger slices functioning as palate cleansers between pieces.

Edamame: Steamed and salted soybean pods eaten by placing majority of pod in mouth and pulling out through teeth, thereby extracting the delicious beans onto the tongue. Served hot or cold.

- Do not confuse your neighbor's ceramic vessel of sake for the pitcher of soy sauce.

Sushi Abstinence

One word. Fugu. It's a poisonous Japanese blowfish that's to be avoided—unless you're in Japan and willing to lay down the Benjamins for a safe version.

Two words. Smelly fish. Fresh fish should smell clean like the ocean, not fishy like a garbage can. If it stinks, skip it.

Virgin's Downfall

The sushi buffet. Reason number one: The fish has been sitting out, getting warm, getting breathed on, and potentially sneezed upon, and probably fingered, thereby breeding unsavory types of germs and such. Reason number two: Those petite morsels of rice and raw fish are deceptively filling. There's no need for all-you-can-eat. Reason number three: Most self-respecting Japanese restaurants don't do buffets.

From Rolls to Raw: A Recommended Progression for First Timers

Squeamish starters. Best to begin with more familiar items. There's vegetarian maki—usually made with cucumber, carrots, avocado, eggplant,

---

BORN-AGAIN VIRGIN

Tempura Toni goes out all the time for Japanese food. Considerate (but slightly squeamish), she responds to offers of ruby-raw toro over vinegared rice with a polite "No thank you." Only when pressed does she divulge her mistrust of sashimi. Never has she uttered her belief that seaweed belongs on the beach and not in her mouth. She admits, however, that years ago she sampled a supermarket California roll with insipid sides of saccharine pickled ginger and chartreuse wasabi, and that frankly she wasn't impressed enough to have another go at it. Toni's trouble: She's never tried the good stuff. Toni is a born-again sushi virgin.

---

mushrooms, daikon (radish), tofu, or a delicious Japanese plum; omelet (*tamago*, really tiny, lightly sweet scrambled egg); smoked salmon (just like the kind you get from the deli). We virgins have had California rolls and, quite frankly, are not impressed by faux crab. But we will submit to boiled shrimp "ebi," which reminds us of shrimp cocktail gone abroad.

Nimble novices. Anyone who's enjoyed a high-grade tuna steak will appreciate the subtle ruby red deliciousness of *maguro* or the coveted *toro* belly piece. Like caviar? Try *tobiko* or *ikura*, salty flying fish or salmon eggs. Next move on to *hamachi*, mild and yummy yellowtail tuna. Mackerel, a silvery, oily fish, is even bolder. Surprising but true: Barbecued eel—called *una-don*—is fully cooked, sublimely tender, subtly sweet, served warm, and especially delicious.

Plucky pros. Sea urchin—*uni*—has the look and consistency of Cheez Whiz, but the taste is nutty and definitely acquired. *Aji* is horse mackerel, often called Spanish mackerel, and is served with onion and ginger paste. For obvious reasons: crunchy abalone, slippery clams and jellyfish, tough squid and octopus, sea snail.

CHEESE & CHOCOLATE ENCOUNTERS

*A cheese may disappoint. It may be dull, it may be naive,
it may be oversophisticated. Yet it remains, cheese,
milk's leap toward immortality.*
—CLIFTON FADIMAN, ARTISANAL CHEESE EXPERT

Forget love . . . I'd rather fall in chocolate!
—ANONYMOUS

*If you are not feeling well, if you have not slept, chocolate will
revive you. But you have no chocolate! I think of that again and
again! My dear, how will you ever manage?*
—MARQUISE DE SÉVIGNÉ

To the reader who turned to this section before all others, we salute you. You, quite obviously, have your priorities in perfect order. Blind dates, money markets, and, most of all, personal trainers can wait until tomorrow. (We love you, tomorrow!)

Right now, it's time to meet two edibles that make life so worth living that we addicted initiates would prefer not to fathom a world without them. We're talking cheese. We're talking chocolate. And if we're talking to one of those marvelously brave minions whose bodies prohibit them from ingesting either or—gasp—both of these most comely of comestibles, we applaud you for your fortitude and forgive you if you immediately move on to the next section.

To the rest of you: Perhaps you're wondering why cocoa and curds are sharing the page.

Reason number one. Good cheese and chocolate have similar aging characteristics—and in-common rules of thumb for buying.

Reason number two. Good cheese and chocolate are highly perishable—and share strict storage requirements.

Reason number three. We love them both so much, we couldn't stand to put one before the other.

As a child, you ate Kraft Singles and Whitman's Samplers. As an adult, you face a confusing—albeit delicious—world of highly evolved, specialized, polymorphic mutations of this familiar fare. Luckily, this same world houses an increasing sisterhood of cheese and chocolate experts. One goes by the name of . . .

GO-TO GIRL

Linsey Herman   Cheese Monger

The day cheese changed her life was the day that Linsey, then a student at the New England Culinary Institute, began her internship at a now defunct dairy farm in upstate New York. "The moment I went to that creamery, there in the shadow of the nuclear power plant on the Hudson, I became crazily obsessed with cheese," she says. From dairy cows to Whole Foods to Food TV to her post as a buyer at Artisanal (the country's preeminent cheese restaurant), Go-to Linsey says the foremost rule of cheese: Get it cut to order—and eat it as quickly as possible. No problem there, Lins.

Buying Cheese

- Find a busy cheese shop or knowledgeable cheese monger (like a butcher of cheese), preferably one that offers samples. Hurrah for free *fromage!*

- When it's possible, ask the person behind the counter to cut the cheese. (Insert juvenile twittering.) Just-cut cheese is always preferable to prepackaged cheese.
- When prewrapped cheese is all that's around, check the packing and expiration dates. The first should be about today; the second, at least a week off.
- The softer and younger the cheese, the faster it spoils. Buy only what you plan to use in the next few days.
- Look at the cheese's edges. If there's browning beneath the rind, skip it.
- Look at the cheese's surface. It should be dry and smooth. If it's powdery or oily under or over the wrapping, skip it.

Storing Cheese

- Plastic wrap is a HUGE NO. Just like you, cheese needs to breathe. Wrap it in cheese paper (as begged for from a cheese shop) or a double layer of wax or parchment paper on the cheese with aluminum foil outside.
- Store it in the cheese drawer or salad crisper of your very own refrigerator.
- Eat it as soon as possible—as if this were an issue.

Serving Cheese

- Variety is the key to assembling a tip-top plate of milky goodness. You have three general categories to keep in mind: texture (soft-ripened, semisoft, semifirm, hard), milk type (cow's, goat's, sheep's), and intensity (mild to pungent).
- Linsey likes to pick odd numbers of cheeses, enough so each guest has a half to a whole ounce of each. Allow more for popular triple crèmes, Bries, or Camemberts.
- Arrange cheeses from mildest to strongest. Label each with tiny chalkboards or paper signs on toothpicks.
- Preslice hard cheeses into thin pieces.
- Serve at room temperature.
- Once relegated to the thankless duty of offsetting predinner tummy rumblings, the cheese plate is, at long last, making the glorious transition to its rightful place between main course and dessert.

Good cheesy accompaniments: Fruit and nut bread (better than crackers), toasted nuts, quince or fig paste, wine jellies scored from your last trip to Europe, dried fruits, olives, honey. Add fresh fruits only if you're not serving wine.

Truth be told, few wines and cheeses really clash. A good rule of thumb is to match younger and softer cheeses with sparkling whites to light reds, older cheeses with rosés to bigger reds, and stinky cheeses with sweet wines.

GO-TO GIRL

Maribel Lieberman   Chocolatier Extraordinaire

Hurrah for Maribel. Five years ago, this savvy entrepreneur traded in her chef's whites to create a line of chocolates as chic and rich as a fleet of Kelly handbags. NYC-based MariBelle Fine Treats and Chocolates come in flavors including lemon, Earl Grey, saffron, and cardamom. Maribel packages them—and her line of Aztec hot chocolate and 60 percent chocolate brownies—in little blue and brown boxes that rival Tiffany's for ooh power. Her mission: Raise America's cocoa bean IQ. "I'd like people to start appreciating where it comes from—Madagascar, Santo Domingo, Colombia, Mexico—each single origin—and how it grows. It's fascinating. And today, people are so hungry to learn about it," she says. Hungry, indeed.

Buying Chocolate

- The fresher it is the better. Translation: Those half-priced bags of Halloween Milky Ways are far from the real deal. Opt instead for chocolate available from specialty shops, candy stores, and chocolate boutiques like Maribel's. One rule of thumb: The bar's ingredient panel should list cocoa before sugar.

- Ask when it was made. Preservative-free chocolate lasts a month, max. Milk chocolate has a shorter life span than dark chocolate. Dark containing a natural preservative like lemon outlasts plain dark.
- Chocolate should have a smooth sheen and be consistent in color.
- If the exterior is opaque or splotched (called bloom), it means the chocolate hasn't been tempered correctly or is old.
- It should smell chocolate-y, not chemically.
- Bad qualities: waxy, gritty, greasy, gummy, lumpy, sticky, crumbly, powdery, coarse, dusty.
- Good qualities: melts immediately on the tongue, is velvety with a long, pleasant finish.

Storing Chocolate

- Keep it in its box. Cover the box in plastic wrap, or place it in a plastic bag.
- Store it in the warmest section of your refrigerator, or a cool place.
- Serve it below room temperature, at 62° to 65° F.
- Most chocolates keep for two to three weeks. Those filled with liqueur can last up to six months.

The Aftertaste

Want to lose your culinary virginity a little bit more every day? Shop at a farmers' market instead of in a superstore aisle. Skip those overfeeding chain Italian restaurants; seek out a mom-and-pop trattoria instead. Keep your eyes peeled and mouth open for culinary adventure at each bend of the road, making pit stops at barbecue joints, pick-your-own orchards, county fairs, and international festivals. Accept free samples. Say yum.

4

DATING

What kind of self-respecting women's guidebook would we be if we didn't devote a chapter to . . . luv? Ah, luv. We first felt the pangs when a blue-eyed boy named Seth was the new kid in our first-grade class. Seth was the fastest runner. And the best speller. He never got pegged in dodge ball. He was from *Colorado*. Unfortunately for our tiny, grade-one hearts, Seth had already found his soulmate. At the ripe age of seven, Seth already showed signs of being deeply in love . . . with himself.

And so it went. Each year, a crush on the new boy in class. Each year, the boy luvved another. David in seventh grade dumped us for a girl who could dribble. Junior year, James passed us over for more boobs and fewer morals. Phil craved a Southern Belle debutante. Frank craved steaks.

How are we, then, qualified to give you advice? Because we know the one, profound secret to finding the partner of your dreams: Stay away from the new boy in class.

INTERNET ROMANCE

Sure, the World Wide Web is great
But you, you make me salivate
Yes, I love technology
But not as much as you, you see
But I still love technology
—KIP, IN NAPOLEON DYNAMITE

A long, long time ago, in a land not so far away, lived a (relatively) young and (somewhat) lonely woman. This woman worked five days a week at an important job. She had many friends, cool digs, superior fashion sensibility, and a hairdresser with whom she communicated virtually telepathically.

Rumor had it she could do the fifty-yard dash in high heels. Still, she wanted more. She wanted a person to dance with in the kitchen, to steal the covers from, to fill the passenger's seat, to push her on the swings, to share large buckets of buttered popcorn and yards of lager.

The problem, you ask? This was, as we mentioned, a long, long time ago. Back in the last millennium, our sweetheart-less heroine's options were meager, chancy at best. She could scope out bars. She could troll religious institutions, scour personal ads or supermarket aisles, seek out a soulmate at driving ranges, WNBA games, the Gap. If worse came to worst, she could ask her parents for help.

Indeed, she tried these methods—and then some. But at the end of the day—or the end of the date—she was zapped. Her naturally positive outlook was starting to fade like a red dress in a sunny shop window. Dating-wise, there was nothing good about the good old days.

Then, on a weekday that seemed just like all other weekdays, she sat at her PC—and saw the light (which was more like a blip, really). It was the blip of the dot-com dawn of Internet dating.

Today, thanks to much tinkering and a general acceptance of this fast and cheap form of casually complete introductions, online dating remains a highly effective method not just for programmers or technophiles, but also for anyone willing to pay a nominal monthly fee to put herself out there.

GO-TO GIRL

Suzanne Schlosberg Fitness Writer, Adventurer in the World and in Dot-Com Dating

If you haven't read Suzanne's book *The Curse of the Singles Table*, but you are reading this, well, you need both. Suzanne's laugh-out-loud memoir recounts her courageous exploration and exploits on Match.com (www.match.com), which she fondly calls "the Starbucks of dating, because you know what you're going to get." For a thousand days and a thousand nights our Go-to Girl lived and loved online, until that fateful date when—wait: You're not getting a finale-spoiler from us, but trust us, she's no longer sitting at the singles table.

Find a Service You Like

Suzanne subscribed to Match.com because it, well, matched her personality. Though Match remains the Internet's most popular dating service, there are plenty more to choose from. Jewish singles find true love on JDate (www.jdate.com). Vegetarians hook up via VeggieDate (www.veggiedate .com). People pretending not to look for dates sign themselves up on Friendster (www.friendster.com). If you want your online lover to come with references (from exes to moms), try GreatBoyfriends.com (www.great

boyfriends.com). If you'd like to date according to your age, religion, ethnicity, sexuality, musical tastes, and/or any other status, you're bound to find a dot-com dating service that's right up your electronic alley.

Most services let you try—or at least surf—before you buy. Almost all let you take time off when you need it. Choose one that suits you personally, and you're already improving your odds.

Your Profile

Many would-be online daters drop out at the prospect of writing what amounts to a personals ad for themselves. That—and choosing photos to go with it.

Suzanne's tip: Give your profile some thought, but not a great American novel's worth. "Your profile shouldn't reveal too much of yourself. Put in something intriguing that makes people want to know more."

Things that are good to hint at but bad to list: your long-term goals, your sense of humor, your energy, your philosophy on life, your number of friends. These aspects of you should come through in details of your life, not just by writing "I am high-energy and career-minded and like to hang out with my dozens of eclectic friends." Subtlety is key.

Also: Employ your sparkling sense of humor, which, BTW, is the best long-term asset a virgin can have. Don't write in clichés. "You have to put something more interesting than 'I love to take romantic walks on the beach,' or 'I love to have fun; I love to laugh.' Who doesn't love to laugh?" That Suzanne is so astute. Some good examples:

"Steely Dan fan with a closeted obsession with 'NSync."

"A knitter—but only when watching *Alias*."

"Paul Giamatti is my ultimate dream date. Or maybe I just like doe-eyed, balding fellows with pillowlike paunches."

Information best left to second or third dates includes emotional wounds and romance-related fears: "I just came off a big breakup" or "Currently seeking someone who won't ditch me for my cousin—again." Bad moves. Instead, reveal the cool little stuff that makes you unique, your favorite sport, taco stand, late-night TV host, or home appliance.

Suzanne's number one profile pet peeve is using the expression "equally comfortable with" to show you're balanced. Example: "equally comfortable painting the town red and staying at home and cuddling," "equally comfortable walking forward and backward," "equally comfortable taking naps and taking my clothes off."

Suzanne's number two profile pet peeve is starting a sentence with "My friends tell me . . ." or "My ex-boyfriend says . . ." Don't hide behind others to seem modest. Just say who you are, and what you like.

Your Photo

"Make sure only you are in it," says Suzanne, who thinks the you-with-friends photo shows little effort. "Post something that truly, accurately reflects your looks. Don't put a one-year-old picture in. Don't put a glamour shot from the one time you had your hair and makeup done."

In other words, you should be selling yourself, not a deluxe—or otherwise altered—version of the true you. If you're not sure the shot works, "have your girl friends help. Gather opinions other than your own." (Suzanne's pals had to talk her out of posting unflattering photos of herself.)

If the site lets you post more than one photo, do it. "I recommend posting three pictures," says Suzanne. "One cute one, one funny one, and one more."

Screening Process

"You have to have some kind of standards, or you're going to spend twenty-four hours a day on the system screening people out," says Suzanne. "Originally, I would try not to pay attention to the photos because I thought that's really judgmental, I've got to look beyond pictures. Then I realized it's OK to look at pictures. It's OK to screen people out. This is my potential mate for life. So I stopped feeling guilty about eliminating guys because of their pictures."

Still, profiles got her complete attention. "So many guys are unable to write in anything but the police report style: 'I'm a single white male, five eleven, brown hair, green eyes.' That's all in the statistics, anyway. So that shows they made no effort."

Big red flags: "Bragging," says Suzanne. "Guys who are like 'I'm often asked if I'm a model or an actor, but I'm more a writer intellectual type.'"

"You want someone who's put some thought into this, who reveals something intriguing about himself, too." The standard "I'm looking for a girl who likes to laugh, who likes to have fun"—"Delete it!" she says.

Nonetheless, the most important part of the screening process is, after a while, to reexamine your weeding-out process. "Change your search criteria every so often. Loosen your requirements. It's good to shake things up. Set your boundaries, but keep an open mind at the same time."

Suzanne's fail-proof system for measuring up guys: "One thing guys regularly lie about is their height. In my experience, guys who said they were six feet or taller didn't lie. You don't lie in the sixes. When you get to five nine or five eight, they're usually lying more. Five nine is kind of a catchall height that guys use. A guy who says he's five eleven is probably five ten. A guy who says he's five ten is probably five eight and a half."

ScreenPals

Your first exchanges with your potential matches will be via e-mail. Please, don't let Suzanne's hundreds of hours of research in this area go to waste.

Number of e-mail exchanges: "Five max—and the last two should be setting up the date." No phone calls (see "Virgin's Downfall," next page). During these brief encounters—because they should be very brief—pay attention. Are you asking all the questions? Does he appear to have read your profile? "It doesn't matter how clever his profile is, how cute he looks, those are not good signs," says Suzanne.

VIRGIN'S DOWNFALL

Emma Match-exchanged four great e-mails with Mike. Mike's photos, profile, and emoticon-free e-mails indicated he was the perfect score. On e-mail number five, he popped the question: "Want to move this to the next level? Emma, will you . . . call me?" The proposition hit the perfect pitch of playful and flirty. Emma phoned that evening. For weeks, the pair chatted their evenings away. They talked about their family and friends, their heartbreaks and hopes. During that last convo, things bordered on steamy. Emma was feeling bold. "Mike," she asked, "isn't it time we take things up another notch?" They met for lunch the next day. Mike, the guy who'd told Emma he'd been depressed for a year when his cat ran away, and Emma, who'd confessed to Mike that after her last breakup she wasn't sure she'd ever be able to love again, were, in the light of day, normal, guarded people. Face-to-face, they couldn't connect. Lesson learned: No phone calls before you meet.

The guy might be a no-go, but there's good news yet. "In the Internet world of dating you don't have to be as polite as you do in person. It's perfectly acceptable to say, 'I don't think we're right for each other,' and 'Good luck!' Or, you can just never respond. You get some e-mails that are just not a good use of your time. Even if you've gone back and forth three or four times, it's polite to say, 'I don't think so.'"

Meeting Face-to-Face: Mission Entirely Possible

Suggest a neutral meeting space. An order-at-the-counter coffee shop is always a good bet: no fuss over the check, no lengthy meal-long conversation, none of the risks of alcohol—and because if all else fails, you can take your cappuccino to go. Arrive on time—early if you'd like to avoid an awkward exchange as you order and pay. Buy yourself a bevvie. Have a seat. Wait.

Suzanne limited herself to fifteen-minute encounters and always said she had a place to be right afterward. This fifteen-minute limit could be shortened for jerks, but never extended, not even for the match of her dreams. The idea is this is a quick hi-ya meeting, not a date. Not even an interview. When you've made nice for a quarter of an hour, it's time to go. The ball is in your court.

"If I wasn't interested, I would say, 'Nice to meet you. Good luck with that report you're working on. See you online.'" Most of the time, it was what Suzanne calls a "mutual zero." So she didn't meet the match of her dreams. At least she pared down the playing field.

"If I liked the guy and wanted to see him again, I would give him my phone number and say, 'Call me.' If I didn't hear from him, I would e-mail, just to make sure—and then I would get the blow-off." It didn't always happen that way. There were the occasional second and more dates. But her high volume of coffee shop dates quickly honed Suzanne's skills. She became an expert at figuring when to pursue, when not to push it, and when—oh, that's right, we're not telling you how her book ends.

Dealing with the Dumps

We don't need to tell you that dating—online and everywhere—is far from easy. It might take months, years to find your mate. So, when you're feeling blue, take heart. "It's fine to take a break if you get discouraged. Remind yourself: The more guys you go out with, the more you eliminate. It's a good thing. It's a numbers game. You're separating the wheat from the chaff."

"I never gave up on the system itself. I just figured I was having bad luck with it . . . I felt like I was in control of my own destiny. Bottom line: You're never going to have the kind of dating disaster that you would if someone else were choosing your date," says Suzanne.

BLIND DATE

Be who you are, and say what you feel, because those who mind don't matter and those who matter don't mind.
—Dr. Seuss

You have to walk carefully in the beginning of love; running across the fields into your lover's arms can only come later when you're sure they won't laugh if you trip.
—Jonathan Carroll

There's nothing like not knowing the person you're about to go on a date with to induce a serious case of the front-of-the-closet freeze. Once the prospect of presenting yourself to a total stranger and potential romantic partner seeps into your head, you're suddenly lost in a swarm of wardrobe options— with absolutely nothing to wear. Your body suddenly appears strangely foreign in the mirror, like that time when you had to spell-check the word "the" because it just didn't look right. Thing is, there's much more to a blind date than what you wear. (This is a good thing . . . we think.) The beauty— and the challenge—of getting through your first such experience with grace is, like the good doctor up there says, is giving your true self a chance.

Le Setup

For us singletons, the mere offense of being romantically unattached is enough to merit punishment in the form of pitying offers from coupled co-workers, family members, neighbors, customer service phone reps— you name it. Do not hate the hitched for their good intentions.

Do, however, take a moment to think about who's trying to mastermind your love life. Pay attention. If you've heard how your secretary's neighbor's brother is a charmer who's new in town, go for it. If, on the other hand, you've heard the charmer has actually charmed the pants off three women in your office so far, stay away.

It's completely kosher to do some reconnaissance before entrusting your free time—and fashion effort—to a near stranger. You should be able to learn the basics from the setter upper. Is your date on the rebound? Painfully shy? A single parent? In town for the week only? You already know your own dating criteria. If this stranger doesn't fit into your must-haves for a partner, don't make the date.

THINGS YOU'LL DO EVEN THOUGH YOU KNOW BETTER (NOT QUITE VIRGIN'S DOWNFALLS)

Google your date

Heck. It can't hurt to find out that he came in 1,207th in the Boston Marathon, is an active member in Mensa, or recently received the cashier of the month award. Just be prepared. We know someone who canceled a date based on erroneous Google-based knowledge and now regrets it.

Drink too much

Dirty martinis taste awesome; we can't blame you for ordering one too many. As long as you're in a safe place—and don't mind a hangover—don't worry too much about it. This is especially OK if you're OK with your date being a one-hit wonder. Then again, your partner for the evening might know someone who'd be perfect for you . . . and might not give you the reference if you end your rendezvous on a blotto note.

It doesn't hurt if you know what your date knows, either. No use fretting about revealing your recent divorce, bad luck with boys, or chronic case of giggles if you know that the setter upper has already spilled those beans.

Le Pre-Date Exchange

This can be via e-mail, land line, cell, or smoke signal. No matter. Just keep it brief.

Our favorite blind date arrangement is those three little words a girl loves to hear: drinks before dinner. (Some folks recommend meeting for coffee. Others think breakfast is a nice, safe, and quick option. We, however, are cranky in the morning and know there's no way we're stressing over what to wear to a Starbucks.)

So, drinks it is. Why not dinner, too? Because afterward, you have dinner plans—also known as an escape route—even if you're planning to head home afterward for a Lean Cuisine and a visit to *Deadwood.* Plan to meet in a fairly popular bar and restaurant that you've been to but you don't frequent, some place where you'll know what to wear, some place with a bar and tables near the bar.

Les Preparations

This may be romance's equivalent of a job interview, but there's no reason to stress. Easy for us to say? You bet it is. It gets easier the more dates you go on, but it's never a cinch.

Employ your best self-knowledge to psych yourself into calm enthusiasm. If you know Vandross's velvet voice soothes you like no other's, crank up Le Luther. If you need to pop a mini bottle of nerve-settling champagne, by all means. Invite a pal over for your prep time, get your nails done, stand on your head—whatever it takes.

One surefire way to fray your nerves: Be late. There's nothing like a dash in heels or sweating behind the wheel to destroy your dating cool. So be early and bring along some ice-breaking reading material. We like *The New Yorker* and British *Vogue*.

Le Rendezvous

So. You've met. You've ordered your drinks. Three sips into it, and you're pretty sure you're not into it. You sip some more. You chitchat, avoiding remotely romantic overtones. You thank Bachelor Number None for meeting you, excuse yourself, and exit. Sticking around for drink number two isn't polite; it's leading the fellow on.

Or. You have your drink. You're very into your date. You think your date may just feel the same way. Well, would you look here? You just happen to be in a great little restaurant, and just happen to have a cell phone to call your imaginary friends who you were supposed to meet for an imaginary dinner to tell them to go on their imaginary ways without you.

Your date may suspect that you never had any plan all along. Your date may mention this suspicion. Panic not. Confess instead. "You're right. I'm sorry. I didn't realize how much fun I'd have with you until we met." Apologize, then compliment. Works every time.

La Conversation

We love a good, fake résumé as much as the next girl. But while this is the time to be on your best behavior, it's not the moment to fluff your stuff.

SETTING UP SINGLE FRIENDS ON A BLIND DATE: YES, YOU CAN!

Do the singles of the universe a favor. Don't set them up on blind dates. Be different.

Yes, we know, this section is a blind date primer. But we thought we'd help out you benevolent and coupled pals out there who are plotting to lose your matchmaking virginity. Instead of trying to create sparks between your two soccer-loving pals or the new person who moved into the apartment across the hall and your number one co-worker, throw a party!

Surely footballers and neighbors aren't your only unhitched friends who could use a date. Round 'em all up at a shindig of your own making—and let them do their own dirty work. Be sure to include couples, too; they'll serve as cover for your deviously romantic designs. The get-together can be big or small, at your place or in a local pub. Need an excuse? What about feting a celebrity birthday, your recent foray into homebrewing, or your new karaoke machine? Make no announcement of your love connection intentions. Your guests will be wily enough to find the love you so subtly set up.

Worried about uncomfortable silences? Subjects that are commonsense conversation starters: blockbuster movies, new restaurants, recent travel, and favorite bands.

Do us a favor: Go easy on the negative criticism. Much cuter to talk about the stuff you like. We're sure you already know this information, but our mothers have so ingrained it into our skulls that we'd feel remiss not to. Please avoid sex, politics, and religion.

Finding that your heart is going pitter-patter? Employ your feminine wiles—the ol' hair toss, the cross-legged ankle roll, the pearly white flash, the eyelash flutter—to show that you're interested. (Now, we didn't have to tell you that, either, did we?)

La Check

Split it. The only case in which it's OK to let the other person pay is when you're gunning for a second date. When your date insists, smile and say, "OK, as long as I can pay for our next dinner together."

FIRST DATE AFTER A BREAKUP

You are broken up. No need to rehash who did the breaking, how long it took, how many friends you have to phone each day just to get by. You are heartbroken. It sucks.

Despite this heartbreak, though, you're going out on a date with someone new. No matter if you're testing the waters mere hours after the split—something that should happen only after the demise of the most casual of relationships—or if you're putting yourself out there after months ruminating on the end of an epic relationship. The same rule applies: The first date after a breakup is all about YOU.

You! Marvelous, brokenhearted you! You may not be completely—or even a little bit—over your last love, but GODDAMNIT, you're not out of the game. Know what? You're going to have a great time to boot.

Speaking of boots, your guide throughout this bold journey is . . .

GO-TO GIRL

Jennifer Worick

Coauthor of the Only Dating Advice Books We'll Ever Read: *Worst Case Scenario Survival Handbook: Sex and Dating* (and, when all fails, *Rebound Rituals*)

To this day, Jen's favorite date remains a midnight rendezvous at a Denny's with a boy from her college. "I love the after-hours diner date," she says. A true woman of the dating world, Jen has survived her fair share of breakups. Her personal, tried-and-true remedy: cocktail-fueled,

(continued)

GO-TO GIRL (continued)

juicy-detailed discussions with her best girl friends. But she also encourages women to write hate mail that never gets sent, consult the tarot, purchase swell new skivvies, travel solo, take up kick boxing, and, best of all, buy a pair of extra-cute "breakup boots." The moral of Jen's story: "Do whatever makes you feel better," she says. (Although she does insist that your rebound rituals remain within the confines of the law.)

Let "It's all about me" be your mantra, because it's a bona fide law of the universe that trying too hard to meet a new mate rarely leads to long-term romance anyway. Plus, chances are, you're not ready to assume the girlfriend role already. You are, however, ready for a good time.

Remember how your ex hated to spring for dessert? Remember how he scoffed at your tastes in music, movies, and just about everything else that mattered to you? Remember how you two would run out of things to say to each other after a quick rehashing of your day at the office, or how the attention stopped coming your way and instead seemed always to be diverted to attractive passersby?

Get ready for a whole new world. A world that spins on the axis of y-o-u . . . you.

The whole point: Get yourself in the mood for some lighthearted fun. If worse comes to worst, at the very least, you'll get "an hour of conversation to distract you from your pain," says Jen.

In the Mood

Jen is of two minds on this subject. Either enjoy the getting ready, or don't worry about it at all.

"I always have the best times when I don't have time to think about my appearance, when I just go out and don't worry about how I look," says Jen. If you're fine with the au naturel look—and the prospect of blow-dryers and eyelash curlers and choosing something dateworthy to wear turns you into a nervous Nellie, then go with this one. "Only leave yourself a few minutes to get ready. Then, just go," says Jen.

On the other hand, if you tend to freak out if you're not recently blown out, polished, and powdered, then by all means take your time getting ready. Just be sure to enjoy the process. "This is no time for jeans and a T-shirt. Buy something new—or wear an outfit you feel dazzling in." (This does not include the one sparkly piece of clothing your ex ever offered you: Keep all relics of past relationships far, far from your body.) Wanna feel extra pretty but look casual? "Wear your most fabulous lingerie. Only you'll know it's there, but it'll give you a boost from the bottom up!"

Another of Sergeant Worick's tactics for avoiding the post-breakup, pre-date jitters: "Call in reinforcements," says Jen. "Have a friend come over to chat with you while you get ready. A good gossip session can take your mind off your nerves."

Daytime Date

Seem to get all weepy after seven? Make a daytime date—one that involves plenty of distractions but minimal travel. Staying near home base is always a smart strategy, especially in case of a sudden, unexpected onset of the breakup blues: "No boating, no hot air balloons, no private jets," says Jen. "No coffee date, either," which Jen deems too in-your-face, too quick, not full-fledged enough to rev up your dating motor. For Jen: "I like the activity dates: going hiking, shooting hoops, going bowling."

Evening Date

This is your big chance to supplant the hours you could be wasting by pining and zoning in front of prime-time TV. Plan something that really appeals, something you'd enjoy doing with just about anyone but your ex. Something new—and possibly kitschy. Roller skating. Karaoke. Korean barbecue. The circus. An amusement park. A tiki bar. "Meet in a location you know and feel comfortable in," says Jen. Needless to say, do not meet at the restaurant where you and your ex went every Tuesday night for all-U-can-eat U-peel shrimp. Go somewhere new but safe, with a manageable crowd.

VIRGIN'S DOWNFALL

If any of the following things happen—you get smashed, you sleep with the date, you experience that unpleasant strain of verbal diarrhea which causes you to talk incessantly about your ex—don't beat yourself up about it. Believe us, MILLIONS of virgins have made much worse dating errors. (We know this to be true, because we have been those millions of virgins.)

Jen also likes the idea of adding an extra, conversation-starting activity into the mix, something you haven't done before: Play quizzo or foosball. Watch a soccer match or a little league game. Visit a science, history, or wax museum.

Her other unconventional wisdom: "Beer goggles aren't necessarily a bad thing." Drinking, while not to excess, doubtless eases that inevitable first date angst. If, on the other hand, you know you're the type who turns into a Girl Gone Wild if you have one too many, line up some lifelines who'll diligently phone you one, two, three hours into your excursion. Their job is to talk you down from the bar top, to meet up with you by accident, or, in case of a martini-induced, in-the-ladies'-room breakup slump, to meet you with shoulders at the ready to cradle a downpouring of tears.

Enjoying It

Afraid you'll lose nerve? "View this date as practice. Flirt, be brutally honest, whatever . . . Treat the date as a little game: See how many times you can get him to compliment you or to kiss you," says Jen.

Remember: Whatever makes you feel good is what's right. Of course, there are certain things that may make you feel good at the moment—and terrible the next day. We think you know what we're talking about, because it's the advice everyone gives at this point: Don't give in to the rebound urge.

Kiss, hold hands, make out, shake your booty to your heart's content. But if you really, truly are dating in order to make yourself feel better in the long run, hold off on the baserunning.

DATE WITH A SINGLE PARENT

Well, it's come to this, has it? One day, you're playing house with the little boy across the street. Today, you're playing with the boy and his little boy.

Or, maybe you're not hopscotching with Junior just yet. Maybe you're not even playing with Senior. Maybe you're just toying with the idea of the whole thing.

Wherever you are with your single parent prospect, it's a good thing to sit down and have a little think before diving deep—or even wading—into this particular romance. And when we say "little," we actually mean think pretty hard. Because as fabulously sexy as it may seem to play Sheryl Crow dating the handsomely calved (and handsome-calved) Lance Armstrong, dating a single parent is a lot like the Tour de France. The ride is awesome—but it's far from a pedal around the park. So let's start you out with a few, basic red flags.

Beware

The my-baby's-mama-just-moved-out-a-month-ago-and-the-divorce-papers-aren't-signed-yet-but-seriously-I'm-ready-for-a-new-relationship parent. Don't believe the hype. You know how insanely long it takes you to heal from a breakup (and if you don't, just take our word for it that it takes at least as much time as all those breakup formulas suggest).

This daddy is nowhere near romance ready. Which means, either he's laying on the lines in order for him to lay his body on yours, or he's so screwed up that he doesn't know which way is up.

If it's the first sex-only scenario, by all means, fling away. Just don't expect a second date. If it's the second, look out. Enter into a serious relationship with this deluded dad, and you're bound to end up where his baby's mama is today. Yes, he may be a great guy. So be a friend. Give him the name of a good therapist, and tell him to call you after a year of sessions.

The here-meet-my-kids-before-we-leave-for-our-first-date parent. This fellow is defying rule number one of parental dating; the law that decrees: No kiddie involvement until the relationship is quite serious. Meeting the kids too soon can make the kids sad or mad and can make you sad or mad, which means that the parent doesn't have either of your interests at heart.

The I-didn't-want-to-tell-you-about-my-child-because-I-didn't-want-to-scare-you-off-and-oh-by-the-way-did-I-mention-I-have-another-kid-too parent. Did he also forget to mention that he's not actually a doctor, that he just plays one on TV? We're not ones to issue dramatic directives—OK, maybe we are—but we've gotta break out this baby pronto: Stay away. Maybe enjoy a romp. But if you're looking for any kind of emotional connection, stay away. Away!

The I-love-my-baby-but-I-hate-my-ex parent. And he expects you to think this is a good thing—and to take his side immediately, based on his ability to carry on a meal's worth of conversation? Honey, didn't his mama tell him that making other people look ugly doesn't make him prettier? And where exactly does he get off insulting the person who spawned his minihim? What's that we smell in the air? Bitter? Looks like a storm's abrewing at yonder other end of the table. Better run for cover.

These are the biggest no-go profiles. Truth is, most single parents fall somewhere between the dating pattern lines. Which is why you ought to know what they might be thinking before you do any wading, diving, or otherwise.

Dating Rules That Fly out the Window, Break on the Ground, and Generally Do Not Apply

Never discuss your personal life on a first date. Usually, the first date is the time to meet, hang out, have a couple of drinks, maybe end it with "Hey, I had fun. Wanna throw back a few more beers at the game on Saturday?" It's casual—at least it tries to appear to be.

But when that first date's with a dad, the devil-may-care attitude can quickly turn serious. Your date may bubble over with love for his kids. He'll break out the wallet-size school pics. He may even get teary. He may admit that he's not the most available single guy on the block. He might even take your hand and say, "But I really like you, and would like to see you at the same time next week." Don't pull back your hand and scream in fear. This is a guy who's been around the block. At least he knows what he wants.

Never discuss your exes with a new love. This cardinal canon breaks PDQ—at least it ought to—in the dating-a-single-parent scenario. There are a few reasons for this, all of which stem from the likelihood that an ex is still part of your new love's life.

The discussion can be nothing but unpleasant, but once you've delved ever so briefly into the ex files, you'll be glad you did. After all, you have a right to know if you're going to be sucked into a bizarre love triangle—or if it will likely be smooth sailing.

It's important for his friends and family to meet you. Friends, fine (as long as they're not part of some evil plan to rat you out to a dastardly ex). But family? Well, make sure it's serious before you (1) fall hard and fast for the little cherubs, or (2) commit yourself to trying, ever so gently, to win over his shy, angry, hesitant, ill-adjusted but otherwise perfectly adorable brood.

Kids can tell if you're nervous. Kids like to say things like "We saw you and daddy kissing in the car last week" and "I know how babies are made." Kids like stability. They are suspicious of strangers. Let Dad lead the way. Don't step in and discipline. Don't take their side just because you think it will help you win friends and influence children.

When you do meet the children, tread lightly. If they become too much to bear, be honest. They are—and should be—the potential deal breakers.

Hear these wise parting words from our model daddy dater.

GO-TO GIRL

Lise Funderburg
Writer, Critic, Intellectual
and Wicked-Good Stepmother

Philly girl Lise knew the handsome architect from the personals ad had a teenage son. But she was meeting and dating the man during the summer, when the boy was clear across the country. The new couple had two whole months, says Lise, "to date like two single people." But with fall came orange leaves, cool nights—and the end to sleepovers. "I actually didn't mind, which may be why the man fell in love with me," she says, advising virgin daddy daters. "When you go into this, if you like the guy, then you'd better sign a noncompete clause with the kid—metaphorically." Her sage counsel: Respect that the child is the first priority—and that when you do meet, you give the kid space by not performing or appearing to try too hard. "One way that I paced myself was to kind of repeat this little mantra: 'We should only like each other if we like each other.'"

WEEKEND GETAWAY

Finding it impossible to concentrate on almost anything in the heat except fantasies about going on mini-breaks with Daniel. Head is filled with visions of us lying in glades by rivers me in long white floaty dress; Daniel and I sitting outside ancient Cornish waterside pub sipping pints in matching striped T–shirts and watching the sun set over the sea; Daniel and I eating candlelit dinners in historic country-house-hotel court-yards then retiring to our room to shag all hot summer night.
—Bridget Jones, *Bridget Jones's Diary*

It's a date. It's a vacation. It's the weekend. It's three things rolled up into one delicious mix of adventure, romance, and the lovely prospect of not having to worry about who's calling or not calling whom the next day, because the next day, you'll be together.

On the one hand, this is going to be great: just the two of you, no home-related entanglements, and a whole new backdrop to play out the next chapter in your own romantic comedy.

On the other, the getaway weekend seems suspiciously testlike. Will you get on each other's nerves? Will the mystery disappear? Will you wind up in a buzz-killing traffic jam, reservations mix-up, or political debate? The vacation-sucking variables seem dangerously unlimited.

Your best bet: Prepare for the controllable—and potentially contentious—unknown outcomes ahead of time.

Before You Go

Planning. This should go without saying, but you two lovebirds really oughta pick a spot that pleases you both.

If you planned the trip together, plan to split the cost. If your partner's done the inviting—and there's no way you can pay your way—explain this ahead of time. Instead, hold your bargain's end by: tipping the bellboy and bartender, picking up the tab for morning lattes and bike rental fees, stocking a picnic basket for your lunch in the park. You get the drift.

GO-TO GIRL

Danielle Burgio

Hollywood Stunt Double for Starlets and Dating Dynamo

When Dani's not running up walls in *The Matrix Reloaded*, kicking villain ass on behalf of Jennifer Garner in *Daredevil*, or doubling for J-Lo in *Monster-in-Law*, she's climbing rocks, jumping on trampolines, and putting dates through their paces at grueling salsa lessons. But when it comes to spending quality time with her guy-of-the-moment, this fall girl takes no risks. She maps routes. She packs light. She makes reservations for rooms with jacuzzis and fireplaces. She leaves on time. When it comes to romantic getaways, there's nothing like a little R&R to bring a couple together. Dani muses, "There's something about just getting out of town with somebody."

Preparing. If your weekends are usually filled with errand-running, take a half day on Friday. Like an early dismissal, leaving work before the bell rings feels as if it has special-privilege appeal. Those Saturday chores—going to the car wash, getting your nails done, running to the Laundromat, stopping by the pharmacy—will take half the time on a weekday, leaving you plenty of time to make extra fun preparations for your trip.

Such as . . . Make an MP3 mix or burn a CD for the drive. Book a table for two for Saturday night. Fill a basket with all the things he'll forget—razor, shaving cream, toothbrush, floss, condoms, a comb, a prepaid gas card (if he's driving), sample-size deodorant (so not cute if he borrows yours), a tube of Chapstick, the latest David Sedaris paperback.

Packing. "I always pack light," says Dani. "One or two pieces that are sexy and fun, a couple that are very casual and comfortable, one pair of good shoes, one pair of flip-flops, minimal makeup and jewelry—and a bathing suit, because you never know when you're going to get a chance to jump into a pool or a Jacuzzi."

Three more things she won't leave home without: her camera, iPod, and a notebook for journaling.

After You Arrive

Precious private moments. You will be tempted to spend every lovin' minute with your weekend companion. Don't. An hour or two apart gives you a chance to collect your thoughts, regain your composure, nap, or work out. Choose a short-term solo activity and let it build eager anticipation for the togetherness to come.

"You shouldn't be afraid to lock yourself in the bathroom for an hour to take a bath. Go down to the pool. Throw on your ear buds and go for a walk by yourself. Schedule a massage," suggests Danielle.

Even idyllic, first times away together can spiral downward when traffic jams, bad directions, lost luggage, or good old-fashioned low blood sugar rudely interrupts the romantic voyage. If escape is possible during this minor glitch in the plans, run with it. Any excuse will do, even something as nonsensical and out of the question as "I'm training for a 10K and really need to go for a run today. Meet you back in the room in an hour or so?"

Even more private moments. You know what we're talking about. You gotta go. For real. Trouble is, he's in the room, watching the OLN, lounging like nothing's doing—within dangerously close hearing—and smelling—range of *la toilette.* Don't panic. You have options.

- The Classic: A move so timeless, so decorous, it's rumoured that Grace Kelly invented it. Announce you're taking a shower. Hope he's so glued to *Fly Fishing the World* that he doesn't remember you already took one today. Enter bathroom. Lock door. Turn on the bath water. Have a seat on lady loo. Do your stuff. Close the lid. If your hair needs no washing, help yourself to the complimentary shower cap. Step into the shower. Get wet enough to appear dewy. Emerge. REMEMBER TO FLUSH!

- The Brochure in the Hotel Lobby. If stage fright or common sense tells you the Classic won't work, dash out on this educational errand. You'll be back in a minute, you say. No, you say, you don't need company. Just popping down for the map of the surrounding historic sites and popping back up again. Keep enjoying the trout show. The beauty of the hotel lobby restroom: It's rarely occupied, always open, and centrally located.

- No Can Poo Because You're in a B&B? Dash out on surprise errand. He can't come along because he'd ruin the surprise. Head to any of the nearest usual public facility suspects—fast-food restaurant, coffee shop, gas station, train station—and remember to pick up a bottle of wine on the way back.

- Humor. Those bold enough to reveal this less sexy side of reality, might as well make it funny. "Hey, do you mind if I turn up the TV? I have some business to take care of in the bathroom" or "You go on ahead: I'm gonna stick around to drop something off in the lav." It won't be your most seductive of moments, but it will sure break the tension.

Additional, essential bathroom etiquette. Remember how he said to you, "Oh, you wear makeup? But you look so natural," and you replied, "Yes, I guess you could say I'm a low-maintenance girl." Now he's gonna find out that your world record for in-and-out morning bathroom time clocked in at just under fifty-five minutes. You could sneak out of bed an hour early, and hop back in, fully washed, brushed, and lip glossed before he notices you're gone. But we sleeping beauts need our Zs.

Here's a crazed notion: Why not skip the shampoo this morning, and wear a cute little baseball cap to breakfast? (You can clean and condition those tresses when he's down for his afternoon nap.) A pre-trip wax job will cut down on shaving time. Still, he's gonna figure out that you're no movie-star rise-and-shiny type. Might as well fess up, be first in line for the shower, and lay off the eyeliner if it's going to cut into your couple time.

5

There's something wholly liberating about walking with purpose through an airport terminal. You have checked in at the ticket counter. Your overhead compartment–compliant luggage trails you on tiny wheels like an obedient pup. As you stride toward your gate, you feel as chic as a circa 1965 Pan Am flight attendant, or, at the very least, a Breck Girl.

What? You haven't felt this level of travel confidence before? You've only felt the panic of waiting in too-long security lines, the pain of the strap from your stuffed-to-the-gills duffel bag digging into your shoulder, and that sweaty, desperate dash toward the gate? Ah yes. We know you.

You're the same girl who freaks out when the drugstore runs out of travel-size talcum powders. You're the one who buys into convenient resort packages and misses out on sipping juice from a just-sliced coconut at St. Lucia's Castries market. You've fought the crowds to see the shockingly small *Mona Lisa,* but you've never had the pleasure of getting blissfully lost in the Louvre. During the annual work conference in Chicago, you retire early to your suite, expense room service, catch up on e-mail, and turn in early. You've never even partaken in the excellently popular trend of extending the traditional girls' night out into a ladies-only week in Brazil.

Girl, you're missing out. It's time to renew your passport, change your oil, call up your classmates and make international connections. It's travel time.

TRIP ABROAD

A tourist is someone who thinks about going home the moment he arrives. A traveler might not come back at all.
—PAUL BOWLES

Certainly, travel is more than the seeing of sights; it is a change that goes on, deep and permanent, in the ideas of living.
—MIRIAM BEARD

We're not big fans of the expression "You had to be there." We find this expression condescending, not to mention envy-inspiring. But we've gotta say, when it comes to taking your first step onto foreign soil, pavement, grass, or gravel, well, you've gotta be there to get it.

The rush at the start of a visit to a new country renews itself each time we do it. Gives us goose bumps just to think about. And, here to back up our bumps are our favorite globe-trotting duo, a pair who so thoroughly rely on their government-issued traveling papers, they named their jet-setting cosmetics company after it.

GO-TO GIRL

**Meredith McGann
and Erin Cotter**

The Travel-Abroad
Broads of Passport Cosmetics

Cute Erin and Meredith were world adventurers before they were makeup artists, and makeup artists before entrepreneur-creators of a plainly luxe line of cleverly packable makeup essentials. These days, the pair keeps busy selling all-in-one cream blush, shimmery shadows, and Lipsticket (tear 'n' go single application lipstick tickets) to Sephora. Nonetheless, they make time to flit to Tokyo, Oaxaca, Pisa, and Rio for regular doses of overseas intrigue. "For me to survive as a person I must take at least one international trip a year," says Erin. "Some people get their adrenaline from jumping out of an airplane. For me, it's arriving some place I've never been before." But where to go, exactly? Meredith says, "Head anywhere that gives you a different flavor from your everyday life."

What You'll Need

A passport. Score an application online at travel.state.gov (where you'll also be able to view the latest version of the government's top ten travel abroad tips). Find paper applications at your friendly neighborhood post office, various municipal buildings, courthouses, and most public libraries.

First-time applicants submit their applications in person. The fee is about $55, plus a $30 security surcharge for a new passport ($12 if you're renewing). You arrange for your own adorable two-by-two head shot (which you can take at any mall photo store). A passport application takes about six weeks to process (two if you pay an additional $60 for expedited service).

A destination. Next, you'll take to the task of deciding where to get your cute little abroad-traveling fanny to. May we suggest a foreign-but-not-too-foreign country? Great Britain's a nice place, very stylish and fun, with pubs and crown jewels and princes and such. Western Europe, in general, is the world's most travel-able continent. Caribbean islands and Mexico in the winter, New Zealand any time at all . . . any country where you have family and friends to take you in makes a great maiden voyage destination.

Since planning (and dreaming of) where to go is a big part of the fun, we'll let you pick for yourself. When you do, however, make sure to find out if you need a nifty l'il visa to go with that passport. (Australia, Kenya, China, and Brazil, for example, require visitors to have visas for even short-term stays. Most countries need to see proof of when you're headed back home. Most any country requires that your passport doesn't expire before your trip ends.)

Not-so-heavy-that-you-can't-carry-it-up-three-flights-of-steps-when-it's-full luggage. "I'm a one-bag traveler, and it's usually a carry-on," says

Meredith. "I have a rule that I need to wear everything that I pack at least once."

Erin agrees. "I would never pack anything in my suitcase that I couldn't wear with more than two things. I have this little black cotton halter dress I bring everywhere it's warm. I wear it to the beach in the day, and dress it up with cute earrings at night." Her favorite take-anywhere item: a silk slip dress by Dosa. "You can crinkle it up into a ball, shove it in your suitcase. If you get it dirty, you wash it in the sink, and it's dry in fifteen minutes."

Both Go-tos rely on layers—and firmly believe in dutifully checking the weather forecast before zipping up their bags.

More must-pack items.

- Large Ziploc bags—Great for sealing up potentially leaky bath and beauty products, perfect for storing still-damp lingerie or swimsuits, perfect for carrying impromptu collections of seashells, postcards, handmade soaps, bits of antique lace. Our number one no-forget item.
- Hand sanitizer or Handi Wipes—It's no fun catching a common cold when you're exploring uncommon places.
- Satin pillowcase—For when you want to preserve your 'do. Also doubles as a washer-safe lingerie bag (just knot the end), laundry sack, and, in times of overshopping, a carry-on.
- A good map—Especially if you're driving and don't speak the language.

- A pocket-sized dictionary—Good for when you're not able to pronounce "restroom" in every language but can always point to the word's entry and nod.
- A superabsorbent towel—Like the hair shammy at blissworld.com. Only you don't have to use it on your head only. This terry baby sucks up water with spongelike power and requires about as much suitcase real estate as two pairs of sweat socks.
- Head scarf for Islamic countries—Essential, though as a woman, you may not be permitted in many mosques.

A friendly bit of advice. As a general rule, the less developed the country, the more you'll need to pack. Bottled water, saline solution—even toilet paper and tampons—are hard to come by in loads of places. Others won't abide women's exposed navels, knees, or hair. So, if you're planning to dive headfirst into sub-Saharan Africa, outer Mongolia, or even Baja California, buy the guidebook. We have only so much room in ours. (Which guide book, you wonder? We polled a bevy of world-traveled women, and the *Lonely Planet* series won the popularity contest.)

Travel Abroad Phenomena

Jet lag. You think it's bad going from Cali to Maui, just wait until you get to Delhi. Everyone who travels seems to have a favorite remedy for jet lag. One is melatonin, a brain-secreted hormone believed to cause drowsiness. Over-the-counter melatonin comes in natural or synthetic form. One 1 mg tablet should do you right, although some travelers recommend a onetime 5 mg dosage to combat serious lag.

Another is valerian, not a Valley-dweller, but a safe, gentle root-based remedy that assists in your transport to the Land of Nod—and doesn't transport you as far as the land of hangover. It's available in powders (one teaspoon in a cup of hot water), capsules (one 250–500 mg dosage), or tinctures (one to one and a half teaspoons).

Fijians have been drinking kava for centuries. Kava root can be used for relaxation (island living is so stressful) and as a sleep aid. How much? A half hour before sleep, 180 to 210 mg.

And a prescription-only medication, Ambien, takes about fifteen minutes to put you out. See your doc for dosage info.

(A word to the wise: Even over-the-counter remedies shouldn't be taken casually. Ask your friendly hippie herbalist or your family doc before indulging.)

But here's the real trick: Take a short refresher siesta upon arrival and force yourself to stay up until the town goes to bed. New-country excitement works wonders for keeping a girl bright-eyed. "It's really important to put yourself on the right schedule right away," says Meredith.

Crazy schedules. "It is critical when you are a tourist to learn the schedule of the people who live where you are," says Meredith. "If you are in Spain and go to dinner at 9:00, you'll be sitting in an empty restaurant. The Spanish have dinner at 11:00. Italians eat lunch at 1:30. Go to dinner in Rio before 11:00 or 11:30, and you won't have fun." In Israel, everything closes on Friday at sundown. In France, many shops close early, or are closed completely, on Sunday. Italian towns pick one day of the week to shut down, and different Italian towns play hooky on different days.

Typical tourist traps. In Paris? By all means ride the elevator to the top of *la Tour Eiffel.* When in Rome, go to the Pantheon; London, to Tower Bridge; Tokyo, to Tsukiji Fish Market. Just don't stick around these places exclusively. The treasures of each city are found in the little side streets. Be careful, of course, just how little and dark the street is—and how alone you are. But by all means, wander!

"It's amazing," says Erin. "You'd think Pisa existed only for the tower. But if you walk five minutes away from there, there's not a tourist in sight. Florence is another one. Start wandering around and find out how the locals are. It's important, of course, to see the attractions. But then leave that area!"

Typical tourist behavior. Travelers—especially American ones—fall into two categories. There are the travelers who don't care that they are known as tourists, and the travelers who want to appear to be local. We sympathize with both sides.

"Don't be afraid to be a tourist," says Erin. "I love to ask locals for recommendations for restaurants, markets, places to see." When it comes to advice, no travel tome can give you the coordinates for the hot new tapas bar that opened last week, or the latest exhibit at an independently owned art gallery. So, the minute you ask a question, you're a tourist. But the minute you walk through the door of the coolest new dance club in town, you're a traveler.

Overscheduling. This is your first foreign vacation, not "the Amazing Race." Take it easy. If you miss one of the ten attractions on your itinerary, don't sweat it. Most of the world thinks Americans are too high-strung. Why not see how the other, less-stressed part of the globe lives for a little while?

Atypical Tourism Ideas

Shopping. Every time Erin and Meredith are in London or Tokyo, they hit the pharmacies and supermarkets for charmingly packaged items that they just can't find back home. (This little trick also saves them the trouble of packing toothpaste and lotion.) They also like to head to locally owned shops. They fell in love with a little clothing boutique in Rio and a shop that made its own bath products in Oaxaca. But they're not above hitting the chains, either, especially in Europe, which still is ahead of the curve on the fashion front. In England, they head to the high streets, where they're sure to find the super-stylish and astoundingly bargain-filled TopShop, among others.

Oh yes. And we think tacky souvenirs are fun. And costume jewelry, since you obviously will not be bringing your own family bling along for the ride. How about a charming charm to commemorate the start of your fabulous life of world travel?

VIRGIN'S DOWNFALL

Adventuresome Amanda had read up. She knew that in Europe, birthplace of Coco Chanel's little black dress, there was no room for color in her suitcase. She packed black jeans, black skirts, black blouses and bras and tights and turtlenecks and comfortable walking shoes. Then she arrived in Amsterdam, Madrid, Lisbon, or Berlin. She looked around. She saw color. Maybe a little more subdued, a little less obvious than back in the States—thankfully, the Red Hat Ladies hadn't wholly invaded the Continent—but there it was, as sure and as solid as the euro itself. She looked at them and saw a smartly tailored rainbow. She looked at herself and saw a stagehand. Lucky for mobile Mandy, there's some fine shopping over yonder.

Museum going. A trick for tackling mega art meccas in new cities? "Rather than seeing the whole museum, I go to an exhibit. Even if you're going to the Louvre, by going to just an exhibit, you're making it more manageable and are more likely to get something out of it. Plus, that's where the locals are going," says Erin.

Movie going. Cinemas in other countries can be a blast—especially the places where they're more like real theaters. Some still employ tray-toting servers who walk around selling snacks at the start of the film. (We love this.) If you're in a non-English-speaking country, make sure the film is subtitled—not dubbed. Or, check out a re-released English-speaking classic: You'll be surprised how many lines you can remember from *E.T.* and *Gone With the Wind.* (Plus, you'll learn how to say "Frankly, my dear, I don't give a damn," in Polish.)

Hotel picking. Meredith's one splurge when she heads far from home? Location. "I'll spend extra money to stay in a neighborhood where I want to stay," she says, "I'd rather pay more to stay in a nice, small, fun, cute hotel than to stay in one by a train station." The safest hotel rooms: the ones on the highest floors.

Ruling the road. If you're planning to rent a car during your trip, learn the traffic laws. Americans are famous for getting into wrecks in Australia, Great Britain, and Jamaica, where the driving sides are switched.

It doesn't hurt to read up on traffic laws, either. Erin's example of a mini Virgin's Downfall: "When we were in Mexico, I turned on my left-hand turn signal to turn left, and when I went to turn, I got hit. In Mexico, the left turn signal means to pass you on the left."

Lesson learned: Spring for the rental insurance.

Topless tip. We are all for the sublimely liberating experience that is upper-half frontal sunbathing. But for goodness sake, don't lay your fifty-percent-naked body down on a beach towel and expect not to attract attention—not if your lovely bosom pales in comparison to your lovely belly, or any of your many other exposed body parts. We have sat on too many French, Brazilian, Italian, and, for that matter, Miami beaches and watched too many American women let it all hang out, then wonder how the local cheeseballs who come to talk to them know they are from out of town.

GROUP VACATION

The great difference between voyages rests not with the ships,
but with the people you meet on them.
—Amelia E. Barr

We women certainly like to go to public restrooms in pairs. Sometimes we go in posses. Sociologists don't know why we do this. But if the magazine reporters are right, we're doing it more and more, and not just to the restroom. They're calling the dozens of new women-only travel groups that have cropped up in the past few years "feminist tour groups."

The Women's Travel Club, Women Traveling Together, Wild Women Expeditions, Gutsy Women Travel, Womanship, Abroad for Adventure, Tribe Travel, Arctic Ladies Adventure—these are just a handful of the groups that'll haul you half across the globe to mountain climb, practice yoga, take private museum tours, and, well, shop.

Still, there's no need to sign up for a package deal if you've got a girl friend gaggle and feel like biking through Thailand. Every girl knows that not only is there safety in numbers, but more than a few can be twice the fun. However, as TV shows from *The Facts of Life* to *Road Rules* have reminded us, sometimes the best of friends don't always make the best of bunk mates. But they do bear a striking resemblence to a . . .

Cast and Crew

The producer/director. Usually, the person who came up with the idea in the first place, the primary mover, shoulders the arrangement-oriented tasks wherever she goes. She might come by her role naturally. She might not. You might want to vote her off the island, *Survivor* style, if she gets too bossy. You might want to give her a break by commandeering the map collection when her human GPS system goes on overload.

Whatever your feelings about the producer/director, make sure she's comfortable doing all she's doing. And thank her for it by buying her breakfast.

The supporting actress. She's the virgin who keeps it zipped when others bicker, who walks away when the gossip bug bites, who always chips in extra when the pot's short for the bill. Not coincidentally, she's the cast member everyone else eventually wants to hang with. She's also the person who, on the rare event that she expresses a strong opinion, will be listened to.

Be the Supporting Actress.

The diva. Aka the Drama Queen. There's one in every group. Walk by a bar with a karaoke contest, and she's dragging you in. When there's a glass worth of champagne left in the magnum, instead of topping everyone off, she'll turn up the bottle and swig it down herself. She can be so much fun—she's brought her collection of tiaras for everyone to wear to dinner, and she makes a great icebreaker when someone spies a gaggle of handsome locals—but she's also the biggest baby when she doesn't get her way.

Enjoy the Diva's outrageous charms, but beware her dark side.

The loner. The opposite of the Diva, this traveler is used to solo exploration. She'll wait for the group to agree to go shopping in town before announcing she's headed for a hike up a mountain. Others in the group will worry about her. But unlike the Diva, she's not being different to score attention. She just needs more time to herself. Give it to her. But ask her to tell you where she's going and when she plans to get back, for safety's sake.

When the togetherness feels too together, take a tip from the Loner: Treat yourself to a walk around the block, or a table for one.

The outsider. The cousin you haven't seen in ages, the neighbor you've always wanted to know better, the friend of a friend who signed up to come along at the last minute, isn't part of the regular posse and needs to

THE CHECK

On a regular old night on the town, we're the kind of girls who don't fret about the dinner check. Sure, we look out for a pal who's trying to save by eating an appetizer only—and, when our own savings are slim, we ask the group beforehand if it's OK if this time we pay what we owe. But for the most part, as everyone from the Etiquette Grrls (www.etiquettegrrls.com) to *Esquire* has told us, when you enter into a dining-out situation, you split the bill. No matter that Janice was the one who ordered the crème brûlée. You took a bite. Make your $2 contribution.

But when you're traveling with a group, the rule is: Make your own rule. Before you leave. Via e-mail. During a getting-devilish-for-Tasmania pre-voyage get-together at your place. Or on the flight. The conversation must be frank. Do you all share the same eating and drinking habits? Good. Plan to split every check. Does Jenelle drink the rest of you under the table? She'll owe extra at each meal. Does Jennifer eat like a bird? She should speak up: It's not fair for her to foot the bill if she's subsisting on soup and salad.

Get the grubby habits out in the open. Make a deal. And stick to it.

feel included. When she's around, skip the shoptalk. She may smile politely while everyone else yaps on about the ins and outs of your in-common office, college, knitting group, or social club, but inside she's asking herself why she came.

Be considerate. Let the Outsider call some shots.

But for the Outsider whom no amount of careful conversation will appease—the man who comes to an all-girl trip, the mom among single girls, the one hetero in a house full of happy gays—consider making room for one matching pal.

The rich one. She has earned her money, and she's going to enjoy it during this vacation, group budget be damned. The funny thing about wealth is that once you have it, you tend to forget that others don't. Don't feel bad turning down her invitation to a four-star restaurant, but don't begrudge her her pleasures, either.

If the Rich One is you, then consider springing for the bottle of wine once in a while. Just do it graciously, explaining that spreading the wealth tickles your fancy.

The poor one. For many of us, the flight and the lodging alone are enough to break the bank. Gals on a budget who aren't apprised of the cost of living—and vacationing—in a new place often set themselves up for disappointment. The best remedy for the cash-flow vacation blues? A good attitude and a backup plan. When the group goes out for a white tablecloth meal, smile, brandish your book, declare you're going to enjoy leftovers from lunch, and that you'll meet them for coffee after their meal.

GO-TO GIRL

Tricia Nelson

From Television Dreamer
to Tribe Guide

The travel bug took its first nibble out of Tricia when she was a regular viewer of the PBS series *Big Blue Marble* and had pen pals all the world over. Now at the helm of emerging travel club Tribe Travel, this L.A. woman has turned that big blue orb into her own, personal oyster—and she takes her pals along for the ride. "Back when I used to travel by myself, it was me trying to think of how to ask directions, trying not to freak out," says Tricia. "When you go in a group if you don't feel like being the leader one day, somebody else will do it." She and her fellow Tribe members have feted an *anniversaire* at the Arc de Triomphe, celebrated a pal's thirtieth in the clubs of Ibiza, sunbathed in Santorini, hung in a time-share in Fiji, and attended a wedding in Thailand (and that's just an excerpt from Tricia's worldly CV). Her mantra: "As long as you're with people you love and you're having a good time in a great location, you can't go wrong."

The Setting

One of the perks of voyaging en masse? Many bodies score better digs. We adore the increasing trend of renting out a ski chalet, beach house, or countryside villa for a week or two at a time. The incredible Internet is an ever-flowing font of these sorts of deals. Be sure to do a background check before you book—which includes finding out the hidden costs of such extras like phone service, utilities, and housekeeping, as well as what supplies you'll need to bring yourself.

Great times of year to travel? Go on Valentine's Day with a group of single pals. New Year's Eve—the king of the anticlimactic holidays—lives to its hype when you're out of town. (Plus, flights between December 25 and 31 can be real bargains.) Those end-of-winter blues seem to float away when you've got Margaritaville to look forward to in mid-March.

Or, Solo Flight

Not in the mood to deal with the group mentality, but not quite psyched to trek the Andes solo? Jet to Paris for a week of classes at Le Cordon Bleu. Escape to Barcelona to learn Spanish cooking (check out www.shawguides.com for resources). Attend The Workshops in Rockport, Maine, where you can take classes in photography, film, and video production by day—and crack up the lobsters by night. Got an itch to summon your inner Jane Austen? How about a writing retreat at one of the Arvon Foundation's rural locations? Pick your pleasure. And then book your ticket.

BUSINESS TRIP

"So, virgin, you want to take on the Vegas account?" your boss asks after you nail another presentation.

"You bet," you answer.

"OK. You're headed to the Nevada office next Wednesday," says boss lady.

"Ten-four," comes your reply.

This is going to be fun: All-night casinos, upscale malls in those casinos, celebrity chef restaurants in those malls, outdoor pools with misters and swim-up bars, shows involving bare-breasted dancers decked out in feathers and sequins. Wonder if Paul Anka will be playing the Sands—or if Siegfried and Roy are planning their big comeback to the Mirage? What was the name of that $12.99 all-you-can-eat buffet with the great lox that Aunt Bertha is always raving about?

Ah yes, we know how you're feeling. This first work-sponsored trip to Vegas—or Pasadena or Miami, or even Cleveland—appears to be an all-expenses-paid vacation.

Up until now, vacation is why you've traveled, right? To do something fun?

This is different. The travel still should be fun—but in a different way. Which is to say, don't brush up on your blackjack or book your bikini wax just yet. The fun part about traveling for work is the opportunities it brings. And we mean professional opportunities, not poolside or slot-machine pleasures.

You say you're leaving a week from tomorrow? Get cracking, virgin.

We're not talking about that PowerPoint presentation you have to give the Western marketing team, either. We're talking about what you're going to do for you—and your career.

What It Is

Trade show. Involves one or more large rooms—often an entire convention center—of booths and people in them. Either the people in the booths are trying to sell you things, or you *are* the booth person trying to sell things. Sometimes you leave the booths to attend a seminar about your job. But mostly, you're near the booths. Going to a trade show for the first time? Make appointments with the people you'd like to deal with beforehand—and prospect the lay of the land before you enter (especially at larger shows).

Convention. Also involves one or more rooms and/or a convention center, but this time, the focus is the seminars, not the buying and selling of goods and services (although that happens a lot, too).

The meeting. Just like in your home office, but this time, you must dress nicely and be on time, if not early. This time, you don't have your file cabinets or an assistant to save you when you realize you brought the Johnson folder, not the Jameson file. You made the effort to get here. Don't screw up the easy stuff.

The Logistics

Flying. This is just the beginning of your life as a savvy business traveler. Find out which airlines are most prevalent at your airport. Find out which ones fly most often to the places you'll be going for work and for pleasure, and if your company has a deal with one in particular.

Use this knowledge to sign up to be a frequent flyer, miles member, winged warrior, whatever. Do it now, because not all airlines let you apply used miles to a new account. (By the way, Amtrak has a frequent traveler program, too.)

Then find out what it takes to become an airline's club member—or whatever it's called—in order to be allowed behind the doors of its preferred travel lounge. Membership is typically tiered based upon your level of frequent flier status, but is usually priced in the several $100 range. Will your company pay for you to join? If not, and it's clear that you'll be logging a significant amount of time in airports, then consider it anyway. These nifty l'il outposts offer perks like faster check-in, preferred upgrades, free coffee, WiFi, newspapers, comfortable chairs, and snacks. Plus, they're a great place to rub elbows with important people.

Beyond that, you'll want to book your flight to arrive with a generous enough cushion of time that you can get there, get settled, and perform a little reconnaissance (more on that later).

Don't assume that just because your company is sending you out of town that you'll be traveling first-class and four-star all the way. Nor should you automatically suppose you'll score brownie points by scrimping and saving and sleeping on scratchy sheets and wilted pilllows at a Motel 6. Most large companies have detailed policies about travel perks depending on your rung on the corporate ladder. If your company has a travel agent, take the time to make nice with someone from that office who can inform you of the ins and outs, and maybe finagle an upgrade or two. If you're on your own for reservations, read the company's travel policies on expense limits and reimbursements, and clear your travel plans with your immediate boss before you go.

Hotel. Again, your company might have the last say on where you slumber. But if the sky's the limit on your corporate AmEx, take advantage of the most stocked hotel in the city's best location—which doesn't necessarily mean most convenient to your office. "Stocked" means it has a twenty-four-hour business center, WiFi or free high-speed Internet throughout, a savvy concierge, and a snazzy lounge.

"Best location" means it's near things that are going on, like restaurants and shops and coffee shops. This is because, while you're away, your number one mission (after showing up on time and prepared for your work obligations) is to meet people.

But don't take our word for it. Believe Jocelyn. Believe Marcelle.

GO-TO GIRLS

**Jocelyn Greenky Herz
and Marcelle DiFalco**

Full-time Go-to Girls
and Authors of *The Big
Sister's Guide to the
World of Work*

According to us, Marcelle and Jocelyn's marvelous book is destined to become the ultimate how-to for working girls. Queens of telling it like it is, these ladies believe in the power of whom you know. (After all, Marcelle got her first big break by writing amazing thank-you notes, and Jocelyn made hers happen by meeting a VIP on a train, remembering the VIP liked her lipstick and sending her a tube.) This pair regards the business trip as networking nirvana. Their one rule when you're traveling for work: "You should not sit in your room. You have to get your butt out and meet people," says Jocelyn.

Networking

How do you meet the influential strangers (other than at that airline club you joined, near the business class seat your friendly travel agent booked for you, and in the lounge of the cool hotel where you're staying)?

Before you go, delve into your Rolodex, BlackBerry, desk drawers, and university alumni journals for names and numbers of professionals who live in the area. Set up appointments for coffee, dinner, lunch. This is why your hotel location is important.

How to know where to go? Call ahead to the hotel concierge and inquire about the hot new restaurants. Pick up a copy of the local glossy city mag when you land at the airport. Check out citysearch.com or digitalcity.com. Ask friends who live in the area. (While we're on the subject of friends: This isn't the time to visit former flames, current cousins, or favorite sorority sisters. If you simply must pay social visits, do it by extending your stay over the weekend. Do not invite your pal Bo to any business event. Jocelyn did this once and wound up with a very drunk friend and an uncomfortable rest of her trip.)

Back to where to go—for work reasons. "Always go to the best places in town," says Jocelyn. "Have a clue about what restaurant to go to. I hate when somebody comes into town and says, 'Hey, where do you want to go?' If the latest something-something just opened in L.A., find out about it, and that's where you're going."

Some concierges have pull at restaurants where reservations are hard to come by. Befriend the concierge. If the desk clerk at your hotel is clueless, go have a drink at a four-star hotel and ask for help there. If Eloise could rule the Plaza, the least you can do is score some free advice.

It's also worthwhile to go the extra mile to ensure that your choice of venue is appropriately targeted to the business associates you're trying to impress. If the hottest table in town features pan-Asian cuisine served up by transvestite waitresses in G-strings, it probably isn't appropriate for a rendezvous with your boss's boss's boss or the chairwoman of the board.

How to pay for all this, if you've yet to score company plastic for your Kate Spade wallet? Use your corporate-given expense account, understanding, of course, that you must get a receipt for every taxi, every coffee, every last bite you consume. "Don't lose your receipts, my friends," warns Jocelyn. "Most companies will reimburse you for under $20 [without a receipt], but you have to find that policy out before you leave."

6

WORK

On a college campus not too far away, in a time not so long ago, you sat on a lawn and complained about your pop quiz. "It's not fair!" you said. "This class is so hard," you whined. "I can't wait until this hellish school is over and I'm working a job that starts at nine and ends at five and I have sixteen hours of free time to do whatever I want and never have to write a paper in a foreign language again."

Meanwhile, just beyond the Frisbee-studded college green, sedans drove by by the dozen. Driving those sedans were hundreds of suit-wearing professionals, some with more suit-wearers in the passenger seats and backseats. As these carpoolers slowed down to ogle the carefree and slightly hungover students lolling about with their book bags and meal plans, they said to themselves, "It's not fair! Work is so hard. We wish we were back in school when we had all the free time to do whatever we want and never had to make another PowerPoint presentation again."

Lesson learned: The grass may be greener on the quad, but office life is rife with the same complaints. Only in the work world, complaints are called "challenges." Here are a few tips on facing those obstacles head-on. And, for when the rat race gets too ratty, we offer a way to get some perspective: volunteering, the work that doesn't pay in checks.

REQUEST FOR A RAISE

The thought of asking for a raise makes you absolutely quiver. There you sit, mesmerized by the screen saver on your laptop, shaking and sweating in your ergonomic chair as if you were about to go onstage to recite your one line in the fifth grade class play. You know you ought to make the move, ask the ask, but, quite frankly, you'd rather eat the last bag of stale Snax Mix from the vending machine in the break room. You'd rather get a paper cut. (Well, maybe not.) But you'd definitely rather eat the Snax Mix.

Why is this happening? After all, you sailed through a gut-wrenching job interview. You survived that initial salary negotiation. Why now is it so hard to go back to your boss and ask for the increase she'd promised so many quarters ago?

Maybe it's because now you know your boss. You two are pals, kind of. At least, you and she share a private joke. You wouldn't ask for money from friends; how are you gonna ask for it from the higher-up who snickered by your side at the company picnic when the VP of sales broke out his disco robot on the volleyball court?

You don't want to seem ungrateful—or greedy.

And you don't need to hear Suze Orman tell you—again—that you'll get nothing if that's all you ask for. We know this stinks. But don't blame us: We love giving things to people who didn't ask for them—like advice. In fact, we're about to do that right now, with a little help from . . .

GO-TO GIRL

Karen Salmansohn   Advice Imparter Extraordinaire

When it comes to workplace guidance, life coach Karen wrote the book. The title—*How to Succeed in Business without a Penis*—made us giggle. The contents made us think twice and twice again, and then moved us to speak up, to take credit, and to ask interview questions like "What do you do to become a vice president here?" and "Do you have any VPs who are twenty-five years old?" Shockingly motivated, those notions of Karen's. Not one to preach without practicing, this Go-to ditched her job in advertising to become an author. "I try to get as many people as possible to quit their jobs," she says. Still, she urges those of us who are happily employed not to stop at happy alone. Instead: Seek promotions, responsibilities, and raises. That last one, she says, is especially important. "If you don't ask for raises enough, you might lose your job because you don't value yourself enough. You might get lost in the crowd."

Timing to Score a Raise

Schedule a meeting with your boss, for in a week or so. This powwow could coincide with your regularly planned review. But it doesn't have to.

Best to plan it just after you've done something professionally impressive. "Do it when your stock value is up," says Karen.

Another smart time to strike out for more gold: When one or more of your office mates has jumped ship, leaving room in the budget for you to score your due. After all, you're loyally sticking around. Who's gonna begrudge you the quitters' leftovers?

Don't, however, spring a caffeine-fueled, spur-of-the-moment, pop-into-the-office-style request, because if you do, chances are you'll make a poor pitch—and your quick maneuvering will be interpreted by your boss as a surprise attack.

Accomplishment Armor

Going in, sitting down, pointing to a calendar, and stating, "It's my turn to get more money," isn't enough. Eventually you might want to mention that the traditional cost-of-living increase has passed by your paycheck, but right now, you want more than that. You want a real raise.

You don't, however, want to reveal any personal reasons for your request. In other words, the Big Boss—BB—shouldn't know what you're planning to do with the risen dough, no matter how noble the cause, how cute the car, how needed the getaway, how desperate the debt. "Your boss doesn't give a darn if you have quadruplets that are home with the chicken pox and you need money to buy them calamine lotion. It's still a company; you have to let them know what's in it for them," says our workplace Go-to Girl.

Instead, you gotta prove to the BB that you've earned—and exceeded—your keep. Make the BB believe the company veritably spins on the very axis of that ergonomic chair of yours (which is to say, that you are the eyes and ears, lips and feet of the organization).

How to do this? Make a list, *bien sûr.* Go through files, e-mails, dusty memories to compile a greatest hits of your accomplishments. Include not only assignments given, created, and enhanced, but also ways in which you've prevented problems. Remember when you talked the prankster IT guy out of distributing an image of the boss's head attached to body of Michelangelo's *David* to the company-wide distribution list, or when you caught a grammatical error—a misspelling of the word "batch," in a press release dealing with the CFO's wife's charitable organization—or convinced HR that substituting the end-of-the-year-bonus with commemorative plaques might not be the direction to go in this year? These count, too.

Think details: Did you work overtime to get a project finished? Did you make employee of the month twice in one year, receive a personal letter of thanks from a client, set a sales record, write the winning proposal, earn any professional awards or recognition, score a big account, drive in the winning run on the company softball team? Include it.

Remember. While doing this, keep track of the monetary worth of each of these achievements. Note the value of each one, right alongside it.

Need help tooting your own horn? Ask trustworthy office buds to offer their two cents. (You'd do the same for them, wouldn't you?)

Type up this list. Print it out. Bring it to the meeting.

Stats of Steel

No way should someone as good as you are at your job make below market value. An after-hours research session can yield a wealth of figures. Check with professional organizations, your college's career counseling service, and online (try *The Wall Street Journal* or JobStar.org, via your favorite search engine).

You might think of asking your co-workers what they earn, but don't. That type of reconnaissance could violate the company policies. Ask HR for a quote of what your position earns. Never, ever go to your boss to tell her that you've found out what your co-workers earn, and demand equal pay. (If you do, you'll reveal that you've broken confidentiality rules, you're the talking-behind-the-back type, or, at the very least, that you're guilty of committing the sin of working for pay, not for the heartfelt satisfaction.)

Look for market quotes that are as specific as you can get. Feel free, too, to estimate your own personal worth in relation to the company's overall earnings and successes.

Type up this list. Print it out. Bring it to the meeting. Hand it to the BB—but only if necessary.

Flexible Figures

Once you've done your homework, you'll have an idea of what to ask for. If you're making average to less, it's easier to ask for an upward adjustment. (Especially since you're such a valuable employee.) If you're making above the average, still ask—but consider whether you're comfortable taking on new responsibilities in order to merit more pay.

After you've fixed on a fair figure, increase it by 5 to 10 percent. "Always ask for more than you think you can get," says Karen. This tactic will leave room for negotiation—and it shows that you're used to striving for the best.

Come prepared to compromise. You ought to know how your boss operates emotionally. Is the BB a woman of few direct words? Is she apt to respond to a healthful dose of pre-pitch buttering up? Think about it. Then, practice your request.

Which should play out something like this. "Hi, BB! Look what I've done! I'm fabulous and by far the best employee ever! Look how much better everything is around here since I came along! Don't you agree that I'm worth at least as much as the person who does my same job at all the other companies that are just like this one? Great! Thanks!"

OK, maybe this is the all-together-too-perky-cheerleader version of your meeting. Point is, you want to emit an enthusiasm that borders on bragging. Vibes to avoid channeling: entitled, immature, unreasonable, threatening (even if you have a better offer from the competition). Be generous. But be firm.

Still feel awkward? Karen says, "Use humor. I once went to a boss, asking for everything. My boss said, 'There's supposed to be some negotiation.' I said, 'Yes. You give, I take.'"

Next, let the BB make the first offer. Reply with "I was thinking along the lines of [fill in a higher amount], which, according to *The Wall Street Journal* and the Organization of National Sachet Innovators, is standard for a person with my qualifications and potpourri-blending experience."

If you think it's appropriate, let the BB mull over your proposal for a day. If the deal is sealed then and there, smile, shake hands, say thank you—and ask for the offer in writing.

If, on the other hand, it looks like no money's coming your way any time soon—and you still want to keep your job—you have three choices: (1) give up for now, but keep on it in the future, (2) ask for something else, or (3) ask the Bigger Big Boss—BBB.

Number one is the easiest. Your immediate reply should be something along the lines of "OK, well, what can I do to raise my value to this company?" You and the BB make a list. You tape this list to your desk. You check off the items as you do them. Then you set up another meeting, return to go, and, barring the receipt of any go-to-jail-go-directly-to-jail cards, you collect your $200.

Number two is for those virgins who believe life's not all about the warm sweater. It's also about the ply of cashmere, vintage buttons, and pretty beading. There might not be a budget for you to get a raise, but you may be able to score:

- A better benefits package
- More days off
- A new office space
- Extra help (like an assistant or new computer)

- Additional training
- The right to work from home
- Compensation for future overtime

Pick any of the above—and any other non-paycheck perks you can come up with—and ask away. Now's the time to do it, because you've got the BB's ear and—can we say this just one more time?—you deserve it.

The last option—going over the BB's head—is for bold-and-sure virgins only. Be sure to let the BB know you're doing this ahead of time (she'll find out anyway) and be doubly prepared for the next meeting, because you'll need to prove your case—and prove your boss wrong.

The Cooldown

No matter what the outcome, thank the BB for her time and consideration. Things will be back to normal in no time—except, we hope, you'll be enjoying an extra cushion in your paycheck.

OFFICE ROMANCE

Is there even a need to set the scene for this one? Must we really describe an inner-office affair that begins with an above-cubicle game of peekaboo? Shall we revisit ye olde cliché that starts with "Excuse me, Miss Smith. Would you please come into my office to take . . . dictation?" Ought we recall one of any millions of movie scenes where a boss and an employee, a salesperson and a manager, a top-secret spy and another top-secret spy turn their 9-to-5 into *9½ Weeks*? No. We'll trust your memories and imaginations on this one.

Suffice it to say that despite decades of sexual harassment suits, despite career counselors' endless warnings against the practice, despite our own faithful repetition of the on-the-way-to-work mantra—"I will not get involved with the person from media relations. I will not get involved with the head of sales. I will not get involved with my manager or my assistant. I will not get involved with my teammate who just came back from vacation in Costa Rica and sure looks fine with a tan and longer hair and that tropical, post-break glow"—despite all these things, the office remains a fertile breeding ground for romance.

Experts who pay attention to such matters believe co-workers' hookups are on the rise because workers are working more hours each day, more days per year, more years per life. Common sense-perts say it makes sense: People with common interests tend to work in common places, and people with common interests are commonly attracted to one another. And us? We think it's just the brain-numbing fluorescent lights. Or maybe the happy hours.

One thing's for sure: There's something about a room full of carpeted compartments, heavy-duty wiring, glowing computer screens, and ringing phones that grows love affairs faster than a petri dish grows bacteria.

Being an advice book, we are compelled by the advice book writer's law to warn you of the dangers of conducting an office romance. Getting it on with your co-workers, boss, subordinate can result in one or more of the following:

Firing. Some companies have official policies that strictly forbid more-than-friendships between employees, no matter what. These policies were most likely written because the company has already had an ugly run-in with office romance, most likely in the form of a sexual harassment claim or decreased productivity. Some such rules aren't as strict as they sound. Some are stricter. Best to find out how your employer operates before you accept an invitation to after-work cocktails with Mr. Costa Rica.

Sexual harassment suit. Yes, you, too, could be slapped with a lawsuit if you date your subordinate. No matter if you dated seriously for one night or one decade. No matter if you were the well-behaved half of the relationship. No matter if you were the one dumped. Enough said.

Dating your boss, however, can result in:

Unrest among the ranks. Maybe you work the hardest of anyone in your department. Maybe your courageous efforts on the air freshener campaign saved the entire second floor of the agency. Maybe the raise/promotion/big office would have been yours even if you weren't intimate with the Big Boss's bedsheets. But date a higher-up, and be prepared to be disliked by your peers. Be ready to face accusations that you earned your privileges not by hard work, but, as they say, by slutting your way to the top.

Think you're off the hook by dating someone your same rank and file? You're not.

A competitive relationship. Get busy with someone who shares your job title, salary, and boss, and you might find yourselves in a race for the same promotion, the same account, the same raise. This is especially dangerous in a sales environment, or in a company fond of downsizing.

A bad reputation. Date a fellow employee with a big mouth, and within twenty-four hours or less of your first date, the entire, gossip-starved corporation will be feasting upon your private life like a swarm of pre-teens at an eyeliner giveaway. You think your co-workers like to talk about *Desperate Housewives*? You haven't heard anything 'til you've heard a breathy version of your first date as retold by Annabelle in Accounting.

A boring relationship. Know how you never want to hang out with Margie outside of work, because all Margie can talk about is work? Dating a co-worker doubles the danger of work-talk burnout. Sure, it might be fun at first to dish, to commiserate, to swap career advice with the one you love, but when the initial excitement ends, when it comes down to it, office news just isn't romantic.

The most painful breakup you'll ever endure. Whereas most out-of-the-office breakups turn your workplace into a shelter, an oasis where you can bury your sorrows in paperwork, an inner-office breakup pretty much guarantees the one person you never, ever want to see again—or, at least, the one person you know you ought not see until your heart mends—is the one person you'll run into all day long. To add to your suffering, Annabelle in Accounting stares at you in pity. She has her own theories about why you and your ex broke up and "just wants to make you feel better" by increasing your seasonal allotment of Kleenex and e-mailing daily affirmations.

So that's it. Those are the risks you run. Feel free to include them in a handy-dandy pros-and-cons list that you write on a cocktail napkin while you wait for Mr. Costa Rica from down the hall to come back from the jukebox on the other side of the bar.

The truth about office romance? All those risks look really small in comparison to the two major gains: good love and really good lovin'.

(A third, not-as-sure gain is the possibility that sleeping your way to the top actually gets you to the top. Frankly, it has worked for some, but it has backfired for more. But enough with the warnings, because we're here to tell you how to get it right the first time.)

The First Step in Finding Love among the Filing Cabinets: Policy Check

Research your company policy. If corporate has a real and serious anti-dating system in place, be sure you're willing to risk your nine-to-five for a little outside-of-work lip action. And prepare to go underground with your romance.

Some businesses have actually created dating waivers—we are not making this up—that co-workers in love cosign to affirm that they've entered willingly into their relationship. Signing such a document protects both parties from sexual harassment suits and the like. It does not protect either party from heartbreak, cheating, bad manners, bad sex, or any of the other annoying things that split up couples in the long run. But, hey, at least you won't get sued.

The Second Step to Getting It On with Your Corporate Honey: Full Disclosure

Agree on how to deal with the new item that is your couplehood within your work environment. Do you work in a place where it would be impossible to hide your relationship? Is it best to keep it undercover until you've completed that project you're both working on? Want to confine your fling to one night? Be honest. Reach an agreement. If you can't, start looking for a new job.

If you can—*phew*—agree and—*hurrah!*—make the leap from teammates to bedmates, flesh out the possible repercussions of coming out of the relationship closet and into the bright light of the break room. Will you be able to handle becoming your office's very own version of Bennifer? Should one of you transfer to a new department?

Next, find a pat answer for inquiring co-working minds who want to know. If you don't, you just might hear Annabelle in Accounting whispering to Jim the Janitor: "Oh, I feel so sorry for that sweet Sue in Product Development. She says Mr. Costa Rica from Marketing and she are serious, but Mr. Costa Rica says they're just friends. I know, Janitor Jim, why don't you ask Sue out?"

The Third Step to Loving the Worker You Find: Putting a Lid on It

Sure, you want to swipe all those reports off your desktop and engage in a good old-fashioned romp. But please. You have a desk at home for indulging such fantasies.

But a little e-mail flirtation is OK, isn't it? No. No cutesy voice-mails either. Yes, it's adorably funny when Bridget calls up Mark Darcy when he's convening an international panel of top barristers. But it's so not adorably funny in real life. In real life, Mark Darcy would have been looking for a new job at a workplace without phones, like as one of those Beefeaters at the Tower of London. Romantic messages transmitted in the workplace have a funny way of getting outed.

The Fourth Step to Making Love, Not Work: Putting a Lid on It, Part 2

Make this pact to each other: "I solemnly swear to discuss exclusively nonwork topics with my office lover." Of course, you won't stick to the pact. You'll absolutely need to bitch about how many smoking breaks your new assistant takes, and about dozens of other workaday details that require out-of-office venting. So you won't stick to the pact. Which is why you'll make a solemn backup pact to limit your discussion of work topics to thirty minutes or fewer each day.

If you happen to be dating someone who works very closely with you, find ways to be apart. Join different gyms. Ride different trains. Hang out with different friends. Be vigilant about this, or risk waking up one day and realizing that you and your office love have morphed into the same person, like Joan and Melissa Rivers.

If you happen to be dating someone who has the same job as you, be honest about your goals at work. If you really want that new account—and your co-equal sweetheart does, too—tell each other. Agree to work hard. Agree to be happy for the other's success. Agree that the account-winner buys the celebratory dinner.

The Final Step to Sleeping Your Way Through Success: Moving On or Moving Out

If it works, it works. Chances are, one of you was going to switch jobs eventually, anyway. Or, if you happen to be one of those miracle couples who loves to spend every waking minute together and plans to climb the corporate ladder of success together, hand in hand, possibly even dressed in matching navy suits, well, all the power to you two lovebirds.

But being pragmatists, we gotta tell you that if it doesn't work, you oughta be prepared for that, too.

First day back on the job after a breakup: Take that broken heart off of your sleeve and lock it in your desk drawer until the day's end. Be ready for your co-workers to find out that you and your ex are exactly that, exes, faster than you can say "Did you get that memo from the head office this morning?" Be ready for them to attempt to talk to you about it. Be ready—of course—for ol' what's-her-name from accounting to offer her circa-nineteen-eighty-four shoulder pad for you to cry on. Thank her for her thoughts. But keep your feelings to yourself. No matter what. Don't expect office mates to pick sides. And certainly don't try to get anyone to side with you, even if yours is the better side. (And, of course, it is.)

Hiding heartbreak is not good for you. But this is your workplace, a wholly different universe with its own wholly different rules. One of these rules is: Share your good news, but leave your woe at home. This is tough. And, for someone who was deeply involved in an office romance, it's nearly impossible. If you find you can't get your work done because you're sad or angry or just plain distracted, it's time to talk to the boss about a vacation, a transfer, and, in extreme cases, a new job somewhere else.

ASSISTANT

Work-wise, you are making it. Your new office is a shiny junior executive–style suite with a skyline view, a door (that closes), paid vacation time, a feather-weight laptop, and—oh glorious work-day!—an assistant. No longer will you affix stamps, fax faxes, collate copies, file files, and answer two phone lines at once. Today, someone just a few, neutral-carpeted steps away will do those and more for you. And all you need to do is delegate.

Delegate = An official-sounding term for bossing someone around.

Delegate = The only way this week's mailing will go out on time, because you can't stuff and send those 750 envelopes on your own.

Delegate = A skill inherited by none, assigned to many, and finessed by few.

There is a giant cherry on the front of this book: Obviously, we're not going to explore any remotely intellectual theories on why bossing subordinates around comes less naturally to most women than it does to most men. Instead, let's just say the following: It's not that we can't do it just as well as the boys; it's just that we tend to do it less automatically. The good news: Once we figure out how to do it right, we do it better. (Don't act surprised; you knew you had a boss inside you.)

GO-TO GIRLS

Caitlin Friedman and Kim Yorio

Co-bosses and Coauthors of *The Girls' Guide to Being a Boss Without Being a Bitch*

As if Kim and Caitlin didn't get enough of our props for repping d-vine Jamie Oliver, aka the Naked Chef, these Manhattan-based owners of boutique PR and marketing firm YC Media also posed in pretty black dresses and pastel pumps on the cover of their first book, *The Girls' Guide to Starting Your Own Business*. Able to foist their chef-clients behind TV cameras in a single bound, capable of spinning a caterer into celebrity status, Caitlin and Kim first realized they had to hire their first assistant when the press releases, media alerts, and magazine clippings overtook their petite office. Hundreds of applicants tried for the position. The one that got the job: a dud. Why? "It was our first time: We wanted her to like us. We became really afraid of delegating tasks to her, and didn't set any boundaries," says Caitlin. "We messed up from the get-go," agrees Kim. Now they know: "Take yourself more seriously, respect yourself more, and put yourself and your company first."

Hiring an Assistant—DIY

If you're a business owner like Kim and Caitlin, you don't just wake up one morning and discover a friendly and assistive person sitting outside your office door, waiting to be told what to alphabetize. Hiring a right-hand woman is as difficult as keeping one. This first step alone will surely renew one's appreciation for the seek 'n' find abilities of a human resources department.

First, figure out how much you can spend on an assistant. Factor in sick days, vacation days, benefits, bonuses, and training.

Second, decide where to troll for said assistant—online or newpaper postings, through an executive search firm, by taping a HELP WANTED! sign (the hardware store kind) in your shop window, through college career centers.

Third, go at it. Shuffle through applications. Set up interviews.

Toss any résumés that are sloppy, or letters that appear to be applying for a job as a trapeze artist when the job description clearly called for a tightrope walker. Whittle the CVs down to your top ten. Call them in for thirty-minute interviews. Don't offer any jobs. Call back your top two or three for more in-depth interviews. Thank the other eight or seven for playing. Do not extend a job offer until at least one day after the interview.

All the while, look for an assistant who . . .

Gets your business's goals. You've made sure the applicant understands what your company is doing by reading his cover letter. The face-to-face interview is for asking "How do you think your abilities match our company's needs?" Or, more simply "How do you describe what we do here?" (If the prospective hire can't answer those, hoist the red flag and bid him farewell.)

Is enthusiastic. Did the candidate arrive on time for the interview? Did he bother to iron his pants, promptly write a thank-you note, seem nervous but excited? Did a happy flush appear on her cheeks when she talked about managing multiple phone lines or color-coding filing systems? In our book, genuine interest and a can-do attitude weigh as heavily as—if not more heavily than—vast experience.

Has work experience. Anyone can pad a résumé or talk a good game. Once you've narrowed the pool down to a few candidates, check references and follow additional leads to more former employers.

Understands the job's duties. This is yours to explain. You're hiring this person to do the daily—and, on occasion, dirty—deeds that take up valuable time you could be spending on bigger tasks. Be up front about your assistant's day-to-day roles and responsibilities.

Example: You know you need someone capable of convincingly saying you're out when you're in. You need someone flexible enough to work one Saturday a month, or late some evenings, early some mornings, etc. You can't offer a huge starting salary, but you can give five weeks' paid vacation in the off season. You'll need him to attend black-tie events— and to add his name to the office cleaning job wheel.

The more you make a candidate aware of duties up front, the more said candidate will know if he'll fit into your office.

Just seems right. Don't underestimate your gut impressions. After all, this is the person who's going to be your in-office caretaker, your backup, and your first line of defense. "Trust your instincts," says Caitlin.

Assistant from Above: HR Did the Hiring, You Get the Benefit

If your assistant shows up in your office without your having had to do all of the above, you still need to be confident he understands his roles and your goals. Even if HR did the hiring, there will be adjusting you need to do. You've got to figure out who this person is, what he will and won't do, and how to treat him fairly.

Who Is This Person? Lifetime Executive Assistant vs. Aspiring CEO Assistant

Both are doing the same job at the moment, but down the line there is a difference. The lifetime assistant is in it for her current job. The aspiring CEO assistant regards her job as a foot in the door, a rung on the ladder, a first step in an upward direction. Make sure you know which one you're dealing with at the get-go, especially if you've hired the assistant yourself.

The lifetime executive assistant. Pluses: He knows where he sits, knows what to expect, and wants to fulfill his current role to the best of his abilities (you hope), which translates to day-to-day operational improvements around the office, like replacing toner in the copier and stocking up on your favorite pens when there's a sale at Office Supplies 'R' Us.

Minuses: Because he does know and accept his role, he can be less willing to pitch in in non-assistant areas, such as offering creative input or to going after new business.

The aspiring CEO assistant. Pluses: He has reason to impress and is more than willing to demonstrate his abilities to function at non-assistant jobs.

Minuses: He can have a tendency to overstep boundaries and might not take his assistant tasks as seriously, because he feels above them and is more concerned with movin' on up than movin' that bulk mailing out the door.

Delegation

To return to our leitmotif: The hardest thing about having an assistant is delegating. The hard thing about delegating is not figuring out what needs to be done and who needs to do it, but telling that person—the assistant—what to do.

The number one trick to reminding an assistant how much she's needed without sounding needy, how to stress a task's importance without acting stressed, how to ask for something without apologizing is first to eradicate "I'm sorry" from the start of your sentences. Be kind. Be direct. Do not be sorry.

What not to say. "Can you . . . ?" and "Would you mind . . . ?" are terrible ways to ask someone who obviously can do what you're about to ask and might mind doing it but has to do it anyway because it's her job.

It's also poor form to personalize delegating with the preface "I need you to . . ." or, even worse, "You need to . . ." Yes, you may need her to answer your phones or need her to type that report by 4:00 p.m., but using "I need" as a sentence starter for a request makes our skin crawl. Save "I need" for requests for first aid: "I need a tourniquet. Do you have one?"

What to say. Instead, ask, "What are you working on today?" Then explain the importance of your request, and work with her to make sure the job's done in a time frame that is convenient for both of you. Be considerate, explain the immediate importance of your request, show you understand how important your assistant's role is—and when you're really, seriously in a jam, your assistant will get it and be helpful. (At that point, use "I need"—but we still don't like it.)

It takes getting used to being someone's boss. But the more comfortable you are with yourself—something that only comes with time and practice—the more comfortable your office will be.

Off-Limit Words and Deeds

Salary. Your—or any other employee's—takings should never be up for discussion with an assistant. Money drives a wedge. If you make big bucks, there's jealousy. If you make little, there's instability.

Your personal life. Talk movies, talk restaurants, talk celebrity gossip. Sequester religion, politics, and your sex life, to the outside, nonwork world (unless your field is religion, politics, or prostitution).

Oh, and also, please don't get drunk in front of your assistant. Not even tipsy. Not even scented of alcohol. If, by some freak accident, you find yourself back in the office after a three-martini lunch, keep a safe distance and put on an Oscar–winning performance of being sober.

The Review

The annual, bimonthly, tri-annual—whatever—review can be as enticing a prospect as a corn removal. But set a schedule for one and stick to it.

Be prepared with a list of your assistant's accomplishments, strengths, and weaknesses. Do not show this list to him. Ask what he thinks he's done well and where he needs improvement. Listen. Discuss. Ask how he thinks you can do your job better and how he can help you achieve this. Consider his request for a raise/more time off/better benefits, making sure he explains why he thinks he's earned what he's requesting.

Get it out on the table. If your assistant feels left out—especially if she's an aspiring CEO-type assistant—remind her how important her job is. Explain to her what she's learning. And ask how she'd like to contribute more. If you know she's not going to be able to move up in your company, break the news gently. "I know you're gunning for a management position. Unfortunately, the company just can't support any more managers at the moment." The truth hurts.

Or, maybe there is some wiggle room. Is she willing to stick around to wait and see? Is there a chance that if she takes on extra responsibilities, she'll be considered for a promotion? Then reassure her. "Right now, you've gone as far as your position will allow, but let's consider a plan that will put you in a better position to move up."

"It's up to us to put people's jobs in the bigger picture. It's really the responsibility of the supervisor to do that for them. If your employees are not aware of how their contributions affect the whole from the get-go, they will feel irrelevant. They'll feel they're not important," says Caitlin.

The Assistant Flub

It's one thing if he breaks the copier or spills coffee on his keyboard. It's another if he forgot to send out the invitations, if he talked back to a client, if he missed the meeting where he was supposed to sit in for you.

Your assistant works for you, but you're in charge. So stand up. Be a woman. He made the mess, but you have to clean it up. It's on you to pay for couriers to deliver the invites, to make amends with the client, to find out what you missed at the conference table.

Of course, behind the scenes—in the privacy of your office, door closed—you absolutely must deal with his mistake. Use a few serious words. Don't harp on it. Don't joke about it. Your assistant's mistake should serve as a reminder of his importance in the bigger picture.

Your Flub

You yelled at the receptionist in front of the entire office. You forgot to clean the toilet when it was your week. You never thanked your assistant for all the extra work she did at home over the weekend. You forgot to take her to lunch on her birthday. Whatever you did wrong, own up to it. Again, don't harp. Just apolgize. "I think if you're a public jerk, then you should make a public apology," says Kim. "And if you're a private jerk, make a private apology."

Caitlin's mantra: "Take the blame—and share the credit."

Virgin's Downfall: One Extreme

Being a good boss doesn't mean apologizing before you ask your assistant to cover the phone lines while you meet with a client. You may not be comfortable asking someone who's your age or older to retype a memo, to deal with four weeks of files, or to stuff envelopes. But get used to it. The more you try to save your assistant from her own duties, the less her job will seem important to her.

Virgin's Downfall: The Other

It's easy—scarily easy—to go from a humble, share-the-wealth, self-sufficient worker to a bloated-headed, greedy, dependent boss who asks your assistant to do things like spend her lunch hour shopping for the marabou-trimmed baby doll negligee you saw in a magazine somewhere and want to wear tonight to celebrate your first wedding anniversary. Your assistant might be the nicest person ever. She might smile and say, "OK!" But she won't like doing it. Soon, she won't like you. Soon after that, you'll be looking for a new assistant.

BUSINESS LUNCH

Um. Haven't you heard? The term "power lunch" is so two decades ago. Not that the midday meal shared by two or more movers and shakers with mutual career-oriented interests itself is over. (Lord no . . . What did you think, that we'd suggest eating a yogurt and a piece of fruit at your desk each day at 1:00 p.m., thereby wasting prime moving-up-the-ladder time?)

It's just that, well, we're now calling this occasion the "business lunch." Leaving the "power" where it belongs—in the land of tools, energy bars, and cardio classes—we are free and unfettered to describe just what goes down when the sun is high and the stomach is grumbling.

A business lunch is an opportunity for you to make a wholly new connection. You meet with someone who has a job you'd like to have, a prospective customer, a possible future employee, or, simply, someone in your field you've heard loads of good things about. You take 'em to lunch. You chat 'em up. You dazzle your way into their long-term memories. You enter the magical world of networking.

According to time-honored tradition, such connections are best made during the midday meal.

GO-TO GIRL

Zoe Alexander

Founder and Diva-in-Charge of Divas Who Dine, Editor-at-Large of *Life & Style*

Zoe was fed up with never being able to accept all the lunch invitations she received from press-hungry publicists. There was always something—

editorial meetings, deadlines, more insistent publicists—preventing her from doing her business lunch duty. Then she had an idea. She accepted five invitations to lunch, all on the same day, all at the same restaurant, and—wouldn't you know it—at the same table. "I decided to consolidate," says the multitasking marvel. She told her five dining companions about her plan. They agreed it was genius. Lunch was a smashing sucess. Word spread. Before she could say "check, please," Zoe had an in-box that overflowed with messages from women wanting in on the lunch gang. In no time, the party of five grew to nine, fifteen, thirty-seven. Nowadays, Divas Who Dine is a members-only club with a group in L.A. and Miami, and three in New York City (one Big Apple group is for gay men who rightly insist that they're divas, too). Most DWD are in media, fashion, or beauty. For an annual fee, they're guaranteed seats at all lunches and other Diva events (such as a regular poker game). Zoe says the vibe is friendly, but really all about the business. "The minute we walk in the door, it's up for networking."

When Not to Ask Someone to a Business Lunch

When it's the boss. The boss really does like you. We're sure of it. Or maybe she doesn't. But one thing's for sure, she's a busy person—or likes to appear that way. If she invites you to lunch, great. It means she's got something to talk to you about. But if you want something from her—to resolve a problem, to ask what you can do to get a promotion, or just to butter her up—don't ask her to lunch.

"It's best to do a [non-meal] meeting with your boss," says Zoe. "If you're trying to get her ear, go into her office with a cup of coffee" and ask for fifteen minutes. "Chances are, your boss doesn't even have time to have lunch with the people she ought to have lunch with."

When it's serious. Got some bad news to break? Got the greatest news to report? Don't do either during a lunch, no matter if the lunch is taking place in your employee cafeteria or at The Ivy's best table. Ditto for hard-core pitches or big deals. Business meals are for getting to know someone, getting a vibe, getting a start to things. Reserve the hirings, firings, and end-of-year presentations for the company conference room.

When you're not up to it. Don't go if you're sick, preoccupied, disinterested, or otherwise not in the mood to spend at least one pleasant hour with your prospective lunch partner. Call well in advance—at least twenty-four hours—to cancel or to reschedule. But be prepared: The next time you ask this person to lunch, she might be unavailable.

When to Ask Someone to Business Lunch

Any time you feel you're ready to begin a working relationship with someone, if you know meeting would be mutually beneficial, if you want to network, to get something done, or just to catch up with someone in your field. And when you're asking, have a date and a time—and a restaurant—in mind.

Getting a Table

The restaurant should be near enough to your guest's place of work. And it's a really good idea to make a reservation at a place where you're a regular. At the very least, you want to have been to the restaurant once or twice before so that you know the lay of the land and which table to request, and where you've already established yourself as an exemplary guest and a generous tipper. (Servers pay attention to this.)

Zoe has an in at Michael's, midtown Manhattan's best known bistro for catering to media moguls. "Michael's is my favorite lunch spot in New York. It's like a school cafeteria." (A school cafeteria where Diane Sawyer lunches with Bill Clinton.) "I love to be in an environment where I know the people dining there, and where the wait staff knows me . . . That way, they put on a show and address me by name."

Not sure your town's equivalent of Michael's will give you the best table in the house based on your two dinners there and your impeccable phone manners? Call beforehand to check. Have as backup an upscale spot with, as Zoe says, "the feeling of business in the air. If you're meeting these persons for the first time, they'll judge you on the restaurant you pick, even if their judgment is unconscious."

Call the restaurant back a few days before your lunch to confirm your reservation and to renew your request for your table, in case the reservationist bumped you to the teensy two-top near the kitchen's swinging door. One business day before your lunch, e-mail your guest or contact her assistant to confirm, leaving your cell phone number so you or she can call if one of you is running late.

Getting Ready

This will be your first lunch together. It won't be your first contact. Avoid awkward so-do-you-live-in-the-city? conversation starters by getting to know your lunch date days before you get to the restaurant. "I try to break as much ice as possible on the phone or by e-mail during the process of setting up the meeting. That way, when I get to the meeting, I know a bit about them and have information about them to build the small talk around. We can talk about boyfriends, husband, or kids, because I will have already initiated talk about them in a prior conversation," says Zoe.

How else to put yourself at ease before the noontime meal? "I just try to look as fierce as possible," says Zoe. "That means I hit the beauty salon for a good blowout the evening before, and maybe get a mani-pedi before work that morning. When you look good, you feel good. That confidence can get you through anything."

Getting In

Bring a credit card, and five singles for the coat check and valet. Arrive fifteen minutes early. This will give you enough time to make sure you're getting a primo table, to give the name of your guest to the host, and to relax at the table with a bottle of water—we repeat, water, not wine. If you know your guest is on a tight schedule, ask your server if he'll take your order a few moments after your guest arrives.

Stand up when she enters. This is a man tradition. But it also applies to women. Exchange small talk. Order.

You know how much time you've both allotted for your meal. Do you have ample minutes to exchange small talk, to tell jokes, to discuss who wore what to the Oscars? If not, recognize your time constraints, and get down to business. "If it's been established that you are having lunch to discuss business, it's best to get the business out of the way first. There's nothing worse than getting to the crucial part of the business talk and the other party has to get back to the office," says Zoe.

On the other hand, if this is a somewhat leisurely affair—you're planning on soups, entrées, dessert—and you really don't have two hours' worth of business to discuss, follow the Miss-Manners-ly guidelines and wait until dessert to get down to business.

Getting Fed

Do you need us to tell you not to order the broiled lobster, spaghetti marinara, bloomin' onion, baby back ribs, roasted garlic salad, or flambéed anything? If it's gonna fly off your plate, stick to your fingers, slide down your blouse, or catch fire, avoid it. Zoe goes even further: "I avoid

OTHER EXTRAORDINARY BUSINESS MEALS

The Business Breakfast

Gaining popularity for its finite time limit and bottomless cups of coffee, the prework meal can be a real pick-me-up. Believers in bagel-time get-togethers are usually morning people, folks who have trouble getting away from the office during the midday rush. They claim that breakfast is the new lunch. They could be right.

The Business Dinner

Perfect for the nonstop 7-to-7er, the business dinner is an opportunity to unwind — and to leave work on time for once. Business suppers also work out well for anyone stranded on one of those countryside corporate campuses where the only lunch spots are the cafeteria—or a thirty-minute drive to the nearest Applebee's. And when you're out of town for a conference, there's nothing like a hearty helpin' of meat 'n' potatoes to kindle a working relationship .

The Group Business Lunch

How to get things groovin' when you're seated at a table for twelve? Start by knowing the guest list before you go. Ask the host or organizer to point out the person you're aiming to meet and approach your target with a friendly introduction and an easy "You know, I'd like to tell you about [whatever it is]. May I sit next to you?" Maybe you don't get to discuss the hefty ins and outs of all that your company can offer your noontime neighbor—and, if you don't want to snub the ten other lunch guests, you probably shouldn't get so deep into your pitch—but at least you'll put a fly in her soup. We mean a bug in her ear.

Missed your chance to speak to the one person you wanted to? Make sure you swap business cards, shoot her an e-mail, and offer to take her to lunch sometime. "Once you make a face connection, you're more likely to take their phone calls," says Zoe.

large animal plates unless the other person is ordering one because they could be vegetarian and put off by the carnage."

What to have? Simple, light food that is fed into your mouth with a fork. "I like a healthy, hearty salad, and a sinful side dish like french fries—something we both really want, but might feel guilty eating a whole order of," says Zoe. (This last move is not recommended if your companion diner seems somewhat traditional, or may harbor an aversion to sharing.) No talking with your mouth full. No elbows on table. Take small bites. Stick to business.

Avoid conversation about "anything that people take sides or can have passionate, negative feelings about . . . religion, politics, or Mets vs. Yankees." Run out of work-related discussion topics? Think of this as a first date and a job interview, rolled into one. Offer your unique insights on the direction of your field. Plumb for common interests: travel, film, theater, museums. You want this person to remember you; and you want to remember this person. Who knows? Maybe the next time she's out of town for an opening night at the Met, she'll offer you her seats.

Be considerate of your guest's schedule. If you're both in a rush, request the check before you've finished the meal.

Stand up. Thank her for coming. Walk her out the door. Offer your business card if you think she doesn't have it. Return to the office. Write a note to say how much you appreciated her taking time to lunch with you, mention your common interest and, if you feel it's appropriate, express your interest in doing whatever it is you discussed would get done at lunch.

If You're the One Who's Been Invited

Congratulations. This means you have something someone else wants. Be gracious. Be clear about how much time you have to spend. Be on time.

Listen to what your hostess has to say. Do not order the beluga appetizer just because you know this person wants your business/advice/corner office/mailing list. Answer honestly to her demands—if you can't help out, at least you won't be beholden to her for fancy fish eggs. Stick to your time clock. Thank her for lunch. Swap cards. Send a thank-you note for the lunch—and reiterate any deals that went down sometime between salad and espresso.

If You Ask Each Other

Let's face it. When you're just starting out, you need all the contacts you can get. If you're the administrative assistant to an advertising executive who's always on the phone with the administrative assistant to the advertising executive's number one customer, ask your counterpart to lunch. Brainstorm about how you can take the next step on the corporate ladder. Exchange creative ideas. Talk about problem solving. Discuss your hopes for the future. It's really easy to turn peer-on-peer dining into a mutual I-hate-my-boss whine-a-thon. Just don't. And remember: eventually the assistants become the bosses.

My Girl, Bill

You noticed how we didn't mention this earlier, huh? It's because there's no one answer to the bill question. You'd think that the person doing the inviting should always pay the bill. She should always offer to pay. For sure. But if the invitee is a higher-up or somehow will profit from the lunch, then the invitee pays. "Generally speaking, the person who will benefit in the end will grab the check and say, 'Oh no, I want to pay,'" says Zoe. "Let them pay."

If, on the other hand, the lunch is between equals who mutually stand to benefit from the meeting, then the invitee pays—or they agree to split the bill. Whatever you do, please don't fall prey to a check folder tug-of-war. It's so not businesslike.

VOLUNTEER GIG

> *Be the change you wish to see in the world.*
> —Mahatma Gandhi

Let's face it. Despite the proliferation of amazing new inventions—lavender MP3 players, cars that don't get lost, men who know how to dress themselves—the world still could be a much better place. Not to be all depressing, but it seems like every time a cure comes along for an old disease, a new disease pops up. For every lucky baby born to an A-list Hollywood couple, hundreds more children enter a world of poverty.

We won't go on with this line of sadness. Suffice it to say that now more than ever people, animals—plants, even—need your help.

The virgin who considers a globe-full of need can get overwhelmed right quick. So many ways to help, so little time. We'll say it again: so little time. You've got your own job to do, your own life to lead. You want to help, but can you?

Take heart, kind maidens of charitable intent! There's plenty of room in your career/social/personal schedule to make the world a better place. The trick is to find the job that fits.

What You Got to Give?

Wanting to volunteer and volunteering are things so completely, comparatively foreign to each other, they can't even perform creative hand gestures in order to communicate on a rudimentary level.

The first big question you must ask yourself—and you must answer honestly—is: How much time can you give? You work two jobs. You can't miss your must-see TV. If you skip Tuesday yoga, you're one cranky chick. You've learned that your weekends are all about you, your pet parakeet, and no one else. These are the next kinds of questions to ask right away:

- Would you rather spend one of your vacation weeks working for an environmental cause in Costa Rica, or does one Wednesday evening a week seem more do-able?
- Do you need to do this heartwarming duty on your own time, or will your employer give you paid time off for volunteer work?
- Will your manager permit you to use your work e-mail account or phone or time to serve your do-good purpose? (More on this later.)

Come up with a number of minutes per week, or hours per month, or days per year you feel you can devote to a cause you believe in. Then halve that number. Got it? Good.

What You Wanna Get?

If you're a virgin who's just starting out in the working world—or still trying to figure out what she wants to be when she grows up—lucky you. Volunteering can offer a host of career opportunities. The most obvious go a little something like this. Like to teach first grade? Ask your local public school how you can lend a hand. Most helping professions—health care, education, child care, pet care—have well-established systems for accepting and training volunteers.

A little less obvious are ways to learn or to sharpen your skills in order to break into one of those catch-22 professions (where you always need to have experience before you can get a job, but the only way to get experience is to have a job). Nonprofits are famous for needing help with fund-raising, event planning, public relations, accounting, community outreach, Web site development, computer repair, graphic design, and writing. The trick is to find an organization big enough to train you or small enough to appreciate you.

If you, aspiring career person, become an essential cog in the giant wheel of volunt-career, you'll earn professional respect, connections, a possible foot in the door—and a definite gold star line for your résumé.

And, if you're already gainfully employed, you can still stand to benefit from the above career perks of volunteering. We know one fabulous former virgin who hated her corporate job, started volunteering at a start-up city green nonprofit, and is now the astounding and content executive director of the project. And it all started just by giving a few hours a week.

Or, if you're happy with your job and just need a break from routine, consider an extracurricular gig: Teach people with disabilities to ski; staff a registration table at the Race for the Cure; or go door to door stumping for your favorite future congresswoman.

You might volunteer for purely social reasons. Nothing wrong with that. Who's going to begrudge you the double pleasure of handing out foil blankets to fine-thighed triathletes, or winking at an agile-footed hottie who's just competed in a dance-a-thon benefit that you helped promote?

Then, there's the big, deep reason you want to volunteer. You want to do your part. Translation: You want to do something good—and you want to feel good about it. Don't feel bad about wanting to feel good.

Just make sure your good feelings are never your main mission.

Which brings us to . . .

Volunteering Is a Job with a Capital J

Ask anyone in charge of volunteers the number one thing she's seeking, and she'll say "commitment." Commitment doesn't mean that you just believe in the cause. Nor does it mean you merely show up on time. It means that you treat what you're doing for your two minutes a day or two months a year at least as seriously as a full-time job.

The cause you're serving needs you—the committed you, not the it's-Saturday-morning-so-I-think-I'll-go-see-if-an-unwanted-puppy-needs-three-minutes-of-my-cuddling you. Treat your volunteer opportunity like the job you've always wanted, and you're halfway there.

Start with an interview. Even an informal one. Contact the person in charge—sometimes this is an executive director, volunteer coordinator, or a member of a charitable board of directors—and ask for a meeting. A face-to-face meeting.

Be on time for this meeting, just like you would for a job interview. Bring a résumé. Yes, a résumé. Be prepared to fill out an application, and to answer a whole lot of questions. And unlike at a real job interview, answer these questions honestly.

You've already determined how much time you have and halved it. Tell this person that number. You've already figured out what extra things you'd like to get out of the experience. Spit it out.

Here's a question the person in charge will ask you: What connection do you have to this cause? Volunteer interviewers ask this question because most volunteers seek out causes that have special, personal experienced–based meaning to them. Most of the time, this meaning serves as a motivator.

But it can also be a deficit. Example: Your grandparents had Alzheimer's disease. You've signed up to be a conversation buddy to residents of a nursing home. Your job there is to be a good companion and talker, but every time you go, you get choked up and can't think of a thing to say. You may mean well, but you have failed at your job.

Then again, maybe you don't have an experiential connection to the cause. Maybe it's just an emotional one. Example: You feel sorry for hospitalized children. And rightly so. But hospitalized children don't need help from people who just feel sorry. And they sure don't need help from people who will treat them differently from other children. They need playmates, listeners, advocates, not pity-partiers. Would you want your own hospitalized child made to feel worse than he already does?

Volunteer coordinators are trained to suss out the motives behind your good intentions. It's quite possible that they'll thank you for your interest but will suggest you approach it from a different direction. Maybe you shouldn't participate in a community cleanup if you're allergic to mold. Perhaps you'd do a better job using your skills as a superior speaker to talk to kids about not littering, or serving on a board of directors, or helping distribute flyers in your neighborhood.

If you do get the job, play by the rules. General ones you'll have to abide by:

Showing up when you're supposed to. Just like at a job, if you show up late or miss a shift, expect to be reprimanded. Do it a few times, and expect to be fired.

Sticking to the script. The more specialized your role, the more you must abide by disclosure instructions. You may be doing what you're doing because of your personal experiences, religious beliefs, or political leanings, but you may not be able to tell any of this background information to the people you're working with. If you want to make a change because of your faith or politics, it's best to seek out a faith-based organization or political group to do it.

Updating your skill set. Even seasoned volunteers have to attend retraining sessions.

Bringing Your 9-to-5 into the Fold

The workplace can be the perfect jumping off point to a successful lifetime of do-goodery. Check with your human resources or community relations department to see what causes your company is involved in. Chances are, you'll be allowed more time to volunteer during a work day if the cause is one the overlords already embrace. (And it can't hurt your rep around the executive washroom if the higher-ups know you're both an excellent employee and an exemplary community citizen.)

Just look how well doing good worked out for:

GO-TO GIRL

Meredith Wagner   Lifetime TV Exec and Workplace Heroine to Women's Causes

Meredith started at Lifetime when cable television was but a prekindergartener. Raised in a family of do-gooders, she saw a world of opportunity at a station devoted entirely to the better sex. Her first project: Enhance a documentary about women and AIDS with grassroots conversations in communities around the nation. Today, she uses her leverage to get national laws to facilitate rape convictions and to make voyeurism a federal crime. Meredith says her job is "all-consuming. I'm not volunteering at a shelter answering phones, but I'm doing it at a different level." Impacting others' lives has made her into a wholly new brand of corporate leader: "It's made me a much more emotional person . . . I have this nasty habit when I speak to our employees . . . I have been known to start to cry. I feel so moved that so many people at Lifetime, that this company is supporting women this way. It's very powerful."

7

THE GREAT OUTDOORS

What do you mean you had us pegged as city girls? Just because we can smell a sample sale a block away, have fallen asleep on rush-hour subways, and love no sound more than the satisfying click of stilettos on concrete sidewalk doesn't mean we're not totally in touch with our earthy sides.

Fine. Maybe we owe the entire contents of this chapter to our back-to-nature sisters, the Go-to Girls mentioned and nameless, who tutored us through woods tinkling and horse mounting, hanging ten, and parring four (not a word, not a word, we know). So, this one's for you birdwatching, backpacking, tent-pitching babes. Thanks for letting us tag along to national parks, putting greens, grassy trails, and sandy beaches. You made fresh-air breathers out of the lot of us.

CAMPING TRIP

We'll be honest. One of the best things about going on an overnight, tent-in-the-woods camping trip is the post-trip appreciation one develops for one's own, cozy home, running water and all. What we were surprised, however, to learn about camping is that once you're out there, alone, ground below and sky above and no one around—except, maybe for the dozens of other campers—there is something thoroughly magical about it. We don't know how to describe it yet, only because we too are so new at it. But trust us. It's worth the investment in  gear, the sore calves from hiking, and the slightly grubby feeling that takes over one's body the next day. If nothing else, you'll never again take your shower for granted.

GO-TO GIRL

Dara Johnson   Chief Camper, aka Education Logistics
                        and Training Manager,
                        Appalachian Mountain Club

Growing up in a family of Boy Scouts, our girl Dara believes in mud puddles, black bears, and bandana baths. She teaches about such natural occurrences—also snowshoeing, backpacking, and cross-country skiing—in Vermont. Dara's taught enough virgin campers to know that bathroom

(continued)

GO-TO GIRL (*continued*)

concerns alone prevent too many of them from exploring nature—and her helpful advice has helped 'em all conquer their pee-in-the-woods anxiety. Among her many words of wisdom: "The more you can stay warm and dry and comfortable, the more you'll enjoy the experience." "It's not the destination, it's the journey that's important when you're out there." And, "Don't put your kid on a moose."

How to Start: Slowly—at Home or in a Park

Those of us generally accustomed to sleeping between walls and under a roof would be smart to take baby steps toward a first forest foray. (No Maine-to-Georgia hikes for you just yet.) Instead, pack a lunch in your backpack, hike into a park, and have a picnic, or pitch a tent in your backyard and have a sleepover. (You know you begged to do this when you were a kid.)

A few minutes' sitting on a big rock will enhance your appreciation for a booty-friendly foam cushion. A night under the stars—even if you're camped out just three yards from the neighbor's jungle gym—might even convince you that a sleeping bag can be downright sexy.

How to Continue: Your Choice

Car camping. Also known as front country or drive-in camping, motoring to a park where you snooze in safe proximity to your car is a good transitional step for a few reasons. First, you can pack all the crap that fits in your trunk, including a fully stocked cooler, adequate reading materials, ambitious crafting projects, and, for the extra cautious Band-Aid addicts among us, plenty of first aid products.

Second, many of these places—especially KOA varieties (that's Kampgrounds of America, Inc.)—offer motel-like conveniences. Call ahead to confirm the presence of restrooms, showers, laundry, a pool, and mini golf. Yes, mini golf. Be warned: The more amusement park-y the place is, the less it offers a true nature-girl experience.

To Bring List

- A friend or two or three
- A tent
- A ground cloth (plastic) to keep you dry
- A sleeping bag
- A foam sleeping mat for between the ground cloth and the sleeping bag
- A camp stove or grill
- Food
- Bottled water
- Bug repellent (look for natural, non-Deet products)
- Unscented sunscreen

Day hiking. Think of this one as an extended stroll in the woods, kind of like a class trip, without the bus ride or the imposed buddy system. A day hike gets you out after sunrise and in before sunset. It also gets you used to traipsing along with your pack on your back. For this, you won't need all of the overnight gear.

To Bring List

- A backpack, one with a padded hip strap that can be affixed tightly
- A small foam cushion for sitting on chilly rocks
- A pair of sturdy hiking boots/shoes (worn-in; new ones are big-time blister givers)
- Layers (Dara recommends fleece, high-tech synthetics, and a waterproof jacket)
- Two pairs of socks on your feet, one thin to wear under one thick (This layering prevents blisters.)
- Extra socks, in case the above get wet
- Moleskin cutouts, in case you get blisters anyway
- Hat and gloves, light- to heavyweight (In warm weather, lightweight gloves can help you climb, and a hat will keep you cool.)
- A garden trowel (We'll explain later.)
- A flashlight, just in case you're out later than planned
- A trail map, with alternate routes in case a bridge is washed out
- A watch (This is important: Plan your trip for daylight hours only. This means designating—and sticking to—a turnaround time. If it's

one o'clock and you haven't reached Scenic Waterfall Outlook #57, you still gotta head back the way you came.)

- Food (ought to include childhood indulgences such as old-school chocolate bars and trail mix)
- Bottled water
- Toilet paper, unscented
- Empty plastic zipper bags to, as experienced campers like to say, "pack out" crumbs, apple cores, wipes, and, well, used toilet paper (see "Nature Is Not Your Toilet, but, Then Again, It Sort of Is")
- Hand sanitizer
- A friend or two or three

(Did you notice how we put a friend or two or three on the list each time? That's because Dara 'n' Co. say camping solo is sheer nonsense. You may want to escape your best friend, worst enemy, nightmare boss, and everyone else in your life. But if you're planning to do that in the wild, get thee to a nature spa. Why? Because. Because cell phones don't work in the wild. Because of *The Blair Witch Project,* for god's sake. Because it might sound like a good idea when you're headed out on the road with the windows down and your womyn-power mix cranked up, and it might even be a blast as you hike up a mountain and pass a few lazy fellas on your way up, but it's not so fun when it's dark and the owls are whooting and the leaves are rustling and you're alone in the woods.)

Overnight backpack trip. Spending a night in nature is a big deal. City girls might find the quiet disturbing. Country girls might feel too confined in a tent. But once you make such discoveries as you're able to get a good night's sleep without a feather bed, and instant oatmeal tastes best when eaten outdoors, you just might head right back next weekend for more.

What you pack depends on where you're planning to sleep. Your options may include a wooden shelter with a decklike surface and three walls, a designated camping area, or just you and the earth. You may even get lucky and pitch your tent near a compost toilet. (Patience, we're getting to the bathroom part.) You'll need everything from both lists—small versions of stuff like the stove, please—plus more.

To Bring List

- All-purpose soap concentrate like Campsuds or Dr. Bronner's
- Water, if necessary, with a purifying system
- An emergency whistle
- Activities: cards, Pass the Pigs, travel Scrabble/chess/checkers
- Clean undies
- Extra food
- Brushup-style tooth wipes
- A camera and journal to document the experience

What Not to Bring
- Scented anything
- Food for the animals

Nature Is Not Your Toilet, but, Then Again, It Sort of Is

The good news: Humans aren't supposed to go in the woods, bear style. The bad news: When you're camping, you gotta do what you gotta do (doo).

Number one: the squat 'n' tuck. Walk two hundred feet (about a small city block) from the trail and also two hundred feet from any stream that's not your own. Remove a minimum of toilet paper from your pack. (Extra credit to virgins who use soft, wide, nonpoisonous fallen leaves instead.) Find a tree. Walk around it until you're facing uphill. Pull 'em down. Tuck shorts/pants behind your knees. Squat so that your butt is right between your heels—but not on the ground, for goodness sake. Hold on to the tree. Tinkle. Drip dry. Wipe if desired/necessary. Pack dirty tissue in plastic zipper bag marked "Dirty." You will be tempted to throw it on the ground or hide it somewhere slightly clever. Do not. Charmin doesn't biodegrade as easily as you think.

Number two: the dig, squat, and tuck. Dara says, this time, "there are a lot more things to consider." We thought she meant a lot more personal issues. But she's talking about the environment, because apparently you can't just go and leave it there (because animals don't take kindly to human poo). So hop off the trail at the first intestinal pangs. Extract your trowel, minimal TP, and that specially designated plastic bag. Go the two-hundred-foot distance. Find a tree, face it uphill. Use your trowel to dig a small hole about six to eight inches deep and four to five inches across, "wide enough so that you can aim," says Dara. Stow your trowel back in the pack. Assume the position. Think happy thoughts, perhaps ones about your brave cave woman ancestors. Still nervous? Whistle. Count trees. Let 'er rip. Wipe 'n' stow paper as instructed above. You're almost done. Use a stick to re-cover the hole. Scatter some leaves over it. Pat down. Use wipes, hand sanitizer, what-have-you to clean your hands. Congratulate yourself. This is a true deflowering moment.

Dara's Further Suggestions for Camping Virgins

Turn wine into water. Empty a box of wine (using the traditional smart consumption method). Remove the silvery bag inside it. Rinse out the bag thoroughly. Fill the bag with water.

Circle in the square. Not quite getting the whole beauty of nature thing? Take a tip from Dara's nature classes for kids: Toss a string ring on a patch of ground and observe what you see. Note, for one, that bugs are pretty darn cool. And that leaves smell like sugar when they biodegrade.

Where there's smoke, there's a cute l'il stove. The Brady family, the gang from Peanuts, and every movie character who ever pitched a tent may have built a mini bonfire and roasted wieners on a stick. But in these marvelous days of environmental awareness, the campfire is *très passé.*

Many sites don't allow campfires at all; others designate specific areas as fire rings, and may require campers to BYO firewood. Still long for flickering ambience? Tote along unscented candles. How about a hot meal? Enter the camp stove.

Where there's a cute l'il stove, there's a one-pot meal. Ever the camper after our own hearts, Dara calls cooking outdoors, "the most exciting part of the camping experience." (She warns it's also the most dangerous, so learn to use the stove at home—outside!—first.) "Keep dishes simple. Pasta is really easy: Boil water, strain it off." Dirty dishes ought to be kept to a minimum; most primitive campsites lack running water.

Where there's a one-pot meal, there's a critter to eat it. Chipmunks, raccoons, and bears probably won't come around while you're cooking and enjoying your deliciously simple victuals. They will, however, show up once you're zipped inside your sleeping bag. "Animals are attracted to dirty and soapy dishes," says Dara. (They'll also munch anything foreign-scented, including deodorant, soap, hair spray, foundation, sunscreen, and Powder Fresh Playtex.) But please, don't feed these furry friends. "They have plenty of natural food out there—and the more they eat your food—including the crumbs you leave behind—the more they lose the ability to find food for themselves." Hang food and garbage—plus sunscreen, toothpaste, and deodorant—in bags from trees, "ten to twelve feet off the ground and six feet away from a major branch."

LEAVE NO TRACE'S SEVEN PRINCIPLES

1. Plan Ahead and Prepare
2. Travel and Camp on Durable Surfaces
3. Dispose of Waste Properly
4. Leave What You Find
5. Minimize Campfire Impacts
6. Respect Wildlife
7. Be Considerate of Other Visitors

This hiker makes frequent stops. "A lot of people go out to hike to get to the top of the mountain. Too many people don't take the time to stop because they're so worried about getting there. Every time you stop and take a break, have a sip of water. Take a chance to relax your breathing and look around," says Dara.

H_2O RDA. "Dehydration is one of the biggest health risks of being in the outdoors. Drink at least a quart of water an hour when you're out camping. Most people on a daily basis are slightly dehydrated. You can tell you are if your urine is yellowish. (It should be pretty close to clear.) If you get lethargic, drink water."

Anti-ascetic. A camping trip is not the time to quit smoking, or to give up coffee, or to adopt a raw food diet. You're already putting yourself in a new situation. Additional change is a bad idea at this point. (A note to smokers: Smoking on the trail is pretty much a jumbo breach in etiquette. Hike off to puff—and pack out your ashes and butts.)

Giving up: Dara's last word. "If the weather is so miserable that you're not having fun, what's to force you to stay out there? I remember camping out with a couple of guys. We were sleeping in a shelter. The mosquitoes were so bad, that at three a.m. we just climbed into the car and left. There's no shame in giving up."

SURFING LESSON

> *Paddle out, turn around, and raise, and, baby,*
> *that's all there is to the coastline craze. You gotta catch a wave*
> *and you're sitting on top of the world.*
> —THE BEACH BOYS

OK. We have a confession to make. A grave one. We spent the greater part of our youth pretending we were surfers. This is not a joke.

We subscribed to *Surfer* magazine and taped each pullout poster of a tan man muscling his way through a curling wave to our bedroom wallpaper. We wore Quicksilver board shorts for boys, Vans, and T-shirts bearing the logo of local surf shops, where we hung out in the hopes that a long-haired clerk would recognize us as the date-worthy subject of the Beach Boys' song "Surfer Girl." We bought surfboard wax, just for the smell of it. We sprayed Sun-In in our hair, and tanning oil on our bodies. When a stranger asked if we knew how to surf, we answered with an emphatic "Um, yeah."

In truth, we struggled to paddle our yellow Hawaiian Punch raft through lifeguarded gullies. We tried the Boogie board thing, but even then we wiped out.

As a matter of course, imaginary surf girl existences eventually give way to a life on the mainland, merely peppered with seaside vacations. Every once in a while, fueled by a surfer documentary or a magazine story about a surfer-turned-model, we feel a memorable pang of I-should-have-done-that. But then it goes away, and we continue our landlubber's lifestyle. Too late for us, we thought. Then we met Bev Sanders.

GO-TO GIRL

Bev Sanders   Goddess of the Waves, Believer in the Cause, Founder of Las Olas Surf Camp

Bev's always been a sport. One of the first women to hop a snowboard for a downhill ride, she tried her luck on a surfboard during a Hawaiian vacation—and has been catching waves ever since. In 1997 Bev and Surf Diva creator Izzy Thiyani founded Las Olas, an all-women surf camp in central Mexico. Today, Bev and her team of world-class wahines (Hawaiian for women surfers) teach women ages eleven to seventy to paddle, pop up, and ride 'em, saltwater cowgirl—between yoga classes and massages, of course. Along the way, if these first-time surfers just happen to regain the happy confidence, the sense of connectedness they had when they were nine, well, it's purely intentional. Bev's words of encouragement to virgin wahines, "The first year I learned to surf was the best year of my life."

Of course, not all of us are going to hop a plane to Puerto Vallarta and plunk down a bulky wad of change just to see if we'll like it. Some of us want to start on our own. Don't. "Absolutely do not try surfing on your own," says Bev. "It's dangerous not only to you, but to other people in the water." (Could be pretty embarrassing, to boot.)

Most towns with a coastline have a surf shop. Most surf shops have a surfing school or instructors attached to it. After all, surf bum-dom doesn't pay for itself. Call them. Schedule a lesson—if possible, with a female instructor.

To get ready for your lesson, do push-ups. This instruction is nearly a cliché among those who teach women to surf. The dreaded exercise— even the girl kind—is the perfect, equipment-free toner for upper body muscles, which is what you use most in surfing.

Better yet, do pop-ups or surf-ups—the push-ups you'll be doing on the board. Here's how. Lie belly down on the ground, your legs out behind you, and your hands flat on the ground beside your chest, elbows bent. Using your feet and hands, jump your feet to where your hands were to stand yourself up and face right if your right foot's forward (called "goofy footed") or face left if your left foot's forward ("regular footed"). Legs are apart. Knees are bent. Once you're on the board, you won't be able to use your knees, or take steps to get into position. The pop-up is one, swift movement. Good luck with that.

Still, Bev's hosted a bunch of women who didn't bother to follow this instruction, and they do just fine, because they: "Do any kind of exercise that involves upper body strength: dance classes, weight training . . . Swimming is a very good exercise for surfing because you're using your arms—and you're getting used to the water. The more familiar you are with the water, the more you can deal with the little panic attacks that start when you're first surfing."

Panic attacks? What?

That's right. The ocean is a big and powerful place that can swallow you up and without skipping a beat spit you out against the beach. The sea seems even bigger when you're trying to paddle through waves to deeper, calmer waters. Bigger still when you try to balance atop a breaking wave and ride it toward shore.

For those of us who have a fear of seas and such, Bev recommends another preparation: yoga. "Being able to calm your mind down is important, because you'll get into situations in the water where you'll really have to relax. Yoga trains you to do that." No surprise that yoga classes come as part and parcel of the Las Olas package.

Next, You'll Need a Few Basics . . .

Board. Remember those cruddy little foam kick board thingies you used to learn to swim in a pool? Well, the clever makers of surfboards have come up with a less embarrassing version for starting-out surfers.

Foam boards are lightweight, easy to maneuver, and, most of all, don't hurt your noggin when they inevitably clock you on the head. If a foam board is not available, choose a nine-foot-or-longer board or a fun board over a short and sporty one. "A longboard is a little more buoyant. It gives you more stability and isn't going to wobble all over the place . . .

it's also easier to paddle out." A funboard is under nine feet but is wider than a traditional shortboard. Once you turn semipro, you'll rely on your height, weight, and skill to determine which board you buy.

Which reminds us: Most surf shops rent boards at low daily or hourly rates.

And also. The number one rule of surfing: Never ditch your board. "The wave is going to want to pull that board away from you. So, think of you and your board as one unit."

Leash. This connects your board to your ankle (not to your wrist or neck). Very important this, because you want to keep that board with you at all times.

Bathing suit. Leave all swimwear involving the words "string," "bandeau" or "crochet," at home. "It is going to fall off," says Bev, who speaks from experience upon experience. "Wear a stay-on bathing suit." You know what this means.

Board shorts. Legs get chapped in no time on a surfboard because rough sand sticks to the waxed surface. Plus, we're sure you'll agree that board shorts are super sporty cute.

Rash guards. Far from the Desitin of your diaper rash days, these silky mock-turtle tops are meant to prevent your upper body from board chafe. They, too, are supercute. Just be sure to get one that fits snugly, like a bodysuit, or you'll defeat the purpose.

Booties. Not exactly the world's sexiest footwear, these are important if there are rocks beneath waves.

Wet suit. Practically mandated if you're surfing in (Northern, or in the winter, Southern) California's chilly Pacific waters—what was Gidget thinking, anyway?—this seal-like neoprene rubber foam one-piece actually allows the water it absorbs to warm to a body's temperature.

Surf wax. This is stuff you rub on your surfboard to keep you from slipping off it. Also acts as a powerful procrastination tool as in "I'll be right there: Gotta wax my board first."

We would add waterproof sunscreen here, but we know you're smart enough to figure that out for yourself.

Where and When to Get in the Water

Wave condition. Choppy, bad. Glassy, good. Waves two to three feet high (waist to chest high on a person five eight) are generally safe for beginners. Waves generated by storms or hurricanes are generally not good. Can't tell by standing on the beach and looking seaward? Phone that surf shop. Ask for the surf report.

Tide. Surfers surf all kinds of tides. Most agree that an hour before high tide offers premium conditions. As for low tide: "If the tide is out, it's going to be really shallow, so when you fall you're going to fall flat. If you think the water is really deep but it's really six inches, you could break an ankle," says Bev.

Riptides. These dangerous, drag-you-out-to-sea currents are the ocean's quicksand: The more you struggle against them, the more they suck you in. Find out if your chosen surf spot has any of these (from a surf shop or a lifeguard) and, if at all possible, move to a safer place.

If you find yourself caught in a riptide, don't fight it. If your feet touch ground, walk out of the current, not directly into the shore, but parallel to the shoreline. If you've lost footing, shout for help, stay as calm as possible, and tread water, tipping your head back, and letting the current drag you out. No one helping? Swim toward shore at a 45-degree angle. Feeling brave? Loads of surfers use these currents to drag them out to better waves, as if the current were a moving sidewalk. Most times, your board will keep you afloat.

Break. Also known as the bottom of the wave portion of the ocean, a break can be sandy, rocky, or, in rarer instances, coral-y. Sandy breaks are the gentlest, then rocky, then coral-y.

Solo. Bev is adamant on this: Beginner surfers should not surf alone. She asked us to put this information in here twice. And we did.

Crowds. On the other hand, it's not terribly clever for starting-out surfers to join during wave-catchers' rush hour. Those paddling into a crowd will panic when there's a surfer headed toward them. Those dropping in on a wave have to cede the right-of-way to the surfer who's dropped in closest to the wave's peak.

Best to stake out a claim in occupied—but not jam-packed—waters. As a beginner, you'll be expected to give up the biggest, best waves to more experienced neighbors. Which should be just fine with you.

GOLF OUTING

Golf is very much like a love affair, if you don't take it seriously, it's no fun, if you do, it breaks your heart. Don't break your heart, but flirt with the possibility.
—Louise Suggs

To all the golfers reading this: We know what you're thinking. You're thinking, Yeah, right.

You golfers say your sport is the most difficult game around. You're probably right. Surviving eighteen holes requires billiards-esque strategizing, the ability to execute dozens of strokes and swings with fourteen clubs, adherence to strict etiquette, the deep pocket to pay famously pricey greens fees—and four to five hours of free time for each round. Oh, and it's a head game, total head game. Which just so happens to make golf completely addictive.

How, you golfers are wondering, do these people intend to explain this most complex of outdoor adventures in one little section?

Just watch us. But first, to all you golfing virgins who are now squinching your eyebrows and thinking you should just skip right on to first lingerie, a word on why to plug on.

Golf's appeal comes not only from the two big facts that we could all use a little more time outdoors, and that holes one to eighteen provide the ultimate networking atmosphere—but because it's a lifelong sport. Start playing (OK, practicing) golf now, and you'll be playing until you can no longer swing a club. Seriously.

But, as with most sports, try to learn it yourself and you'll develop bad habits that will be doubly hard to break. Plus, with golf, it's go all the way—or don't go at all.

GO-TO GIRL

Sally Hammel   LPGA-Certified Teaching Pro
and All-around Good Sport

Sally took up golf in junior high, played on her Kansas high school team, and won a full golfing scholarship to Mercer College in Macon, Georgia, where she's now head coach of the women's team. Between holes, she's skydived, scuba dived, toured Europe, earned her MBA, taught hundreds of private golf lessons, and learned to play tennis. Though this southern gal is proud that women are increasingly joining in the golfing fun, she also recognizes her favorite sport is still considered a gentleman's game. "One of my biggest pet peeves is to see women not playing," she says. "I'd rather see a woman out there, spending time with her husband or girl friends, being willing to embarrass herself and to laugh at herself."

Sally was more than enthusiastic about giving us some pointers to pass along.

Find a Teacher

On this first point, Sally is insistent. Look for a PGA- or LPGA-certified instructor—a pro with ample experience teaching women. "Look for someone who's warm and friendly and encouraging, someone that you have a good rapport with. That's half the battle." You can find an instructor through the LPGA, the Executive Women's Golf Association, or through a private club that allows nonmembers to take lessons with their pros on staff.

Expect to pay anywhere from $45 to $125 per hour for a private lesson. "The average is about $75 per hour." Seventy-five bucks seem a little steep? Sign up for a ladies' beginner clinic, or get together with two or three friends for a semiprivate lesson, which usually costs about $100 an hour for the group.

Find Time

It's likely you'll start out with a weekly lesson for one or two months, and then move to biweekly appointments. But that's not all. It's also important to find time to practice on your own. "Take two or three hours a week, and you'll improve pretty quickly. You can pretty much take your own balls and do it," says Sally. Since it's likely you'll first learn your "short" game—which means shorter distance shots, like putts and chips—you can even practice in a backyard or park. Many courses offer discounts during twilight hours, and you can usually save bucks by passing on a golf cart and walking the course instead (although some courses are carts only). Save the driving range for down the line.

Don't Buy Anything

"Whatever you do, don't go out and buy golf clubs," says Sally. Each club fits specifically to your size, skills, and game. "Most teachers are going to have equipment for you to learn with."

When you are ready to spring for your five starter clubs, involve your teacher in the selection process. A full set of clubs—fourteen—runs around $800. So wait and see if you like the game before investing in it.

"You don't have to have golf shoes either," says Sally. "It's fine to learn in tennis shoes." Attire etiquette bans jeans or denim and calls for a collared shirt (we'd call it a polo, but since we're talking about golf . . .) or a fitted knit shirt with modest shorts, khaki pants, or a cute l'il golf skirt, maybe one with l'il embroidered golf tees?

Be Patient

"You need to commit three to six months to learn. That doesn't mean you can't go out on the golf course in those months; I hope you do. But if you want to go out there and participate, to be part of a team for a company outing, for example, I would say, give yourself six months. I would not suggest going out with clients or business associates unless you know how to play. You don't want better golfers to be waiting for you, because it will become more of a frustration and less of a social thing."

This last bit of news sounds discouraging, but Sally assures us that those few moments of beginner bliss on the greens far outweigh the

FAKING IT: TALK THE TALK

Since, as Sally says, "You can't fake knowing how to play," the best way to break into the golfing scene without actually golfing is to learn the game. "I've met so many people whom I have nothing in common with except the sport, but that alone gives us so much to talk about."

A few terms to kick off your designer impostor career in golf (thanks, Sally):

Par: The score an expert golfer would be expected to make for a given hole. (Score is measured in number of strokes it takes to get a ball in, so the lower the par, the easier the hole.)

Fairway: The closely cut, well-kept portion of grass between the teeing area and the putting green.

Teeing area: Often called the tee or tee box, the starting point for each hole on the course.

Bunker: A depression where the turf or soil has been removed and replaced with sand. It is a hazard. (Commonly, but improperly, it's called a "sand trap.")

Putting green: All the ground around the hole being played.

Drive: A long shot played from the teeing area, usually with a wood. (A wood is a kind of club.)

Putt: A rolling shot taken on the green.

Chip: A shot originating just off the green that begins with a tiny hop and ends by rolling.

Pitch: A shot that originates off the green and remains airborne before rolling a short distance.

Birdie: A score of one stroke under par for the hole. (A good thing.)

Eagle: A score of two strokes under par for the hole. (A better thing.)

Double eagle: A score of three strokes under par for the hole. (We know, we know, the math is bad on this one; just go with it.)

Bogey: A score of one stroke over par for the hole. (A bad thing.)

Double bogey: A score of two strokes over par for the hole. (A worse thing, but, hey, we're all laughing at ourselves, right?)

Fore!: A warning shouted to let a person know that a ball in flight may hit or come close to her.

bloopers. "It's when you hit that first big shot that you become addicted to it," she says. "That first time the ball comes off the club face correctly: You can see it. That's your instant gratification. Even if you go out and hit fifteen bad shots, that one good one feels like getting a hundred on an exam in school."

Handling those fourteen poor putts requires being able to laugh at yourself. "If you're not comfortable making a fool of yourself, then don't pick up the game," advises our resident golf pro.

Going Along for the Ride

Another great way to get a grasp on the flow and etiquette of the game: Tag along for nine holes of a more experienced pal's game. "Watch what the golfers do: where they put their clubs, how they put the flag stick back in the hole. If you're dressed properly, most places are going to let you ride along or walk along," says Sally.

The Perks

"There's a saying in golf: 'Who cares how well you play as long as you look good and can eat lunch afterward?'" says Sally, adding, "for women, you get to buy new clothes and shoes. How bad is that? . . . After your game, you get to sit around and talk about the shots you hit, laugh about the stories, and have a beer. That's the really nice part."

HORSEBACK RIDE

The best thing for the inside of a person is the outside of a horse.
—WILL ROGERS

Some of us grew up horsey girls. As soon as we were able, we swindled our parents into signing us up for riding lessons. We played with equestrian Barbie. We wore velvet riding helmets to the dinner table and cried for days after watching the final scene of *Black Stallion*. Others of us went through a horse phase where we did all of the above—except the riding part. And, yet others of us just went through a horse phase in appearance only, which we thankfully grew out of by age fifteen.

We're not sure what it is about us girls and horses. Romance, power, speed, and grace—and a giant animal that loves you like the family dog but can take you places the family minivan couldn't fathom.

But horsey love follows us well beyond our days of dolls and parental permission. No longer are we the fearless small fries whose bruises and boo-boos are badges of bravery. These days, instead of jumping up on the first pony at the party shouting "Hi-ho, Silver!" we want to know a little more before we take that midnight ride—or, as the case may be, a ride on Midnight.

GO-TO GIRL

Elizabeth Rufenacht   L.A. Rider

Elizabeth's riding career began as a bribe. She remembers around age seven: "I told my parents I'd take piano lessons if they'd let me take horse riding lessons, too." Between her childhood act of cunning and her career in equine brokerage, our Go-to competed in equitation, jumpers, and dressage. These days, she's a full-time editor for film and TV in Hollywood who keeps her horse phase alive by riding and competing with Hope, her Danish Warmblood. She says riding is "kind of like meditation. I don't think about anything else. It puts me instantly in the zone: I don't think about the traffic; I don't think about relationship problems. I don't think of anything else at all."

Tacking Up

The pants. Going English style? "Get a nice pair of Harry Hall's—you may even have a pair from a couple of years ago when they were in fashion," says Elizabeth. If Britain's favorite jodhpurs are a little out of your price range—they run around $150—spring for any elasticized pants that won't rub when you ride.

For Western trail blazers, beware the wrath of denim! Jeans may seem like cowgirl classics, but, says Elizabeth, "that place in your jeans where

HORSE TALK

It might help if we knew a few riding terms, too:

English style: Smaller saddle, reins give cues, more elegant outfits.

Western style: Larger saddle, body gives cues, Texas-lookin' outfits.

Walk: Slowest gait. Walking, little or no bounce.

Trot: Next speed up. The horse moves from one diagonal pair of legs to the other, with a period of suspension in between—a two-beated gait.

Canter: First one hind leg strides, then the opposite diagonal pair strides. Last goes the opposite foreleg—a three-beated gait. In Western riding, called "lope." Faster still.

Gallop: Each foot touches the ground separately—a four-beated gait and what racehorses do around tracks. The fastest.

Aids: Signals or cues the rider gives to the horse. Voice, legs, hands, and weight give natural aids. Tensing up, squeezing, and gripping are called driving aids (not good things these).

Bridle: Belt-y contraption worn on the horse's head that connects the bit in the horse's mouth to the reins in your hands.

Tack: The trimmings—OK, equipment—used for riding (saddle, stirrups, etc.).

Zony: Cross between a zebra and a pony. (Obviously very useful information.)

the seams meet can be a horrible thing when you're riding the horse. It's going to hit you in the crotch and . . . Ouch!" When you're picking out a pair, go for elasticized jeans tailor-made for riding—or at least something with a little more coverage. Low-rise styles creep embarrassingly low once you're saddled up. "Don't go riding in a pair of Lucky jeans," advises Liz.

The boots. English riders will need traditional tall boots with small, square heels. "If you don't have your calves protected, the stirrup leathers are going to pinch, and you'll end up with bruises all up and down your calves." The boots' heels are to prevent your feet from slipping out of the stirrups.

Western riders should know that your adorable Durangos are OK, but the taller the boots, the better. No sneakers, no sandals.

The jacket. "Choose something that has a vent in the back so that it's flexible on the hips."

The helmet. Although you may not be required to wear a thing to protect your noggin, it would be pretty silly not to borrow a helmet from the stable or to buy one that fits well. "The best helmets on the market are Troxel. They're designed by a doctor, and there's an inexpensive trail riding version and a really expensive competition riding one. I think they're the best helmets out there."

The bargains. "There's some great used tack on eBay, and tack stores often sell secondhand tack. Anyway, for a first-time rider, worn-in boots are much better than a brand-new pair of stiff boots."

The Ride

If you're planning on signing up for a guided ride through the countryside, "Find out what kind of riding you'll be doing before you saddle up," says Elizabeth. "Are you going to be walking the whole time or galloping? Ask what level of riding is expected." Trail rides are usually in comfier Western saddles with easygoing horses who know the way. Equestrian holiday rides—for example, a jaunt through the Irish countryside that's the equivalent of a pub crawl on horseback—might require you to dive into ravines and to jump over creeks and small cars (an occasion for which lessons are definitely in order).

"If you're going out into open nature, you should feel comfortable asking to be taken into the arena where someone can help you walk, trot, canter, gallop, and stop the horse so you feel that you're comfortable making a safe transition from a canter to a gallop or back to a walk."

If you've made certain that you can handle the gait and the terrain—and you're still nervous—don't be afraid to ask for a slow-and-steady horse. There's nothing wrong with riding "the baby-sitter, the old guy who's probably going to ignore everything that you do. This horse knows his job, knows when to turn around, and knows how to go back home," says Elizabeth.

But if you do go for a jumpier model, try to remain calm at all times. "Adults tend to hold, squeeze, grip, and pull back on the reins—which, ironically, will make the horse run away," says Elizabeth. Instead, "Think of sitting in a chair, and whenever something seems out of control, relax and exhale, and the horse will relax, slow down, and exhale, too."

Be prepared to be bounced around during—and to experience sore thighs after—your ride. If you know you're extra stiff in the hips, it's a good idea to prep beforehand with riding-specific exercises. "You've gotta have really good balance. Doing Pilates and using a balance ball are great ways to prepare for the trip." Yoga works well to prepare those inner thigh muscles for the serious stretch they'll get on the horse.

Great Horses for Beginners

- Andalusian. "Highly trained, and extraordinarily comfortable to sit on."
- Peruvian Paso Fino. "Like sitting on a couch. All their legs move, but they don't use their backs much for movement. They're bred to be comfortable, literally to trek around the Andes on."
- Norwegian Fjord Pony. "Really small, and has a pretty, smooth gait."
- Icelandic Horse. A peaceful, docile breed known for its five-beated gait.

So You Want More?

Check with the American Riding Instructors Association (www.riding-instructor.com) to find a certified teacher. Good news for virgins: Novices pay less for lessons—private sessions last thirty minutes or one hour, and prices vary widely, averaging $25–$50 for a half hour and $35–$85 for one hour (less if you happen to own your own horse).

8

Arts events can look so intriguing from the outside. Watch theater-goers file into a lavish opening night. Peer through glass windows of an art gallery to view a bohemian mix of models and critics, sipping champagne and strolling among sculptures. The world of living arts is all so glamorous, so hard-to-reach.

On the other hand, maybe not. Maybe, we're simply in need of a little background information fortification. Maybe just a few pages away lie the secrets of finding your fabulous place in the art world.

GALLERY OPENING

We have. You see. This "friend." She's a nice enough girl. Cute, too. She just goes to those free openings at art galleries for all the wrong reasons.

This friend of ours likes to get dressed up in her finest, edgiest frock and heels. She paints on her shockingest lip color. She enters a roomful of perfect strangers, helps herself to complimentary hors d'oeuvres and champers, and every minute or so strikes this sort of art gallery pose that involves placing herself in front of a painting, a drink in one hand and her jutting-out hip in the other, squinting her eyes, and nodding ever so slightly. Sometimes she cocks her head. On rare occasions, she says, "Hmmmm."

When she's had a drink or two, she moves on . . . to another gallery. We have reason to suspect this friend has never bought an actual piece of art during one of these shows. We have further reason to suspect that she attends these events simply for the fun of it. Whatever shall we do?

We'll say it loud and proud: It is OK to go to an art opening just for the fun of it. Especially if you received a personal invite. Especially if it's one of those early-evening, all-neighborhood gallery crawls that cities and towns are shin-digging these days. Still, there are a few simple things to know before you, yes, go.

And, surprise surprise, we have just the person to teach them to you.

GO-TO GIRL

Liz Kinder

Potter and Observer of and Victim to Opening-Night Angst

"My artist friend was talking about her wedding. She said, 'Do you know what getting married is? Getting married is like having an art opening. But at your wedding, there's no art; there's no one to talk about the art: They're all there to talk about you,'" says Liz. An international potter who earned her fine arts BA in painting at Amherst, her MFA at the Royal College of Art in London, and currently roosts in Philadelphia, Liz has played the role of featured artist and invited guest at more openings than she can remember. For the record: She prefers the role of guest. Why? Because the artist is as much on display as the art itself. "People are not just buying my pottery. They're buying me," she says.

Art Opening Basics

When to go. Fashionably late, if you'd like to blend in with the crowd. On time if you'd like to meet the artist.

What to say. "Trying to talk to the artist at this point, other than to say, 'Your work is fabulous,' is faulty," advises Liz.

Still, if you'd like to learn more, asking "Who's your influence?" is always good, or, "What other artists do you like?" or "Where did you study?"

"Don't ever ask an artist how long it took her to make something . . . You've got some old potters who'll say, 'Fifty years! I've been doing this fifty years, and all fifty are in that piece of work!'"

"If you feel snubbed by an artist, chances are he's just socially inept. . . . Realize that the artist is vulnerable—and quite possibly drunk, because all the attention is on him."

Hold your criticism until you're out the door and out of earshot. Not only is an observation that "my four-year-old brother could have done this" quite rude, it's also a cliché.

If the artist is your friend. Go early and offer to be her wing woman by refilling her glass, steering her toward a bejeweled couple who seem to have fallen for her latest work, and, when it's all through, taking her out to a relaxing meal.

How to buy. Many citizens of the art world advise against buying a piece of artwork—and especially a first piece—during a gallery opening, because the swirl of drinks and excited Parker Posey look-alikes and more drinks harm aesthetic sensibilities—and common sense.

But if you'd like to check out the prices, ask the gallery owner for a price sheet. Any piece with a red dot next to it—or on the price sheet—means it's already sold or not for sale.

If you've fallen for works that are way out of your price range, ask the gallery owner if the artist ever does smaller commissions, or would consider selling studies or sketches. "Artists often want to get rid of sketches and that kind of thing," says Liz.

At certain openings—student exhibitions, for example—the artist might not be ready to talk cost. "That's sort of delicate," says Liz. "In that scenario, it's always good to say, 'I'm really interested in this piece. I don't see a price. Here's my card. Call me.' You want to make it as easy as possible for that person."

No photos, please. Most galleries absolutely do not allow photography. But if you'd love a shot of yourself and Liz, for example, ask permission from the gallery owner. Ditto if you'd like an image of one of the works. (The owner can provide slides or prints.)

Please touch. If the show is of functional art—furniture, pottery, ceramics, textiles—you may be welcome to handle the works. "Unless a chair says 'You can't sit in this,' you can ask. How would you possibly assess something like that unless you could try it?"

Please bring a date. "It can really give you something to talk about. It can even be fun to hate things. In fact, that can be even more fun!"

ART PURCHASE

> *The purpose of art is washing the dust of daily life off our souls.*
> —Pablo Picasso

"Hello there, sexy," says Mark Wahlberg, his Calvin Klein underpants peeking out the top of his jeans.

"Bonjour!" shouts the pretty lady from the pastis poster.

"Welcome to the Rockies!" announces the stretch of beach/mountain range taped above your bed.

"Let's kiss!" says Usher.

"My oh my. What a darling collection of *art* you have, darling," observes your friend, who's just in from her first year living in Manhattan (where she developed an affinity for the word "darling").

"What's wrong with my posters?" you ask. As soon as the words leave your Juicy Tubes lips, you know the exact answer to your own question.

Your bedding is made of crisp linen the color of sea foam. Your dressing table is a family heirloom. Those pretty beads on your cat's collar? Genuine freshwater pearls. But, honey, you've got to do something about your, um, wall aesthetic.

You know, you know. This isn't your first worldly friend to make a comment. But give you a break, right? You studied *accounting* in college.

The last time you set foot in an art gallery, well, have you ever set foot in an art gallery? You know you've been to a museum—on class trips—but you're not quite sure you've actually entered an actual, art-for-sale gallery. An art gallery seems so, well, intimidating. Kind of like a Gucci store. Someone might look at you and realize you're faking it.

Of course you like art. It's just that there's so much of it. And it's so expensive. How could you afford it? Where would you start?

Virgin, have we got good news for you. Actually, our pal Laura has the good news.

GO-TO GIRL

Laura Satterfield Multitasker, Art Student, Art Dealer, and All-around Nice Person

"The art world is there for you to grab." This is how Laura starts a conversation. We are intrigued. Then we learn the co-owner of South La Brea Gallery spends her spare time working as a docent at L.A.'s Hammer Museum, doing marketing for the performing arts, majoring in art, and still finding time to effuse about her passion for art. Her sparkly outlook is enough to convert us to art lovers in a wink of the *Mona Lisa*. The mission of Laura's gallery: "To help not only emerging artists, but also emerging collectors. Collecting for the first time can be so intimidating. So, we've built ourselves around being a place that can be more comfortable." Oh yes. Laura is our kind of Go-to Girl.

There are two places to start your first exploits into the art world. You could consult your bank balance. Or you could consult your surroundings. We think the latter is a whole lot more fun.

Ways to "Get" Art

Look around. "Take a look at the design of your house," says Laura. Sounds simple, right? If you live where you live because of the contemporary, classic, or antique-y setting, there's your first clue.

When you're out and about, "just keep your eyes open for the things that you're attracted to. Even if you're in the mall." Aha! Going to the mall is now a cultural event! If only we'd known this one when we were fourteen and went there to try on cheap miniskirts and to chase skater boys!

Enter those galleries. Really, they're much more welcoming than you think. (In fact, we have it on good authority that gallery owners are trying desperately to attract people just like us.) "Visit a lot of different types, and soon you'll be able to pinpoint what you're attracted to."

Browse a bookstore. "Flip through art books and take notes on what you like," says Laura. "Maybe pick up *Art Forum* and pay attention to what artists say their influences are."

Take a class. "Major museums and university extensions have classes you can take that can help guide you," says Laura. Some of these classes take trips to gallery districts, where you will step into actual galleries. With the protection of the professor, of course.

Join an art museum. The benefits of a basic, annual, reasonably priced membership: invitations to art openings, curator-led tours, and lectures from special guests. "You can even set up private tours with you and a couple of friends. Sometimes museums charge a fee for this, but sometimes they don't. Once you hear someone talking about artwork while you're seeing the work in person, you begin to get a grasp of it."

Go to auctions. To look and to learn, not to bid and to win (at least not yet). Find the world's largest through Web sites like artnet.com and artfact.com, and closer-to-you auctions through local galleries and museums. Art auctions typically cater to an exclusive batch of experienced art collectors, consultants, and other Thomas Crown types. "I wouldn't recommend a formal art auction for a first-time buyer," says Laura.

Do all these things, and you can't help but start to get a sense of what you like—and what you can afford to spend.

The Deal

But how much does good art go for these days?

"There is no specific price range," says Laura, "You can get original artwork from $10 to $40 million. If you're starting out, there are a lot of options—a lot, a lot of options. Maybe start out with a print, or an original lithograph by the artist," usually in the range of $100 to $500.

"You can look to spend up to $1,500 to $2,500 for a piece. You can go down as low as $300 to $500 for pretty incredible original artwork. Different galleries cover different price ranges: More emerging, young galleries will have the lower price range than the more-established, blue-chip galleries."

Once you've found a piece you can afford—and love—joyously alert the gallerist. Make no attempts to bargain. If necessary, however, work out a payment plan—most galleries will let you do this. Schedule a delivery for near to after the date when the show comes down. Arrange to have a representative for the gallery come install it in your home. This will likely cost extra; it is worth it. Do not plan to install art yourself. Please.

Go home. Un-tape the posters from your wall. Save them: One day, they, too, may be considered blue-chip art.

List your recent purchase on your home owner's or renter's insurance. "You can get a special policy for artwork. The larger galleries

UNUSUAL PLACES TO FIND ART

Flea Markets and Garage Sales

Best for kitschy finds, these collectively culled bazaars are fun to explore—and even more fun to drag home funky stuff from. Just be prepared to defend your purchase to your guests and family. Feel free to remind them, as Laura reminded us, "Diane Keaton collects clown paintings." Some of our favorites: Portland Expo in Portland, Oregon; Rose Bowl Flea Market in Pasadena, California; Cignancourt in Paris, France.

Estate Sales

A step up from a typical garage sale, these whole-house cleanouts can yield interesting pieces.

Student Art Shows

Go to the art school to check out MFA and undergrad shows. Kids these days are producing great, great art.

Charity Events

A lot of museums, arts organizations, nonprofits, and all of the above raise funds via auctions and silent auctions, many of which happen at annual balls, cocktail parties, and dinners. (So if you don't come home with a great work, at least you'll come home well fed.)

will provide you with some form of documentation: a slide, a digital image, a photo, as well as a detailed bill of sale and the artist's CV. Sometimes a piece might have been sold a few times, and you'll receive a list of provenance. The more documentation, the better," advises Laura.

Art World Myths: True or False?

1. Money. You'll need a whole bundle—at least a couple thou—to start a collection.
2. Smarts. You'll need a whole bundle—at least a degree in art history—to start a collection.
3. Van Gogh. You'll need a shiny brass plate with the name of a famous European artist—or at least a French native—to start a collection.

(Answers: 1. False. 2. False. and . . . 3. False.)

Oh, and one more myth that's more an aberration, actually: There is a certain, small population of people who purchase art as investment alone. They buy original pieces of gifted persons' souls as if they were stock for monetary—not aesthetic—value. We're willing to bet these people stockpile Cabbage Patch dolls in their original boxes, age wine beyond its time, and judge a book by its cover.

Buy art because you love it. If it earns interest over the years, good for you. But it's your long-term interest in the piece itself that really counts.

OPERA

> *Opera is as it is because we fundamentally crave romance.*
> *We want plumes and velvet somewhere in our lives.*
> —Mary Fitch Watkins

In the world of theater-going, amid movies and ballet, Broadway puppeteers and Alvin Ailey, Hollywood blockbusters and indie flicks, Shakespearian reincarnations and avant-everything, opera remains the big O.

And if you think we mean O as in Out-Of-reach, ObsOlete, or Otherwise tOO Old wOrld for anything you'd be interested in, well, we love you, but, darling, you're wrOng.

The big O means just what we're insinuating—and more. Like: Outstanding, Outrageous, Oft-Overlooked.

This centuries-old art form isn't all

horned-hat-wearing Brünnhilde types and tearful, chest-out tenors. It's romance and comedy, spectacle and intimacy, song and dance, costumes and lighting, drama and tragedy—all wrapped up in a gorgeous package that's far easier to appreciate than nay-saying stereotypers would have you believe.

The truth is, understanding opera comes down to a few essential elements. The rest is all about how it makes you feel.

Talking the Talk

Leaf through any Opera 101 text, browse most opera Web sites, and you'll likely come across a lengthy list of operatic vocabulary. There are literally dozens of mostly Italian and German words to describe every single detail of operas (most of which are sung in Italian or German).

But when you're starting out, it's enough to know ten terms, of which one is a gimme. And, if you've ever done anything remotely choruslike, you already know six. So you really have only three to learn.

Libretto: Means "little book" in Italian. In English, it means the words to the opera, which are all sung.

Arias: The songs. In Italian, literally, "air." Like in a musical, the songs represent an emotional reaction to what's going on, often a character's unspoken thoughts and feelings, the equivalent of a diary, set to music.

Recitative: Also sung, but more like dialogue. The recitative represents action, conversation. (Recitative + Arias = Libretto)

Soprano: Highest women's voice range.

Mezzo-soprano: In-between women's voice range.

Contralto: Lowest women's voice range.

Tenor: Highest men's voice range.

Baritone: Middle-range men's voice range.

Bass: Lowest men's voice range.

"Bravo/Brava!": The gimme. Congratulatory exclamation shouted at the end of the opera when the performers take their bows. Extra points for remembering to shout "Bravo!" for a male performer and "Brava!" for women.

One more thing you oughta be prepared for: "Supertitles" (which so doesn't count as a vocabulary word). A while back, audience-friendly opera innovators realized their guests would appreciate live translation. Their solution: Project the translated words above the stage's proscenium. Subtitles (like those used in foreign films) go below the action. Super ones go above it.

New York City's famous Metropolitan Opera goes one step further. Its supertitles run across each seat back, visible only to the one person facing them, like a personal news ticker. We think this is super indeed.

So, that's about it. Really. Well, not really.

More difficult operas do require mild preparation. Like a Shakespeare play or a Fellini film, they're best enjoyed if you already know and understand the story (or if you at least see the movie version) before you go.

"Operas are like anything that you're going to go see: You can benefit from preparation. A lot of people like to read the synopsis of the story before they see it. But if you're going to see an opera that you really don't know, I say, why not go into there and be surprised, just like you were going to the movies. Read a capsule to find out if it's a romance, a war story, or a spectacle. But then go in and let yourself be surprised by the ending," says our Extra Amazing Go-to Girl, who, by the way, might like to be introduced by now . . .

GO-TO GIRL

Cori Ellison   Dramaturg, New York City Opera,
                              Dreams in High Notes

Cori was a wee gal of seven when she found two red vinyl 45s (um, records) that belonged to her grandfather. Though the red vinyl first got her attention—"All the other recordings I'd ever seen were black and opaque"—it was the man on the albums who transformed an innocent first grader into a lifelong goner. Tenor Mario Lanza "just knocked me out," she gushes. As soon as she was old enough, Cori was hopping the Saturday train to the Met, where she'd snatch up standing-room-only tickets for the day's two performances. Today, her job at the world-renowned New York City Opera is "the literary and musicological and linguistic point person." Translation: She's in charge of publications, education, supertitles, research. She also consults with designers and conductors, travels, sings—and is nonetheless happy to spoon feed the basics to a first timer. Cori believes anyone at all can fall in love with opera: "It just hits you on all eight cylinders."

Starter Operas

Anything by Puccini: **La Bohème, Madame Butterfly, Tosca.** All boast scores of incredibly beautiful music and are "packed with hit tunes," says Cori. Their pacing moves more like movies, moving in real time, more naturally and less stylized. And, says the expert, they're short enough to "get you home before the eleven o'clock news."

Carmen *by Bizet.* Pure entertainment, chock-full of drama, romance, intrigue, and comedy, with the same movielike quality of Puccini, plus that amazing finale scene. (For prep, rent the film *Carmen Jones,* starring Dorothy Dandridge and Harry Belafonte.)

Hansel and Gretel *by Engelbert Humperdinck.* (The original Engelbert, not the pop singer who took his name.) The fairy tale of two lost siblings, their candy cravings, the witch in the gingerbread house, and the chicken bone that saved them is one of Germany's easiest-to-understand operas.

Porgy and Bess. Gershwin's great American opera has gone from classic to controversial and back to classic. You'll laugh. You'll cry. You might wince, but you'll never want to stop singing "Summertime."

Contemporary American opera. Not long ago, opera god Jake Heggie earned rave reviews for his operatic version of _Dead Man Walking._ Like the film, it's not exactly a laugh a minute, but it is undeniably beautiful. Another contemporary opera you'll recognize and adore: _Little Women,_ adapted from Louisa May Alcott's classic by composer Mark Adamo.

An Opera for Every Mood

Need a good cry? Itching to nourish your inner drama queen? Craving inspiration? Just want to get lost in a story? Here's a fast 'n' fab guide to picking an opera when you're craving . . .

Romance. _La Traviata,_ about a love-shy party girl. _La Bohème,_ whose starving artists live and love in Paris's Latin Quarter.

A Good Cry. Like _Thelma and Louise_ during the French Revolution, _Dialogues des Carmélites_ by Poulenc. (But the above two will work, too.)

Overall happiness. Donizetti's _L'Elisir d'Amore,_ about a Love Potion No. 9 that works high-jinxing magic. _Don Pasquale,_ with no war, no blood, just a goofy uncle who gets caught up in a love story.

Woman power. *Aida*, Verdi's Egyptian-Ethiopian love triangle. Tchaikovsky's *Eugene Onegin*, a reunion of would-be lovers. *The Magic Flute* by Mozart, a mystic, mythic world where the women make, break, and learn the rules.

Bleakness. *Peter Grimes*, twentieth-century composer Benjamin Britten's who-done-it about a fisherman and his apprentices.

A good scare. *Turn of the Screw*, Britten's opera of the ghost story that's *Nanny 911* gone terribly wrong.

Hopelessness in love. *Aida*, and *Lucia di Lammermoor* by Donizetti, a super-bleak tragic romance set in a bleak Scottish castle (makes *Romeo and Juliet* look like an Adam Sandler movie).

A sense of history. *Boris Godunov* by Mussorgsky, in which tzarist ambitions and ghostly power-plays make modern-day government intrigue seem comparatively ho-hum.

Horned helmets. Last of all, for the Xena-like Valkyries (the helmets-with-horns-wearing women), the second opera of Wagner's seventeen-hour *Der Ring des Nibelungen* aka the "Ring Cycle."

What to Wear (Hint: Not a Horned Helmet)

"There are certain opera houses in the world where people really do dress up," says Cori. Germany's summer Salzburg Festival, for example (where one of the theaters is carved into the side of a mountain), or to opening night at the Met, or to the Glyndebourne, a summer festival that takes place on an English noble family's estate, where gowns and tuxes are de rigueur for afternoon picnics alongside the sheep and cows on the lawn.

During regular operations, however, most opera houses are happy to host comfortably attired audiences. "In the U. S., the trend is come as you are," says Cori. Still, it's always smartest to call ahead to the box office—or to the opera company itself—to inquire about a dress code.

Our suggestion: Why not concoct an elegant getup to complement Grandmother's jeweled opera glasses? After all, in this setting, dressing up just seems natural.

Whatever you wear, whatever you see, "be open," says Cori. "That's the best advice I can give."

9

FASHION

I s there really any need to entice you into this chapter? We—you, us, the woman over there poured into her $300 jeans—are fashion addicts, slaves to style, lovers of garments both homemade and haute, trendy and timeless, cheap and not anywhere within our budget.

Some of our tenderest moments take place in quaint boutiques. Some of our greatest victories transpire amid the sales racks of T.J. Maxx. We brake for flea markets.

Still, it's a big, fashionable world out there—and we've only begun to explore.

FASHION INVESTMENT

This section is not for the virgin who entered this world with a Gucci bag on her wrist. Nor is it for the virgin who recently received a full set of Louis Vuitton luggage for her birthday. Have front-row seats at Fashion Week? Employ multiple personal shoppers? Turn loose. The rest of us have something to discuss, and it doesn't concern you. Off with you to "Volunteer Gig," page 230. (Paris, Nikki, go make yourselves useful.)

Virgins of the real world, it's time to unite against a common enemy. Together, we can conquer our predilection for shopping according to our desires to (in no particular order): cash in on sales, follow trends, stock up on "maybes," fill our forearms with paper handle bags, and, more generally, fill our closets to overflowing with spur-of-the-moment purchases whose tags we never remove.

It's high noon for treating our wardrobes in the same manner that we treat our cars, homes, and relationships. Time to score clothes that last through this year, next year—and might even hang around until our granddaughters raid our closets and beg to borrow them.

It's time to invest in fashion.

GO-TO GIRL

Tracy Reese Does This International Style Setter Really Need an Introduction?

Fabulous fashion designer Tracy is truly a virgin's virgin. Born to a mother who made most of her clothes, the creator of Plenty and her own eponymous line devises feminine clothes according to her own tastes, not what looks best on supermodels. Back when our Girl was at Parsons, she decked herself out in vintage coats and self-stitched styles. Today, she's the toast of upper-crust fashion circles. But look in her closet, and you won't find a flood of pricey designer labels—not even a de rigueur collection of stilettos. In fact, only a couple of years ago Tracy splurged on the much-ado-ed-about Manolos. "I'm a little Victorian about how I buy things and wear things," she admits. "It wasn't until I was thirty-something that I started to care about quality and having a few better things . . . I believe you have to have something to look forward to."

Fashion investment is, like Tracy suggests, relative to one's economic status and career needs. The whole point isn't to overspend on one item; it's to make a purchase that will bring a return on your expenditure.

Blow all your savings on a Chanel suit for that chance encounter, and you're playing an expensive lottery. But spring for a multipurpose, eye-catching silk scarf that classes up your basic interview separates—and you're investing in your future.

Still, even silk scarves are out of most of a first timer's price range. "When I first started working, I couldn't afford good things and I would buy vintage. It might have been a little bit smelly, but that was the best thing I could access," says Tracy. "I went low chic for years and years."

Our Suggestions for Stylish Starter-Investments

Vintage. Affordable, timeless, and impeccably constructed, vintage suit jackets, wool coats, pencil skirts, and beaded sweaters boast an endurance that far outlasts the one-night-stand fashion that fills modern strip malls. (We love you, H&M, but there's no way we're considering those mauve $12 culottes a long-term investment.) Plus, when you wear a circa-1950s gathered taffeta skirt, you won't see yourself everywhere you go.

Shoes. If Manolos and Choos are the kicks you covet, save up and go for it. Just be sure to pick up a classic pair in a color you can see yourself living with for a while—and in a style you can actually walk in for a block or two. If those over-referenced designers are out of your price range, go for wearable designs by Via Spiga, Donald Pliner, Kenneth Cole. Choose never-go-out-of-style styles: ballet flats, strappy sandals, to-the-knee leather riding boots.

Lower-end designer lines. How benevolent of Marc Jacobs, Donna Karan, Ralph Lauren, Isaac Mizrahi, Calvin Klein—and, of course, our girl Trace—to design less expensive lines for those of us still in the initial stages of style induction.

Extras. Tracy's first-time investment advice? "A lot of times, it comes down to fantastic accessories." Avoid the trendy piece of the moment—unless you've always been into it. The basics we consider timeless: over-sized—but not too much so—hoop earrings, non-logo but big-name bags (think Birkin or classic Coach), pretty belts, and sparkly barrettes. Pashmina-style wraps have endured far beyond all fashionista predictions. Snatch one of these, too.

Jeans. Nice ones. Which means, no holes, no whiskers, no strategically placed faux fading. No studs, rhinestones, inked messages, or star-shaped back pockets. Butt cleavage is so three years ago. Long legs left to drag and fray at their hems never should have happened. And if you're even for one moment thinking about one of those pairs with the cutout sides and built-in denim mock thong? Go splash your face with some cold water. Non-faded jeans that look like slacks, however, fit in most everywhere.

One cashmere sweater. In a color you'll wear all the time, like black or navy blue or dark brown. BTW: Pay a couple dozen dollars more for this, and you'll be pleasantly surprised at how little it pills and how long it lasts. One-ply cashmere is short-lived. Look for two- or three-ply, by designers such as Autumn Cashmere. We long for pullovers by Lucien Pellat-Finet. But honestly, Lands' End does a great job on theirs.

Winter coat. Those of us dwelling in the top half of the country may intensely dislike winter, but we needn't punish mother nature with ugly outerwear. One decent, camel-color, black, or white wool overcoat that reaches just below the knee will serve you very nicely. For more fun styles, follow Tracy's advice and go vintage.

Tailoring. So this isn't really a piece of clothing. But it's one of the best bits of advice we've ever gotten. Find a good tailor. Someone who will shorten your jeans and reattach your original hems. Someone who will replace the worn-through lining in your coats and skirts. Someone who, when you walk in the door, will smile and grab a pincushion.

Tracy's famous last words on fashion investment: "Do it for yourself more than you do it for anybody else. You'll always feel good when you present yourself well."

LINGERIE

There are first times—and then there are first times. There's the first time you ate instant oatmeal—and the first time you ate caviar. Your first coffee ice cream—and your first double espresso. Your first friend who was a boy—and your first boyfriend.

Of all the firsts you'll forget and the firsts you'll remember, there's nothing— and we mean nothing—in a girl's life like her first lacy black bra. Sure, your first bra was a big deal in itself (and one that you might prefer to forget). But the first sexy bra, well, THAT was a revelation.

This is because the black bra has secret powers: When you wear it, you feel like you have a pretty little secret all to yourself, even if your bottom half is draped in regulation white cotton briefs. The black lace top somehow transforms you from the skin inward, not unlike the way your Wonder Woman Underoos made you feel superheroic.

GO-TO GIRL

Rebecca Apsan   Owner of La Petite Coquette

If it's true that a girl is only as old as she feels, then Rebecca must be an eternal twenty-two—twenty-three at the limit. After a quarter-century reign as New York City's lingerie queen, she remains as charmed as ever by balconette cutout bras, see-through boy shorts, silk stockings with garter belts, and black thongs worn with black boots. Nonetheless, her famous Greenwich Village lingerie store (whose name means "the little flirt" and which holds the distinction of being the first stateside shop to sell the pearl thong) practices fit before fantasy. Staffed by salespeople for whom "seeing naked bodies is their business," the shop has literally transformed the busts and bums of thousands of grateful clients, simply by offering them foundations that fit. Her number two piece of advice for lingerie shoppers, after, of course, finding the proper fit: "Leave your mother at home."

Boob Basics

Does your current bra fit? "The band should be snug—but not so tight you can't fit a finger underneath," says Rebecca. It should not ride up the back (meaning it's too big) or create rolls of flesh above and below the side wings or in back, around your shoulder blades (meaning it's too small). A back clasp that comes undone when it shouldn't calls for a smaller band size. An underwire bra should lie flat against your chest, and should never sit on top of the chest tissue itself, creating an unsightly under boob effect.

Cups half full—or half empty? Wrinkles in the cups indicate you need to go down a cup size or switch bra styles. Cups runnething over call for a larger cup size or a full-coverage bra.

Shoulder issues. If you're constantly playing push up with your straps, be sure to adjust them after each washing, switch to a T-back model, or purchase a nifty strap cincher band, similar to a back belt for your straps, available in most specialty lingerie shops for $15 or less. If straps pinch, leave indentations, or—this can happen to you—create neck pain or headaches, a more supportive bra is in order.

DIY measuring. Place a measuring tape just beneath your bust and around your back to form a perfect circle around your rib cage. Don't have a tape? Use a piece of string and measure that with a yardstick. Cups are more challenging: Women usually think they're smaller than they are. Virgins: Don't be modest!

When—and How—to Shop for a Bra

Go when your boobs are their normal size. In other words, don't go when you're bloated, like during the first day of your period. If you've just gained or lost weight, if you haven't been fitted for a bra in the past few years, if you're having or have had one or more babies, if you haven't bought a new bra in a year—it's time to go shopping.

Find a shop like Rebecca's near you. We prefer the personal touch of little owner-operated boutiques, but any department store staffed by one or more lipsticked lingerie mavens will do. If at all possible, avoid lingerie-only chains. Buying a bra from an independent boutique or Bloomie's costs a little bit more—usually about $10 to $20 more than you'll pay at Victoria's Secret—but the fit and quality pay for themselves.

Next: Leave your modesty at home in the drawer with your Lanz nightgowns. Bring instead an open mind and a sense of humor. Your boobs and butt are about to be sized up in a wholly new fashion.

Don't be surprised if, when you walk in the place, the owner immediately stares at your chest and declares, "Honey, you're wearing the wrong bra," for all Main Street to hear. This is why you're here. To get a new and better bra. This is only the beginning.

First she'll push you into a dressing room. Then she'll measure you and stare some more. She might suggest tossing your current model. Chances are, she'll start by giving you a variety of basic, everyday samples. (No worries: You'll eventually get around to a new, improved version of your black lacy number.) You'll try them on. She'll bust back into the fitting room.

She'll look at your boobs again. She'll readjust the hook. (Tip: Brand-new back-hooking bras should fit at the outermost hook. As they stretch out with wear, you move to tighter hookage. When front-closure bras stretch out, they ought to be replaced.) She'll readjust the straps. Straps, like hooks, should start at the biggest size. They'll stretch with wear, and you adjust the l'il buckle to make them smaller.

Next, she'll pull a move that you didn't know existed. She'll reach into your B cup and move your boob up and over. (You probably could do this yourself if instructed, but go with it. The twins are crying for professional intervention.) This move is the starter cousin to the famous supermodel shake, the one where Naomi Campbell leans over, pulls out her bra straps like suspenders, shakes, and stands up, her boobs miraculously appearing a full cup size larger. Most shop owners prefer the hand-to-boob move. They claim it's more precise than the supermodel shake. Whatever gets the job done.

Your boobs should fill out the cups. They should not spill out from the bottom or overflow at the top, forming the dreaded quadruple boob. There should be a clever l'il cleavage cleft running down between them, but no space between the fabric and your chest at the center. They should appear lifted and perky.

There you'll stand, looking in the mirror at your boobs, looking at a virtual stranger looking at your boobs, and wondering if it's over yet. It's not.

You next want to try on the bra with a shirt. Some shops provide a basic white tee to see how it looks. You might want to bring a T-shirt and a blouse of your own just in case. Add the shirt. Witness your new, uplifted shape and likely improved posture. Take a moment. Ask yourself: Do I like the shape of what's going on? Does the bra fabric show through, and, if so, does that make me happy, sad, or other?

The good thing about becoming intimately acquainted with the salesperson: Once your nipples have been prodded and moved about by a stranger's hands, you'll feel surprisingly uninhibited about expressing your own opinion. Don't like the little bow where the cups meet? Speak up. She'll find you another model.

P.S.: Different manufacturers fit differently. "You may be a B cup in one designer, and a C cup in another," says Rebecca. Ditto for panties: Just 'cause you're a large in Cosabella thongs, doesn't make you a large in a pair by Hanky Panky. Try 'em all on, no matter what (making sure to use those disposable thong thingies the salesladies give you) . . . and when you find a great fit, buy more than one, for goodness sake!

P.P.S. A note on bra color: If you're planning on wearing a white or light-colored top, match your bra to your skin tone. If you're planning on wearing anything dark on top, wear something dark underneath.

Contour

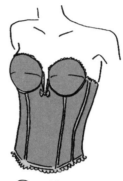

Bustier

Convertible

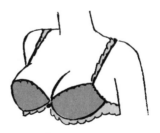

Demi

Bra Terms

Balconette: A demi bra with extra padding.

Bralette: An unlined, underwire-free, soft cup bra, best suited for small chests. (Mom used to call this a "training bra.")

Bustier: A hip-to-bosom corset, often with boning, lace, detachable garters, and a lace-up closure. Very boudoir.

Contour bra: Distinguished by cups that retain their shape even when empty. Always padded. Always with an underwire. Provides protection against any "Boy, it must be cold in here" comments.

Convertible: A work of ingenious adjustability, with straps that can be moved to change the bra into one that's conventional, halter, one-shoulder, off-the-shoulder, crisscrossed, or strapless.

Cookie: A padded, inedible insert for a bra cup. Great solver of the uneven boob dilemma. Definitely a vast improvement upon stuffing your cups with tissues.

Corset: The boned lingerie that played a starring role in an opening scene from *Gone With the Wind.* The supportive, bust-smooshing, waist-cinching top extends from the bust to below the hips, usually with garters at the base.

Demi: A sexy half cup that reveals the top portion of the breasts, great as lingerie for bigger-boobed gals, great every day for perkier persimmons.

Full coverage/Full support: The only way to go if you're D or above. Extra banding under the cups, reinforced side *wings,* and two times the hooks keep those girls in line.

Minimizer: Just what it sounds like. Used to rein in larger busts, usually made of strong microfiber.

Padded push-up: All-time confidence booster, with fiberfill or cookie-filled cups that lift those babies for extra cleavage.

Shelf bra: In lingerie, it's another word for demi bra. In swimsuits and yoga tops, it's the extra layer of cloth and elastic band built into a top.

Strapless: Always seems to be the most challenging variety, with the greatest tendency for slippage to the waist when you're wiggling on the dance floor. If you're buying a strapless bra to go with a specific piece of clothing, bring the clothes to the shop to try them on together. Look for a snug-fitting model with silicone edging on the inside, triple hookage, and a higher fit in the back than in the front.

Wings: Side panels—usually in larger cup sizes—to provide support under arms and in the bust.

Satisfied with your new, improved upper half? It's time to ease on down.

Thankfully less complicated than its upper-more counterparts, the derriere suffers nonetheless when drawers don't fit. Because most trouble occurs quite literally behind our backs, we often don't know it's going on. Panties should not bind or dig into your skin. Rebecca says, "The fit should be close to the body, but not so close that it creates bulges. Nobody wants underwear that's too close for comfort!"

Rebecca's Three Rules of Knickers

No visible panty lines ("VPLs"). "Your panties should smooth you out completely—there should be no lines whatsoever."

No wedgies. "Your panties should be 'budgeproof'—that means they stay put where your cheeks meet your legs."

No front wedgies ("vedgies"). "Your panties should have the right length rise for you—this is the key to a comfortable and smooth fit."

French Cut

Boy Brief

Tap Pants

Panties Terms

Bikini: Waistband goes below navel and on hips, usually with high-cut leg line, varies in bottom coverage.

Boy brief: Tomboy style, in the shape of boy's drawers.

Boy leg brief: Hot pants–style shorts with a low waist and legs extending to thigh.

Brazilian back: A little more coverage than a thong, a lot less than a traditional pantie. Think Giselle on the beach.

Brief: Waistband at or below navel, full coverage in back, sometimes with high-cut leg line.

Control brief: Shaped like a brief, designed to flatten the tummy and add shape to the rear.

French cut: High-cut brief.

G-String: Strings around the sides, string up the back, for minimal coverage.

Gusset: The crotch lining, usually cotton. At least, it ought to be cotton, especially if you're susceptible to bacterial invasions in the nether regions.

Hipster: Lower waistband and lower leg cut than bikini, great for low-rise jeans.

Hot pants: Short shorts that fall just above or at the bottom of the cheeks.

Tap pants: Short shorts with a small flair at the hem.

Thong: The buttock-exposing cure for the panty line blues. Don't knock it 'til you tried one that fits properly.

Thong Boy: The pool attendant straight out of our Wham-style fantasy. Just kidding. Boy brief with a short thong back that allows a cheeky game of peekaboo.

The Good Stuff: Sexy Lingerie

The good thing about the fancy stuff: You don't have to pay a fortune if you're wearing it to bed only. Nonetheless, tops and bottoms should offer the same, snug-but-not-too-snug fit as your everyday undergarments—and they deserve the same gentle care.

Other thing to remember: This stuff is for pure fun. There's no point wearing something for pleasure if it hurts or makes you feel uncomfortable. That said, sexy lingerie often requires an extra dose of confidence to pull off. The good news: If you've put on the lacy combo in order to impress a special someone, the effort itself will surely make you irresistible in your observer's eyes.

Shops like La Petite Coquette offer an almost

CARE

Most lingerie shops sell extra-mild detergent specially made for hand washing undergarments. No matter what, never, ever, ever toss bras or good panties in the washer without a lingerie bag, and never, ever, ever, ever put them in the dryer. A half-hour soak in sudsy, lukewarm water, a gentle rinse in cool water, no wringing, and an afternoon on the drying rack are all they'll need. To store bras: Do not push in or fold cups to make them fit into a drawer. Better to give them a little more space, or to hang them up on hooks or hangers. Very important: Rotate bras, giving them a rest every other day, and replacing them when they become stretched out (usually three to six months for everyday bras, six months for panties).

---

overwhelming array of jaw-dropping, extemporaneous unmentionables. Have an idea of what you'd like to wear beforehand so you don't wind up in a pair of crotchless panties beneath your new minidress, or Rebecca's shop's famous pearl thong on a Sunday bike ride through the park. That said, most lingerie salespeople have developed a knack for picking out pieces that will complement your body shape, skin tone, and hair color.

Our advice for sexy lingerie: Whatever you do, buy the whole ensemble. If you're going for the eyelet baby doll nightie, pick up matching tap pants. If you've lusted after a marabou-trimmed chiffon shortie robe, by all means, get the high-heeled slippers to match! That said, mixing lacy styles or bright colors is fun and fine: Just don't wear your prettiest Cosabella bikinis with your rattiest old Champion Jogbra.

One word of warning: A lot of the prettier pieces just don't work underneath going-out clothes. Consider changing into your getup, Superwoman style, once you're back at home.

Keeping It Up: Athletic Undergarments

Howard Hughes may have been freakishly fanatical when he insisted his lady friends be driven at two mph in order to avoid bumps or jars that might damage their delicate breast tissue. But he was sort of right: Once your beauteous boobs experience enough gravity-induced jostle, there's no natural way of fixing them.

Bulletin: You virgins who jog, aerobicize, kick box, jump rope, moon bounce, or get as excited as Venus Williams after a Wimbledon win, please wear a bra that prevents your boobs from hitting you or your fitness instructor in the nose. We say this not to offend you, we simply would like to assist in the postponement of the inevitable southward vacation your marvelous bosom will one day take.

A health note on the downside: We don't blame you for not wanting to take a post–spin class shower at the gym. But do your crotch a favor: Change out of sweaty drawers as soon as you're able. Infections and other ickies fester in moist places. A quick panties switcheroo can save you a trip to the gyno and a $20 tube of Monistat.

These days, women-friendly sportswear companies—manufacturers, stores, catalogs—rate sports bras for cup sizes and activity ranges. Some of our favorite places to find the latest and greatest: Athleta (www.athleta.com), Title 9 Sports (www.title9sports.com), and Lululemon Athletica (www.lululemon.com).

BLACK TIE

You're going to a wedding, not joining
the witness protection program.
—Cynthia Rowley and Ilene Rosenzweig

There is nothing in this world as silly as The Prom. When viewed through the twenty-twenty lenses of hindsight, this awkward adolescent tradition—on perpetual rerun at the finale of umpteen teen flicks—is actually le dorkiest of formal fetes. The prom—aka Prom—is nothing more and nothing less than the confluence of poor dress-up, ridiculous up-dos, carnation corsages, raging hormones, Breathalyzers, photos you'll regret, and So Much Hype, So Many Tears leading up to it, you'd think it was your own Presidential inauguration.

What? You say your prom was actually the apex of your life so far?

Come back to us in a few years. Better yet: Peek your head into your local high school gymnasium/conference center ballroom/inexpensive cruising company on prom night. Train your eye to the dance floor. Behold how silly you recently looked.

But just because your puffy-shouldered self and your tails-wearing date looked slightly to extremely ridiculous way back in the eleventh grade doesn't mean you're destined for a life of flubbed formal wear. When that heavy card stock arrives in the mail, all engraved with pale and pristine letters, requesting the presence of your company at this or that society wedding or charity ball or Buckingham Palace affair, don't toss it in the recycling. Use it as an opportunity to redeem la petite fiasco that was le prom.

Cracking the Dress Code

How to determine the scale of dressing up? Chances are, if the invite comes on paper that's thicker than a business card and as colorful as an early Fellini film (black and white) and includes an extemporaneous sheet of sheer tissue, then you're in for a swanky soirée, sister.

Other more obvious clues: The invite includes the words "white tie," "black tie," "ultra-formal," or "formal." Or if it's coming hand delivered by a soldier of the Queen. Or if it involves the possibility of your accepting a shiny gold, globe-shaped award in front of a television audience of millions.

Rules of dress:

- White tie or ultra-formal: floor-length gowns or ball skirts
- Black tie or formal: the above (but also fancy enough cocktail-length frocks in summer months)

Cocktail dresses, BTW, used to mean dresses that go from knee to ankle. Today's cocktail dressing can go a bit higher, especially if you're attending an event in a fashion-forward metropolis like New York City or L.A. Cocktail dresses are traditionally dressier than the little black linen dress—although glitzed up with the right jewels, bag, and shoes, certain LBDs do in a pinch.

Oh well, we might as well include these rules of dress too:

- Black tie optional: cocktail dress
- Creative black tie: cocktail dress
- Semiformal: cocktail dress
- Cocktail: you guessed it
- Dressy casual: A step up from business clothes (Flowy pants with a sequined halter. Those day-to-night work ensembles magazines are always advocating. For example: Take a simple black sheath, add chandelier earrings and gold heels, and go!)

GO-TO GIRL

Holly Dunlap

Dashing Designer of Various Adornments
We'd Love to Wear Formally,
Informally, and Generally All the Time

Manhattan fashion designer Holly of "Hollywould" shoes, bags, and dresses has been going to formal affairs as long as she can remember. "I started really young, going to black tie balls with my parents as a child." Shirley Temples, live bands, and, on one occasion, "a one-shouldered dress which was way too grown-up for an eight-year-old and frankly, very tacky" (but that she thought made her look like Diana Ross) fueled Holly's love of live dress up. These days, the designer attends "no less than twenty formal parties each year." How does she keep from repeating dresses? Easy: She designs them herself.

Make no mistake: This section isn't going to tell you which fork goes with what (see "Four-Star Restaurant," page 94) or how to score an invite to the Met's annual Costume Institute Benefit (see "Charitable Donation," page 364). It's going to tell you how to gussy up and how to behave gussied up.

Ahead of the Curve

The big day is one month, more or less, away. Start getting ready now. Open your closet. Reach your hands to the back, where you've stowed the fancy gowns you've worn in weddings, inherited from Grandma, bought on sale, and splurged for in the likely event that Prince Harry phones to invite you to a dress-up dinner with the Parker-Bowles-Windsors.

Try on each getup you'd consider getting into for the big night. Too small? Reject pile. Too big? To the tailor, if it's not too out of date. Embellishing doodads such as sequins, beads, and fringe have a sad way of abandoning a frock, and dresses that haven't been properly laundered can develop odd stains in strange places. Test your potentially head-turning garment in ample light, with multiple mirrors, and, if possible, under the watch of a superstylish pal who is honest enough to tell you that there is no way you can get away with a merlot-mottled satin at a swanky soirée.

When to Shop

The absolute last thing you want to happen is to be stuck the day or week of the event having to rush out to find something—anything—to wear. Some formalwear boutiques require shopping appointments. Many offer in-house alterations—as long as you have at least two weeks before the affair. Snazzy shoes are famous for requiring a day or two of professional steam-stretching (this is one of Holly's favorite tricks). Fashionably late, after all, applies to your arrival at the fete itself—not to your last-minute shopping spree.

What to Spend

Set aside at least $100 for a dress (which will usually require you buy it on sale). Good places to find a fancy bargain: sample sales (see page 321), vintage shops, consignment stores (especially ones in neighborhoods studded with the biggest, oldest houses and the pristine lawns), department store sale racks, bridal boutiques. We know one formal-dressing girl who visits Loehmann's back room every month or so to see what she can find for less than the cost of a haircut. We are also absolutely smitten with J. Crew's black tie line—almost nothing is over $200.

Exceeding one's means is super easy when it comes to fancy dressing. (Anyone looked at a *Vogue* photo caption lately?) Set a limit for yourself. We think you can find a very nice frock in the $300 range. Allow yourself a little more if you're the star of this event, a little less if you're relinquishing the spotlight for the evening.

As for the shoes, bag, and hair thingamabobs, shoot for under $200 and aim for items you'll be able to wear again, dressed down with jeans and a white blouse on more casual occasions.

Spend over your budget, and expect prom-style disappointment.

How to Shop

Smart stores often stock their dressing rooms with shoes of various heel heights so you can see what you'll look like on the big occasion (usually two inches or so taller). But not all stores are smart—and not all shoppers like to try on used shoes. So, BYO stilettos. Walking around in your own shoes will also give you a sense of how a hem might catch—or how you're going to need a more comfortable pair of strappy sandals.

What to Buy

Most advice givers love to say how you can never go wrong by wearing black. Most advice givers want you to play it safe. Fine. Black looks good on almost everybody, but wear it, and expect to look like at least 75 percent of your fellow female guests—and 99 percent of the guys.

Other colors and patterns and what they say to us: Red is sophisticated and slightly vampy. Pink is sweet and fun. Yellow is happy but can hint at jaundice on fair-skinned virgins. Deep green is understated, classy. Purple is quirky and bold. Deep blue is a runner-up to black, but morphs into dangerous prom territory upon approaching the royal blue family. Etiquette books say no white to a wedding. We say, no white to any occasion that involves colored drinks and a dance floor.

We adore formal frocks of playful prints. Plaids during the holidays, cabana stripes in summer, petite to grand florals all year round really make a dress stand out.

Swingy spangles are great for the dance floor. Tightly sewn beads require a gentle touch. Sequins and crystals work in moderation, but border on beauty pageant overload when applied in excess. Lace is both old-fashioned and sexy. Ruffles. Well, be careful with ruffles.

The Styles

A-line: A silhouette that's narrower at the top than at the bottom (like the letter A). A classic style, usually understated and comfortable.

Backless: Where there normally is a back, there isn't. Often ties at the neck, often dips just above the posterior.

Ball gown: Usually a corset style on top, with a full, gathered skirt that flows to the floor. Like Cinderella's. Flattering to most figures.

Ball skirt: The bottom half of a ball gown, gathered, full, and twirl-inducing, looks great with a pretty cashmere cardigan, chubby, or shawl.

Handkerchief hem: A dress whose bottom edge forms points instead of a straight line. Very showgirl.

Mermaid: Hugs everywhere except below the knee, where it flounces like an upside down flower. Best for supermodels and Jessica Rabbits.

Sheath: A contoured but waistless dress that usually hits at or above the calf.

The Details

Basque: Dips in the center at the waist to make a V or a U.

Bustle: At the back of the waist, this extra gathering of fabric lends a whole lot of help to those of us who could use a little enhancement in the derri-area.

BIGGEST FORMAL OCCASION PET PEEVES

Ours: Removing shoes during the event. Flower girls—small flower girls—may do this. Grown-ups (anyone over thirteen) may remove shoes only for a post-party stroll on the beach, or toe dip into a pond. Otherwise, keep your shoes on. Keep 'em on!

Holly's Hose. "Just because it's cold doesn't mean you need hose. If you're wearing knee-length, chances are your dress will look better with color hose, fishnets, or bare legs, but nude hose should be avoided at all costs. Also no hose with sandals—ever," she says.

Drop: Waistline below the waist, at the hips. Think Annie Hall.

Empire: Pronounced "um-peer." A waistline that's above the waistline and can go as high as just beneath the boobies. Can look très chic in a Jane Austen way, but can also look very maternity.

The Shoes, the Bag, the Outerwear, and the Chicken Dance

Of course, the dress is just the start. As soon as you're frocked, get thee to the shoe department—bringing along the dress if possible, if not to try on, then for color coordination's sake.

SMALLER FORMAL OCCASION PET PEEVE

Breaking out the latest dance as displayed on *TRL* while you're all decked out like Princess Anne. There is something innately wrong about trying to bust a move while you're dressed like a diva. If you're at a formal wedding and the happy couple want the DJ to play "YMCA," by all means, get up there and form your best body letters. But booty shakin' just shouldn't happen when the word "ball gown" is involved. Waltz, slow dance, have a little fun, but don't attempt to krump. Remember the Prom!

A word to stiletto initiates: Don't schedule your first stroll down the red carpet to coincide with your first steps in three-inch cigarette-heeled Choos. A woman can be well-heeled, but if she's wobbly, she's not so wonderful. "It is crucial to always wear shoes that are comfortable to black tie events, so you can dance the night away and not be in too much pain. If I'm planning to wear new shoes, I have them stretched by the shoe repairman before going," says Holly.

Bags often match the shoes, but they don't have to. Stash your over-the-shoulder sisters at home. Opt instead for a dainty clutch. Use it to stow the essentials: cell, compact, comb, lipstick, mints, and feminine products.

The one thing most often overlooked when dressing for a formal occasion—not the blowout or the nails, the pearls or the strapless bra—is the coat. As unfashionable as it is to arrive shivering and coatless at a swank soirée, it's not much better if you cover your couture with a puffy parka. Think ahead and score yourself—or borrow—a pretty pashmina or cashmere wrap for this night. It might look so good you'll want to wear it inside the party, but don't. Coat checks are for safely stowing your preferred method of keeping warm until the party's through. Leave chair backs and forearms for their original purposes.

MOVIES WITH FORMAL PARTY SCENES TO GET YOU IN THE MOOD

The Thin Man (and all the fabulous sequels)
The Philadelphia Story
Sabrina
To Catch a Thief
The King and I
High Society
My Fair Lady
Dangerous Liaisons
Strictly Ballroom
Sense and Sensibility
Shall We Dance (the Japanese version)
Shakespeare in Love

SAMPLE SALE

Show me a Manhattan girl who'd rather watch Don Giovanni *than shop Chanel at Target prices, and I'll renew my membership at Equinox Gym on 63rd Street and actually start going on a semi-regular basis.*
—JULIE BERGDORF, *Bergdorf Blondes*

Friends don't let friends sale goggle.
—DANY LEVY, ON THE IMPORTANCE OF BRINGING
A CLEAR-HEADED PAL TO A SAMPLE SALE.

Imagine this: You, dressed comfortably in an outfit that includes modest but pretty undergarments. A wad of cash tucked safely into your Le Mystère push-up bra. A rack and more racks, a cardboard box and more cardboard boxes, a table and more tables all full of your absolute favorite designer clothing, so deeply discounted that you stand there, agog, unable to move at the enormity of this ideal shopping reality.

But you're not still for long. Your reverie receives a rude disruption in the form of a sharp elbow and a shove, administered by a beady-eyed, crazy-haired woman who emits a shrill, "Are you going to keep that cami?"

Your senses return. "Yes!" you proclaim, clutching the top to your chest, "I am!"

And you have at it. Scanning, grabbing, running to a communal dressing room—or simply stripping down to your skivvies right there in the middle of the sales floor—you eyeball other shoppers' unattended piles of cashmere, leather, and silk and ask yourself, Would it be wrong to shanghai that lady's stash?

Welcome to the sample sale, shopping's most competitive sport, the equivalent of a forgotten game show's glass chamber of blowing money, retail's version of a heaven and hell party. The bargains, of course, are the heaven. The rest, however, can be hell.

First, a bit of sample sale history. As far as we can tell, this mass retail hysteria originated—where else?—in New York City. Began as a way for Manhattan designer showrooms to get rid of the clothing, shoes, and accessories that had been shown to stylists, photographed in magazines, hung in displays, taken on sales calls. The stuff had been used, but not purchased.

Those original sample sales were unannounced and private, open only to friends and family members of the people who worked in showrooms.

That is, until word got out.

Suddenly everyone—from battalions of high-end hunters to gaggles of bona fide bargain adventuresses—wanted to be "on the list." They begged, they pleaded, they schmoozed, and they shouted.

Today, sample sales are the shopping Olympics. Except these retail events occur more often than the Olympics. And some are even harder to get into than the Olympics.

There are sample sales and then there are sample sales.

GO-TO GIRL

Najwa Moses   Style-aholic and Sample Sale Lone Ranger

The first time we heard Najwa on our car radio, we had to check the station reading. What was a chick so chill, so stylish, so absolutely with-it doing reading smart and sassy fashion commentary . . . on public radio? We didn't get it. But we liked it. The marvelous Ms. Moses lends her style savvy to both NPR's *Day to Day* and "The Closet," a multifaceted, multifabulous, NYC-based happening that's a sale of wares of up-and-coming designers, a showcase of international female DJs, and, of course, a rockin' cocktail party. Naj has been to her share of sample sales and says her favorite is the one at Triple 5 Soul, because, well, if the clothes fit . . . Her favorite ever sample sale score? "Electric silver spandex biking pants that were once worn by Aaliyah."

The Sales We Dream Of

The Chanel sale, the pre-sales at Sigerson Morrison and Manolo Blahnik are about as easy for an outsider to enter as the insider-est insides of the Pentagon. Truly, only the very best customers—plus a few select members of the couture press—are welcome at these invitation-only events. That said, there are always tales of the interloper who waltzed into Aeffe like she belonged and made out like a couture bandit. We say, whatever it takes. Another little hint: The later in the day it gets, the slacker the admission policy becomes. Why not come armed with a smile, a bag of doughnuts, a tray of coffees—or a flask of cosmos—for the folks at the door? By the end of the day, they just might look in the opposite direction when you sneak in.

The Sales That Charge a Cover

Late last millennium, a few sample salesters came up with the brilliant idea that shoppers will actually pay an admission fee in order to score a chance to get big discounts. Ah, the all-American phenomenon of spaving (spending to save). Once you're over the shock of this fact, you'll be shocked again to learn that some of these pay-to-play events are actually worth the dough.

Our favorite: Billion Dollar Babes: Thought up by two adorable Aussies, this L.A.-born phenom is the Super Bowl of sample sales. It costs $100–$200 to get an opening-day invite. But it's worth the entry fee to be welcomed into a world—actually, the Hollywood Palladium—of Plein Sud and Catherine Malandrino. In recent years, the BDBs have spread their discount love to the rest of the country, starting jumbo sales in NYC, San Fran, and Chicago (www.billiondollarbabes.com).

All the Rest

These are the ones we can deal with. Open to the public—although many of them also host invitation-only presales a day or a few hours before the public opening—these are, thankfully, the most common, the most fun, the most adventure-promising of the sample sale bunch. Even better: They seem to be multiplying across the country, cropping up wherever a shopper loves a bargain (which, of course, is everywhere).

The sample sale has also extended its scope far beyond what was once considered sample sizes (yesterday's size 6, today's sizes 0–2). Today's double Ss often include last season's unsalables, this season's overstock, irregular or damaged or fixer-upper pieces, and—our favorite—designer originals that never made it into the official line. Sample sales aren't the same as warehouse sales, but these days the two seem to overlap more often than not.

Though sample sales are definitely year-round occurrences, more of them happen in fall. Many offer a small preview of next season's wares and, like we said, last season's glorious leftovers. But most sell what's wearing right now, which is good news for those of us who live for the immediate gratification.

Remember, too: A sample sale is like an open-air farmers' market in a fabulously exotic country: You don't know what you'll find, so don't go looking for something specific. If you find yourself daydreaming about all the great places you could wear that brilliant pink spring suit by Nanette Lepore, then save your dollars and buy the darn thing at full price. If you wait for it to appear in a sample sale, well, chances are it (1) won't be there, (2) won't be available in your size, (3) will be there, but will be in poor condition, or (4) will be snatched up by the shopper who queued three seconds before you.

One last note before you're recruited into sample sale boot camp: Some sales combine designers, like Billion Dollar Babes and Barneys. Others thoroughly follow a theme, like all accessories or everything's coming up bridal. If you're shopping for a white wedding, Google bridal sample sales, and eat your Bridezilla heart out!

So. You think you're all set to shop? Think again. The fun's just begun.

Getting Ready

The city of New York alone hosts hundreds of sample sales each year. Even though you'd like to go to all of them, you just can't. Reserve your energy for your favorite labels. (For example: if you can't squeeze into the D&G duds at Saks, you won't fit into them at the sale either, so skip it.)

Finding the ones you want can be as easy as hopping online to sites like www.dailycandy.com or *New York* magazine's Web site www.newyork metro.com. Naj likes to stop by showrooms and stores to sign their mailing lists. Phoning these places works, too. Of course, it doesn't hurt to be a loyal Flight 001, Cassina USA, or Vivienne Westwood customer to begin with. Nor does it hurt to pay heed to the sample sale rumor mill: In every flock of events involving serious discounts, there are sales known to be major time wasters.

However you approach the reconnaissance portion of your mission, be sure to find out if a sale requires an invite—and ask what it takes to get in the presale, if there is one. Hint: Some places say you need an invite but don't bother with a guest list the day of the sale. Better hint: Ask around for tips. Find a trustworthy sale pal who'll share her plus one, and you're set for your sample sale life.

Getting Set

Two hours early is a good ETA for a moderately popular sale. If you simply must get in the door with the first wave, find out how early the line starts forming. If you're going just to check out the scene, an hour might be enough—as long as it's not a lunch hour. Lunch hours are notoriously the busiest times at sample sales. Everybody thinks she'll just pop by on her lunch hour. Nobody ends up both getting in the door and getting back to the office before 3:30.

Clean underpants and a presentable bra. Modest? Wear a bodysuit and leggings under your outfit. Most sample sale dressing rooms are communal. Many sample sales don't have dressing rooms at all.

Correct payment. Though credit cards fly at most sales these days, as Naj says, "cash is king" at a few others, especially sales featuring smaller labels or indie designers. Find out first, and bring the right stuff.

A big bag. Take a cue from Ikea. Bring along your biggest, lightest weight tote—empty, please—so you can shop hands free.

A friend. A good one. Not one whom you suspect of what Najwa calls "competitive dressing," which means she'll tell you that Palm Beach-y Lilly shift doesn't complement your hair color—and will then take it for herself. Instead, bring a candid someone whose taste you trust, whose endurance is that of a three-time marathon winner, and who will guard your pile of maybes with the vigilance of a mama bear guarding her cubs—while you dash out in search of a smaller-size cocktail skirt. Of course, you'd do the same for her. You'd better. Oh. And don't bring a shopping-bored boy.

Breakfast. Yes, scoring a Badgley Mischka gown does require you get up at the crack of dawn to get in the sale's line by 6:30. But since you'll be waiting in line for three hours for the door to open, you must feed before you frenzy. No time? Line up, smile gently to the person in line behind you, and ask if she'd save your spot if you run and get the both of you lattes and scones. Or, bring a friend who'll save the space for you.

Go

"Everyone knows in the sample sale, it's everybody for herself," says Najwa. True that. Understand that there will be eagle-eyed shoppers there just waiting for you to turn away from your carefully culled Max-Mara separates in order to filch a few pieces from your pile. There will be pushing and shoving. There will be shoppers who seem to have woken up on the wrong side of the bed every day for the past decade. There will be tears. There might be blood.

Knowing all this, you have a choice: Join the mad masses—or rise above.

Some believe that it's shop or be chopped, that the sample sale is the extreme fighting of below-retail events. You'll likely survive if you succumb to the mania, but be sure to keep a sense of humor about it—lest those crazies get the best of your own, sane brain. Then again, if you're getting hitched in a month or two and another woman is trying on what is obviously Your Wedding Dress, by all means, hit her with the "anti-sale." "It all depends on your moral values," says Naj. "I know for me personally I'll try to do an anti-sale for someone in a heartbeat. Don't swipe [something you want] from a pile, but definitely ask, "Do you want that?" If they're not sure, push 'em to the other side. This is the lowest you ought to go."

Others believe in sample-sale karma. Steal from a pile, and get pickpocketed on the way home. Convince a fellow shopper she looks terrible in the denim of your dreams, and interview with that shopper when you apply for a new job. Keep it in perspective: "It's not war. It's not raising children. It's just clothes," says Naj.

Score

There's a delicate balance to strike just before you make your way to the register. Are you buying those Gucci sandals just because they're dirt cheap? Do they fit? Are they in good condition—or repairable? Broken zippers, unhinged seams, missing buttons, sagging hems are easily remedied with a trip to your favorite dry-cleaning seamstress. Stains, holes, tears in fabric, fraying threads, and missing beading are harder to fix.

If the fit's wrong, skip it. Sure, those Sigerson Morrison pumps are a steal, but if they're a size 7 and you're an 8½ on a good day, they're best left on the rack and out of your closet.

You just can't resist snatching up a shockingly reduced Tocca shift— even though you know you'll never, ever wear it, for whatever reason. Buy it for a friend who'd love it. Sample sales—especially ones put on by department, furnishings, jewelry, or accessory stores—are great places to gift shop, understanding, of course, there are no returns.

In case you missed it in that last paragraph. There are No Returns. None. You walk out the door with it, it's yours for life. Then again, there's always eBay.

PRECIOUS JEWELS

Beauty is a great pleasure, and it's the best investment.
—SIMON TEAKLE, CHRISTIE'S NEW YORK

We might as well be straight up at this point. When we're talking about precious, dripping, blazing adornments for our necks, earlobes, wrists, fingers, and—why not?—noses, we're talking about diamonds. Rocks. Fire. Ice. Bling. A Girl's Best Friend.

Don't roll your eyes. We know what you're thinking. There was once a time when we, too, wouldn't dream of going for anything so, well, predictable. An engagement ring? Mmmm, we preferred princess-cut cornflower blue sapphire. Elegant post earrings? Brilliant pink rubies sure are nice. A big, hulking stone to shock the class of '01 at your next reunion? Why waste money? They'll so fall for a CZ (cubic zirconia).

Then, somewhere between H&M and Balenciaga, something changed. We got it. Sure, there would always be desert sand soirées for draping ourselves in turquoise and silver, Caribbean cocktail hours for decking out in coral and mother-of-pearl, country club benefits for being demure in strands of pearls and 14-karat add-a-beads.

But when we're sitting in the back of a taxi, dashing through a mall, gazing across paperwork and out the window at the neighbor's landscapers, sneaking seconds of the dulce de leche, Googling exes, or waving to adoring fans from the red carpet—these are the times when diamonds are truly a virgin's best friend.

By the way: We were not paid off by international diamond conglomerate De Beers to bring you this special message. (Not that we'd turn down a three- to four-carat thank-you gift, either.) What got us—other than the stone's go-everywhere invincibility—was the science of it. And the symbolism. Not to forget that diamonds—unlike designer jeans, high-tech gizmos, even other gemstones—retain their value long after everything else has disappeared from the fashion scape.

Diamonds are the true gold standard. Sparkler-believers of the world over put more trust in rocks than in paper currency. They're the final frontier. Maybe because they're so durable. Maybe because we humans are inexplicably attracted to all things shiny and happy and perfect, like fireworks and sparklers.

You're still not convinced? Don't fret. This section will also help you out with precious metals. But diamonds are our lucky stars.

GO-TO GIRL

Elaine Tse   Jewelry Designer and Diamond Self-helper

Philly bauble-making babe Elaine spends her days twisting black freshwater pearls and gold wire into floral-looking spangles for a clientele of mostly "women who are buying for themselves." Taking a cue from her own customers—and ignoring her friends' warnings that "your husband is the one who's supposed to be buying you diamonds"—this single sister used her thirtieth birthday to give herself five carats' worth of ice. "I wanted to start my third decade buying things I would keep in my life for a long time." Neither too big nor too flashy, Elaine's b-day bracelet is something she wears both to black ties and on casual shopping trips. "The concept is well loved and worn often . . . The person you're going to be with for the rest of your life is yourself, so you might as well treat that person really well." Know what else she says? "I don't think the woman has to wait for the man for anything—especially diamonds."

From Bling to Eternity

Buying diamonds is a little like buying art. You start by paying attention to what you like. Leaf through magazines, peek at other women's hands, bump your nose on the thick glass windows at Tiffany's, cross the threshold of your local jeweler: In no time, you'll know exactly what kind of diamond girl you are.

But play before you pay. Doesn't cost a thing to try on. And, as Holly Golightly discovered half a century ago, the nicer the jewelry store, the nicer the sales staff working in it. Remember: The clerk wearing the scintillating chandelier earrings may look like a princess, but she's really just modeling the bling 'til the shop closes. Smile nice at her and she might even let you give those babies a test drive around the store.

This, your "just looking, thanks" phase, is the perfect time to start understanding the basics of those much-discussed four Cs.

The Four Cs

Cut. This one's actually pretty simple. It means the depth, width, and uniformity of the facets. In other words, the cut means what the little notch-like surfaces covering the rock look like. Cut applies to all gemstones, not just diamonds.

Modern diamonds tend to fall into three cuts. (And one of them is so simple.)

1. Brilliant. This means the facets are shaped like kites or triangles. The most popular brilliant diamond is the round. (We're assuming you know what round looks like.) Modern round brilliant diamonds must have fifty-eight facets. Vintage round brilliants vary in their number of facets.

   Also popular in the brilliant style: princess. Princess means square at the face. We think this is funny.

2. Step. Think of step farming. Or, for that matter, steps. Step facets are sloping, with four sides cut below the face of the stone, and running parallel to the edge of the fattest part of the stone (called the girdle). Trust us, this is a whole lot more complicated than it reads. The step cut is basically like four or more staircases, all leading to the same, flat floor.

3. Mixed. A combination of brilliant and step faceting. Very popular for colored gemstones, too.

There are other cuts. But basically, they're just a variation of the first two. For example, an emerald cut is a classic, rectangular step cut stone with the corners cut off. Old Mine Cut has a higher crown than the brilliant cut. An Asscher—hello, Reese's fourth finger on her left hand—is emerald cut but square, with wide step facets and deep clipped corners, so it looks like an octagon.

The whole idea behind the cut is that it's the first thing that allows light to reflect off your rock, making others blink and you smile. If a cut is too shallow, the light filters downward, into a well of no return. If it's too deep, it escapes out the sides, like the contents of an overstuffed sandwich. If the cut's just right—which means the proportions are perfectly placed; the facets perfectly symmetrical, the surfaces perfectly aligned—light bounces in and bounces right back out at ya. This is called an "ideal cut." An ideal cut produces scintillation. Scintillation is what you want.

Clarity. Simply put, the fewer the internal and external flaws, the better the clarity or clearness. All of you who spend way too much time looking for teensy defects in your own face, you've got nothing on the gemologists who inspect diamonds. They have a whole vocabulary for the faults so small they have to be viewed by a magnifying glass called a loupe. And their grading system makes tenth-grade geometry seem cinchy.

There are two basic kinds of flaws:

1. Inclusions: Tiny spots, cracks, colored or uncolored crystals inside the diamond
2. Blemishes: Exterior flaws, usually caused by cutting and polishing

There are many kinds of clarity grades:

- FI: Flawless inside and out (extremely rare)
- IF: Internally flawless (therefore slightly imperfect on the outside)
- VVS1 and VVS2: Very, very slightly included; teeny-weeny flaws on the inside, very barely visible to an experienced grader
- VS1 and VS2: Very slightly included; teeny flaws on the inside, barely visible to an experienced grader
- SI1 and SI2: Slightly included; flaws on the inside that are visible to an experienced diamond grader
- I1 and I2 and I3: Obvious inclusions, visible to the naked eye, even yours

The mid range for clarity is actually in the latter half. Some flaws in clarity are remedied by positioning a prong or setting in one area. Others can be improved with cosmetic procedures. (The stars spotlit on the *Star*'s "Knifestyles" page aren't the only ones who get work done.) Laser treatments can help remedy some inclusions, though lasers often leave a trace.

Fracture filling is a semipermanent solution that involves filling cracks with a colorless substance.

Color. Enough about the rare pink and yellow diamonds already. The true measure of a diamond's color is its absence of color. (Fine. We'll get to the pastel-colored ones in a minute.)

Color, like clarity, is subject to a complex grading system. An alphabet, really. An alphabet that starts with D and ends with Z. D through F are the most colorless—and therefore most coveted—of the white diamonds. G through J are very good, too. S through Z are visibly tinted, usually yellow to brownish.

Part of the color comes from the shine a diamond makes—called fluorescence. Diamonds can fluoresce yellow to blue, depending on the kind of light source they're subjected to. This is why it's important to view diamonds in several types of lighting—at least fluorescent, incandescent, and natural—before you buy. The highest quality of diamond fluoresces white. White light coming from a diamond is called "brilliance."

Note: Both clarity and color ratings are included in Gemological Institute of America (GIA) certified diamonds. GIA-certified diamonds are like purebred poodles: They come with papers. And, like show dogs, they're more expensive than unpedigreed rocks. Buy a diamond with papers, and you're sure of what you're getting. Buy one without, and you might save money, but you don't get a guarantee. If you want to make a major, non-papered purchase, consider bringing along a third-party appraiser—someone with GIA credentials—to check out the stone before you make the commitment.

Carat. Of course, the big one, the one diamond owners are supposed to brag about. Will you be surprised when we tell you size doesn't matter? No, of course you won't. Because size sure does matter. But it's not everything. Generally, the bigger the rock, the rarer the rock, the more expensive the rock. But that's only generally.

One carat equals two hundred milligrams, for what that's worth. One carat weighs about as much as a carob bean. Two carats weigh two carob beans . . .

One hundredth of a carat is called a point. Points are used to describe smaller diamonds. A fifty pointer is half a carat.

The abbreviation for carat: ct. The abbreviation for the weight of all the diamonds in a tennis bracelet, or around the shank of a ring, is ct tw, which means carat total weight.

Now don't you feel smart? Wanna feel even smarter? A 1.9 carat rock costs a whole lot less than a 2.0 carat rock, simply because somebody decided that's how it oughta be. Buy a pair of stud earrings that weigh a total of 1.9 carats, and we won't tattle if you call them a "one-carat pair."

More price tips: If you want to compare similar pieces, calculate their prices per carat. You do this by dividing the cost by the carat weight. The smallest number is the best buy, carat-wise.

The Purchase

"For me," says Elaine, "the hunt is part of the fun." Then again, Elaine walks around Philly with a jeweler's loupe in her bag.

After you get chummy with the darling diamond hawkers at Saks, after the navy-jacketed representatives at Tiffany's have taken to shouting out your name, "Norm" style, when you enter their hallowed store, that's when the real work begins. Figuring out how much you want to spend is no little matter, especially if you ought to be reading the "Credit Card Debt" section of the money chapter, page 351.

But, trusting you've got your savings in place, your rent paid, and your cat fed, you ought to spend with your head—but not too much. "If you're buying a big gift for yourself, it should hurt a little bit," says Elaine. "They say three months' salary for an engagement ring." Three months may be a bit excessive, but a paycheck or two—plus birthday money—seems pretty smart.

Where to buy? As much as we love, love, love the l'il blue box, those ladies at Saks, and anyone at all involved with words that drip like hot fudge: Cartier, Van Cleef, Harry Winston, we must confess that a virgin pays a whole lot more when she pays retail. Even more when your gem's setting is lovingly stamped with a squeal-worthy name.

The upside of the big, glittery store: uniformity of pieces. Tiffany's, for example, grades and sizes all of its stones, so that every sparkly piece is uniform. Saks offers a thirty-day return policy for jewelry. Some stores permit customers to "trade up," which means buy it, wear it, and, when you're feeling particularly flush, exchange it for a pricier model that's at least twice the value of your first purchase.

The upside of your neighborhood jeweler, the one who's been at the same address for forty-some years: You're not paying for the label. Their diamonds glitter just as brightly as the ones from the wouldn't-go-in-there-without-dressing-up-first stores. Smaller boutiques offer the same friendliness of the big stores, too. They can also keep an eye out for loose diamonds—which, incidentally, cost less to buy separately and then to have set. They might even cut you a break on the price if you become a regular shopper and tell them you need to treat yourself to a l'il some-thing-something because you and the love of your life just called it quits.

Wherever you go, be sure your jeweler has GIA certification, and is a member of the Jeweler's Association. Doesn't hurt to ask your most sparkly and savvy shopping pals where they pick up their weekly bling, either.

When you're there, ask to view your prospective gem through a loupe, ask if it has papers (which give official grading of the four Cs), ask any-thing at all that you want to ask. This is your big deal for yourself. No jeweler worth his weight in carats will hit you with the hard sell or will poo-poo you when you double check the rock under a halogen.

The Investment

Yes, diamonds will retain their value after you purchase them. Their set-tings—which get banged up, erode, and likely go out of fashion—may not. Count on your cherished jewels to be worth the stone's value alone.

Jewelry does not produce income like stocks, bonds, or real estate. Al-though diamonds—like gold—fluctuate in market value, they generally don't lose their worth. If you happen to have an art deco piece by Cartier, then, yes, it will bring far more than Great-Great Auntie Eloise paid for it eighty years ago. But don't rely on Dad's mall-bought pinky ring for a nest egg.

While diamonds remain a consistent, reliable investment, natural, un-treated gems—especially ones whose world supply is running low—are considered today's best financial investment. Want to gamble on a crowned jewel? Blow your surplus savings on a Burmese ruby or a Kash-mir sapphire. Just make sure the stone is verifiably all natural, untreated by any cosmetic type colorations or operations.

Still, diamonds hold the most consistent, long-term value. And, as you now know, value is not based on carat alone. (If you're investing, think clarity and ideal cut over carat: Medium-size diamonds tend to be an eas-ier sell than hulking stones.)

Colored Diamonds

Perhaps the most complicated and controversial of the diamond sector, colored diamonds seem to increase in visibility in proportion to the increase of gossip mags in supermarket checkout aisles.

What you need to know: Diamonds also come in pink, yellow, green, blue, and red. Not often.

The most common color on the fancy diamond spectrum is yellow. The rarest are blues, then pinks, then reds. Two things cause white ice to turn pale pastel. In the natural world, it's nature: trace elements like nitrogen (turns diamonds yellow) and radiation (turns 'em green). In the synthetic world, it's a treatment that combines irradiation and high heat.

How to tell an earth-made from a person-made color? Papers. Another clue: If you can afford it, it's probably been treated. Colored diamonds are nice, but like we mentioned before, we wouldn't turn down a simple, one-carat pair of plain old clear-diamond stud earrings.

Speaking of Carat: Gold

Gold's quality is measured in k-karats, not c-carats. This time, karat measures the percentage of pure gold in a piece. Its abbreviation: kt.

- 24-karat = 100 percent gold
- 18-karat = 75 percent gold (or 18 out of 24 possible karats)

- 14-karat = 58.3 percent gold (or 14 out of 24 possible karats)
- 10-karat = 41.7 percent gold (or 10 out of 24 possible karats)

Anything less than ten karats is not considered solid gold in the old U.S. of A.

Twenty-four-karat gold sounds really swell, too, but it's actually very malleable, and so not ideal for everyday wear. The more common 18kt and 14kt are more durable. The metals added to gold are called "alloys." They're used to make the gold more durable, to make it last longer. They also can change the color of the gold. Add palladium or nickel, and you get white gold (and, BTW, if you happen to be allergic to nickel, you also get dermatitis). Rose or pink gold comes from adding copper. Silver makes gold greenish.

Other gold incarnations. Gold-filled means gold filled with another metal. So the gold is the cannoli shell, and the other metal is the ricotta filling. The markings on the piece should indicate how much and what kind of gold is in the coating. For example: 1/10 12kt means the piece is one-tenth 12kt gold. Too little gold, and it'll rub off.

Gold-plated has an even thinner coating of gold that wears off with moderate wear.

Gold-washed has the thinnest coating that dissipates with minimal wear.

Silver

Like gold, silver is usually served best with an alloy. That l'il 925 on the back of all your silver bangles? It indicates they're made of 92.5 percent fine silver, and 7.5 percent copper. Now you understand why silver tarnishes so easily, just like your favorite lady statue. It's the copper.

Whereas gold's value comes from its purity and weight, silver is priced by the work that went into it, and the name of the designer.

Platinum

Ah. Our favorite. The most durable of the natural wearable metals, pale silvery platinum is also the purest, rarest, and heaviest of the bunch. It'll scratch but it won't splinter. It'll develop a gentle patina but resists tarnish. All that, and it's hypoallergenic.

The white luster of platinum complements diamonds—and is said to bring out the brilliance in rocks at the far end of the alphabet color scale. The best possible platinum is 95 percent (5 percent iridium or palladium alloy) and marked with 950 or 950 pt. Next up: 850 pt or 850 (85 percent platinum).

10

Welcome to the—ugh—money chapter. We say ugh because we mostly agree: Money is great to have, fun to spend, but, quite generally, a bore to read about. No wonder we left it until the end of the book.

Still, we've busted our business to fill this quite important portion with as-fun-as-we-can-make-them *mots* on how to handle your *argent*. Because your coin is quite a big deal. We promise we won't sound like infomercial extremists or Bloomberg analysts (as if that were a possibility). We may scare you a little, but, hey, that's what it's all about.

Let's kick it off with the facts, ma'ams. (Courtesy of www.msmoney .com and Go-to Girl Tiffany Bass Bukow—bio below.)

- Women live longer than men—on average, seven years longer than men. (Lucky us, right?)
- Women earn less than men—on average, a third less. (Not so lucky.)
- Women work fewer years than men—on average eleven years less. (Not because we're on vacation—but because we're working without pay, à la June Cleaver.)

What does this mean? Women have got a lot of saving to do . . . because we sure as shootin' aren't gonna miss our afternoon shuffleboard tournament followed by the early bird special when we're living in the lap of our luxurious golden years.

It's hard to think about being old. We're young! We have parties to attend! Jobs to do! Attractive persons at the end of the bar to kiss! We don't play shuffleboard! We eat beer nuts and Caesar salads! What do we care about old?

Well, since you asked, we'll tell it to you straight: Seventy-five percent—that's three-quarters—of elderly American women are living below the poverty level. These women are not worried about shuffleboard. They're not catching the early bird and the early show. They are old. They are poor. They are us, if we don't start thinking about our future.

GO-TO GIRL

Tiffany Bass Bukow   Founder of MsMoney.com,
Hand Shaker of Hillary Clinton,
and Person Who Makes Us Want to
Play the Market

Tiffany—by the way, so our favorite name back when we were little gals playing glamorous grown-up—is the San Francisco dynamo behind the Internet's most successful money empowerment site. Hailing from a family where Dad was a Green Beret and Mom was household CFO, our girl T.

learned PDQ that moderate living and wise investing paid off. (The proof: Mums and Pops are now blissful millionaires.) In college, Tiffany realized not everyone is born into financial planning greatness. "Most of my girl friends got into credit card trouble in college. They'd been given credit cards when they were young and didn't understand how to use them. What started as $2,000 in debt when they were twenty-one ended up to be $20,000 in debt when they were thirty-one." Smarty Tiffany's mission: Tell the mass of misguided Ms.es how to save, invest, and retire happy, shuffleboard stick in hand.

Tiffany's First Pearl of Wisdom: Give Up the Cinderella Shtick

"Typically, women are thinking there's going to be a man to come into their lives and help them manage their money . . . Women are thinking: I'll be married. My money will be my husband's money. But when your husband comes into that marriage with a preexisting retirement account, that's his money. Women should stop thinking that Prince Charming is going to take care of them."

In the mood for some more disturbing facts?

"Women do far worse in divorce than men." For those who remain married for life: "The average married woman is widowed at age sixty-six. A quarter of those widows are broke in twenty-five months."

"I don't know who sold us the dream of Prince Charming. But it's a terrible dream." Deep down, the knight-on-the-white-horse fantasy lurks inside of most of us, no matter if we grew up in a single-parent home or had the Huxtables as our television role models. There's only one way to squelch this nightmare-coming-true: Commandeer your own financial future.

To help you along, we offer up this rabble-rousing rally cry from our Go-to Girl: "Do we strong, powerful women want to succumb to that Disney dream? Or do we want to say, 'No, I can take care of myself! I can take a few months to learn how to invest wisely. And when I'm seventy, I can be proud. I can live just as well as a man?'"

Of course, there are a few small matters to handle first. Like that credit card debt. Or opening a savings account. Read on, because you may be virgins—but you're no wimpy Cinderellas!

Second Marvelously Wise Pearl: Do Not Budget

"Budgets don't work, because people can't stick to them. People are very, very busy. Keeping a budget seems like a chore, like scrubbing the toilet." Right on, Tiff. Instead, figure out how much you need to live. Figure out how much is left over, and save and invest as much as you possibly can. Read on, brave, non-toilet-scrubbers!

ACCOUNTANT

#%*#@:&#%#%#!!!! This is how we feel about taxes.

Not coincidentally, #%*#@:&#%#%#!!!! also describes our emotions toward tax codes, tax audits, sales tax, and using a calculator for anything other than spelling upside-down messages SHELL.OIL and BOOBLESS.

Don't get us wrong: We have much respect for our sister CPAs. In fact, we applaud anyone who can read up on accounting matters and not come down with instant influenza. Equation solvers and government mumbo-jumbo comprehenders, thank you for untangling our messy numbers for us. Thank you for organizing our finances to neat documents. Thanks for turning our tax forms into a matter of submitting receipts and signing at the "X." Having you in our lives is even a pleasure on those off-years when we have to enclose checks with those papers.

Do You Need One?

Not everyone needs an accountant. If you have one job, rent your home, are single, have no kids, have invested no money, aren't looking for a new job, live in a city and state with simple tax codes, don't work at home, use your car for commuting and pleasure only, have all your medical expenses covered by insurance, balance your checkbook flawlessly, don't make much in the way of charitable donations, and have no outstanding loans, then you just might not.

But as soon as one of these elements change—and chances are, one will soon—it's time to find someone to help you out. Preferably prior to April 14. Preferably prior to January 1. For that matter, why not right about now?

Rule of thumb: The more complicated your career, the more expenses you have, the more you need an accountant.

How to Find One

Really, truly, word of mouth works best. Ask other people in your field and in a comparable financial position for recommendations. Your parents' accountant may be a great dude, but he may not be the best choice for a person of your means and needs. Ask yourself: Do you want someone just to fill out your tax forms, or to offer sound financial advice too?

Then turn around and ask those same questions to at least three CPA prospects in separate, informational meetings. And while you're there, you might as well also ask:

Who exactly will be undertaking my work? (Because you may meet with one face and work with another.)

What are your fees? (Because some accountants bill by the hour; others charge one flat fee per year.)

Compare your prospects. Eliminate any that give you the creeps, seem out of your league, or can't offer any references. And there you have it.

How to Work with One

Someone else may be crunching your numbers to suit the snarly, gnarly tax code, but you still have to keep up with your stuff. Have your accountant explain to you what you need to keep track of—including work-related expenses, medical bills, pay stubs, and a dozen more varieties of other uninteresting bits of paper—and create a filing system that's as elementary, as outlandishly simple, as possible. Use bright folders, scented markers, and hearts and bunny stickers, if you'd like. Just put those papers in their proper places so that you can yank them out in the beginning of the year, add 'em up on that trusty l'il calculator of yours, and turn in the results to your new, friendly CPA.

Other things your accountant can do for you: Advise you on your retirement savings (since IRAs and 401(k)s are often tax-exempt), advise you on making charitable contributions, and help you figure out how you'll be able to afford the cute fixer-upper around the corner.

BUT. Even though your taxes are now out of your hands, in the all-seeing eyes of the government, you're still responsible for them.

CREDIT CARD DEBT

This is not the time for us to dillydally with a clever summation of the love-turned-to-hate saga that transpired between you and your gold card.

Nor is it currently apropos to remind you of the importance of reading the fine print when an overfriendly credit card representative offers you a 0 percent first-year interest rate, a plastic bank account with a $2,000 limit, and a beach towel.

No need, even, to explain the basic axiom of credit card companies: The reason they ask for minimum payments only is that it earns them big bucks over the years it takes you to pay them back.

We won't rehash these details, because . . .

1. You did not turn to this page with vague interest, thinking to yourself, One day, maybe I'll sign up for a credit card, and see if I can mount my debt miles and miles above my means . . . because you've already done that.

2. You are precariously positioned above a deep vat of what boils down to noxious goo consisting of sticky IOUs and highly toxic interest rates that will make you pay for your twenty-one-year-old indulgences into and beyond your golden years.

3. This vat has already started eating away at your credit rating, and will soon—if it has not already—kill all your prospects of buying a car or a house, getting a mortgage, renting an apartment, scoring a loan of any kind, and, quite possibly, ever having the life you'd envisioned for yourself.

So, you see, this is no time for clever commentary. We are here to help.

Know Your Enemy

We're big believers in knowing what you're up against before the battle begins. Come 'n' git your credit reports today.

There are three major agencies that offer three different—and all essential—credit reports: Experian, Trans Union, and Equifax. (Add ".com" to names for Web addresses.) Since each place offers reports from the other two, there's no need to shop around. The cost is about $35 for the three, more if you seek counseling from these companies.

This is something you should do yearly—more often if you're worried about it. (A tip: One month each year, there's no charge for this service. This freebie month varies in different areas of the country—look on the above agencies' Web sites for when it applies to your neighborhood. Oh, and if you're unemployed, on welfare, have been denied any kind of credit, or have fallen victim of credit card fraud, you qualify for a free report.)

The cool thing about these reports: They let you track your progress as you reduce your debt, in the same way that a scale reveals how well your South Beach diet is progressing, or how gold stars on a bulletin board show who's behaved that week.

Divide and Conquer

Ditch all cards but the one with the lowest interest rate and lowest fees. By ditch, we mean cut them up, just like in your worst nightmare. And by keeping one, we mean, one. *Uno. Une.* This applies to all sorts of cards: your Neiman's charge, the AmEx Daddy said was for emergencies only (which you took to mean any time you really needed MAC lip gloss).

You'll see: Cutting up plastic is actually sort of fun. Just pretend the cards aren't yours. Pretend you're the snooty salesperson who's doing this to you.

But make sure you save the statements. You'll need those.

Gather the Troops

Round 'em up. Stack 'em up, highest interest rate to lowest (the card you're keeping). Make note of each card's annual fees, late fees, or any other extra service fees, too. Can't find a statement? Piece back a couple of those cards for the customer service number on the back, call 'em up, and request a copy of your last statement. Now you're cooking with gas.

Forward, March!

Some debt repair women say to transfer as much money as possible to the lowest interest card. Others say pay as much as possible on the highest interest card, and make minimum payments on the lower interest cards.

The best strategy: Do both. Consolidate as much as you can on the card(s) with the lowest rates. Each month, pay well over the minimum fee on the card that charges the most interest and has the highest fees while continuing to pay at least the minimum on the other cards (even a few bucks over the minimum helps). When you're done with the highest interest card, concentrate your efforts on the next highest.

Why pay more than the minimum? Because that initial $2,000 charge will triple—and will take thirty years to pay off—if you keep paying the minimum fee only. That's why credit card companies can afford the big offices! You're paying their rent!

Stay the Course

One major aspect of debt reduction that your friendly credit counselor doesn't so much like to discuss: You'll have to make sacrifices. They could be small. A year of making coffee at home and bringing it to work in a nifty retro thermos can save you $500—or $1,000 if the vente skinny caramel mocha has been your daily get-up-and-go. Other sacrifices may be more daunting—getting a roommate to share your apartment,

VIRGIN'S DOWNFALL

Indebted Isabella knew there was no way she'd figure out the tangled web of her student loans, car payments, and credit card bills. She thumbed through the phone book to get help from one of those nice, nonprofit credit counseling agencies. Look: There's one just down the street from her place! And the folks there love to smile! They sort through her paperwork, assure her they'll take care of everything, and come up with a payment plan that requires Issy to write one, simple check to them each month. What sweet Isabella doesn't know is while her payments will get easier, her new counselor's interest rates are even higher than the ones she'd been paying on her debts to begin with. We thoroughly understand the need to call reinforcements. We just wish Issy had checked to see if the service she used was a member of the National Foundation for Credit Counseling or the Association of Independent Consumer Credit Counseling Agencies, or checked with the Better Business Bureau or her state attorney general's office. Just like she should have looked into her credit cards before she'd signed up for them, she ought to have asked questions before diving in headfirst.

Or, if she didn't want to use a service, she could have asked an accountant or a financial adviser for help.

carpooling or taking public transportation to work, meeting friends in the park instead of at a restaurant, or—gasp—going single process on the highlights.

The whole concept of eliminating debt: You've gotta spend less than you make.

The best bet for a lifetime far, far away from that bubbling toxic debt vat: Always pay cash or check. Never charge anything you can't pay back right away. Cash. Check. That's it.

Credit-burdened virgins, hear our cry: Cut those cards! Consolidate that debt! Pay 'em down! Get them out of your life for good! (We promise, it will be as satisfying as completing a marathon—just as hard—but just as triumphant.)

SAVINGS & INVESTMENTS

Now that we've got your psyche and credit straightened out, it's time for the so-easy-you-wonder-why-you-didn't-do-it-while-you-were-still-into-boy-bands ways to make your money multiply.

What? Excuse us? You skipped right along to this section and missed our witty money pep rally? You passed right over the whole, well-worded woe-is-you credit counseling session? Fine. We won't blame you. Truth is, we're just glad you're here. Let's get down to it.

Save It

Savings accounts are the safest, slowest, and most liquid of ways of getting your dough to rise. (Liquid, BTW, means you can deposit and withdraw money easily.)

So your first step, if you haven't taken it already: Open a savings account. One with a low minimum balance and a nice, reliable 2 percent interest rate. Feeling lazy? Do it at the same bank where you have a checking account. (While you're there, order some new checks; you'll need them since you're not going to rely on that credit card of yours to get you through the day.)

This account should contain just enough to cover emergency expenses and short-term financial goals. For single, childless women, three to five months' salary should suffice for possible emergency expenses—emergencies, by the way, have nothing to do with running out of Cristal at your first cocktail party. For short-term goals, tally up any big expenses you plan to incur in the next one to three years—a down payment for a house, a trip to Hawaii. Use this liquid account to save up for these goals.

Tip: Make depositing money into your savings a habit, like depositing your paycheck or making withdrawals from the ATM.

Retire It

The next step: Put as much money as possible in retirement savings, most usually a 401(k) or an IRA (individual retirement account).

This, as you carefully read at the beginning of this chapter, is a vital step for everyone—but mostly for us ladies. Here's how they work. (Then we'll get to how they're different.) You make a yearly contribution to the account—both have limits, depending on your annual salary. You get this money back at age fifty-nine-and-a-half, at which time you discover you've earned a nice bundle of bucks.

The short-term rewards. You don't pay taxes on the money you put into an IRA or a 401(k).

The short-term limitations. You get heftily penalized for withdrawing money before you're nearly sixty. (There are certain exceptions, however, for first-time home buyers and returning students, for example.)

The long term. Not only are you not eating cat food by age seventy, but you are eating fresh fish you just caught off the starboard side of your private yacht anchored just off Turks and Caicos. (At the very least you'll be able to enjoy the early bird special.)

The difference between 'em. A 401(k)—which got its catchy name from a section of the 1978 Internal Revenue Code—is arranged through your job. In fact, that big, bad boss might even show her soft side by matching up to a certain percentage of your contributions. You want to make sure you contribute the maximum amount that can be matched so that you get all the free money you can.

An IRA—short for individual retirement account—is arranged through a bank or a credit union. This is most popular for self-employed types who can't benefit from 401(k)-style matching programs. There are different kinds of IRAs geared toward different income levels.

Where does the money go, exactly? Good question. Pretty much wherever you'd like to put it: stocks, bonds, money markets, mutual funds, each with its own level of risk and reward. The 401(k) and IRA are more about the amount you invest—not where you invest it. The good news about such long-term planning: The earlier you invest, the more you'll get back.

Smart investors—even starter-outers like you—ought to do much more than have bank-based and retirement account savings. We'll let you in on some of the options in order from low-risk and low-return to high-risk and high-return.

Bond It

A bond is a loan to the government or a corporation that offers interest to you, the lone loaner. Bonds are issued for a fixed period of time—one year or longer. Most are low-risk, except for the high-risk—and potentially high-yield—junk bond, which, we think, is an awful name.

Mutual Fund It

The next step up. Very, very broadly, mutual funds are a diverse group of diversified investment portfolios shared by a diverse group of people. Before you get all head-scratching about that, we'll back up: A mutual fund is a collection of a bunch of different kinds of investments—like stocks and bonds—packaged together, for the investing pleasure of many persons.

The philosophy here: In finance—as in life—there's safety in numbers. Or, the more, the merrier. Mutual funds offer a modest return without much risk. They're managed by fund managers—clever, huh?—who can buy, sell, trade, etc. while you sit back and watch your little nest egg grow and grow.

How to choose, since there are more mutual funds than stocks on the New York Stock Exchange? Go to a big-name firm. Smith-Barney, Charles Schwab, and Vanguard are tried-and-true go-to firms of the mutual fund market.

Mutual funds are the gift basket of the investment world; chances are, there's going to be a scented shower gel in there that doesn't appeal, or a smoked cheese that you know you'll never eat, but overall the good goodies outweigh the downward trending duds.

Stock It

Stocks are a little like gambling, but with much better odds. You'll need a working knowledge of the market, a positive outlook—and a strong stomach—because most individual stocks take five to ten years to produce a return on your investment.

The very basics: Stocks represent interest in companies. Other words, you give your money to a company. The company uses your money to

ANOTHER STOCK OPTION—AND IT INVOLVES COSMOS

Here's . . . Tiffany! Ms. Bass Bukow, the Go-to Girl who greeted you at the start of this chapter, advocates quite a wily way to combine the classic girls' night out and investing in stocks. It's called the investment club. It's the money-making cousin to—actually somewhat the combination of—a poker posse and a knitting group. The investment club comprises you, three to five of your responsible but fun gal pals, and some smart talk.

First: You'll need a working knowledge of stocks. One or more of you should be in the financial services industry, or should have at least attended a class on investing.

Second: Test it out. The ever-amazing Internet offers a variety of free, portfolio-building simulators and games, such as Stocktrak .com, smgww.org and virtualstockexchange.com. You log on, make up a silly name for yourself, pick a few stocks, and watch what happens. With nothing to lose.

Last: Ask your friends to come up with the names of a few companies they love—Louis Vuitton, Revlon, Estée Lauder, Target, Apple Computers—get together, and discuss. This is where your stock knowledge will come into play. Go home, do a little more research on these and maybe a few more companies. Meet again, choose a few shares of each stock, pick a contribution amount that you feel comfortable with, pool your dollars, and get to investing.

FOR THE VIRGIN WHO'D LIKE
EXTRA HELP: A FINANCIAL ADVISER

"I think everyone should have a financial adviser," says Tiffany. "A good financial adviser will sit down with you about your life goals. For example, a person who is an artist and is not considering buying a fancy car will require a very different strategy than someone who's going to get their MBA and plans to work in a corporate world."

Tiffany recommends hiring a certified financial planner who charges an hourly fee instead of an adviser who bases her fees on the deals she makes. "Fee-based financial advisers are just there to give you good, solid advice" [and don't gain any back-end advantages by trading certain stocks].

---

earn more money. The company turns around and gives you a cut of its success—in the form of a dividend check. The risk enters when the company fails to earn or loses money since it doesn't have any obligation to reimburse you for your original investment.

Stocks are generally the best option for virgins who aren't afraid of a little risk, are willing to learn a little, or are getting started somewhat late in the game and need to kick up the retirement savings.

Buy low, sell high. This means invest in a company with great potential when the company is still small, and you'll stand to earn the most when your superior judgment pays off down the road (think Google's IPO). Buy when a stock is high, however, and you're destined for a downhill cruise.

There are a bunch of tricks to learning about stocks. Some come with nifty, chicken-related sayings. One general rule is to diversify your portfolio—to invest in a variety of stocks, to spread the wealth: Don't put all your eggs in one basket. Another, to be patient: Don't count your chickens before they've hatched (again, five to ten years).

But that's really the tip of the stock trading iceberg. If you want to go it on your own, why not take a crash course at your local community college? If you want to be a stock owner but don't want to deal with the trading part, find a reputable broker who's not prone to panic attacks. But still, you want to learn a bit before doing any kind of stock marketing.

CHARITABLE DONATION

It starts in the second grade. You bring an extra cupcake to school for your best friend, and your teacher tells you you'd better have enough for the rest of the class too. You don't understand. But you obey. Later that year, you feel the effects of being the only girl not invited to a birthday party—and, in a flash of wise-beyond-your-age-eight understanding, you comprehend the law of the cupcakes.

Now, when a neighborhood Girl Scout comes knockin' on your door, when a trooper from the Salvation Army rings his red bell outside the supermarket, when your local public radio station holds its fund drive, when your office mate is collecting contributions for an organ donor fun run, when it's time to renew your membership to the natural history museum, or to give spare change to the local humane society, when your alma mater jauntily inquires if it can expect a little something from you for its annual fund, you are kind. You say yes.

Good for you. The world could use more givers and less takers. But lately, you've been wondering . . .

Is it wise to spread your wealth in this manner? Or, is it better to concentrate your giving to one great cause?

How much can you afford to give—how much can you afford not to?

GO-TO GIRL

Veronica Chambers
Awesome Author and
Perfect Phyllis-anthropist

Call Veronica fabulous. Call her a hottie or sweetheart or a smarty-pants. Don't, however, call this L.A. author, screenwriter, and Simon's Rock grad a philanthropist—even if she is one. "Philanthropist" is just, so, well, not the girly-girl we know and love as Veronica. So, when our V. told the dean

(continued)

of her Massachusetts alma mater that she'd endow a library renovation in her grandmother's name, she became what we'll call a Phyllis-anthropist. "I'm a girl who grew up in the age of labels—Jordache jeans in junior high, Donna Karan in my twenties. I wanted to put my grandmother's name on something," says this Go-to, "I committed to $5,000 and began making a monthly contribution of $140. Sometimes I was late with payments, but I made them all—and it was so satisfying. I knew exactly what my money was paying for." Veronica's lesson: A larger sum to a single place packs more of a punch—and might even score you a place on the board of directors of your old school, to boot.

What It Is: A Charitable Monetary Contribution

Karma-wise, a charitable contribution is any money you voluntarily give to a worthy cause without expecting anything in return.

Internal Revenue Service–wise, it's money you voluntarily give to a qualified charity without expecting or receiving anything in return.

So, the first question to ask yourself before you donate: Do I want to get a tax break for my contribution?

If so, those Thin Mint cookies won't be much help. Nor will the money you spend to attend benefit dinners, enter raffles, or pay board dues or association fees. Basically, if you receive a good or a service in exchange for your contribution, you can't deduct it. On the other hand, if you paid more than the item or service was worth, you can deduct that extra part.

The name for charities that qualify as tax-deduction-worthy: 501(c)(3)s (yet another IRS-generated term with the sparkling personality of a, well, tax collector). "Nonprofit" does not necessarily mean 501(c)(3). "Tax-exempt" does not indicate your contribution will be tax deductible, only that the organization itself does not pay taxes. Other non-qualifiers for tax deductions: foreign charities and political lobby groups.

Where to Donate

Not all good causes are quite as pure as they first appear. Beware the smaller ones, the ones who tug a little too hard on your heart—and purse—strings, any organization that solicits door-to-door, on the phone, or online.

Research the charity first. Start by double checking the charity's name: Some of the bad guys try to fool you by imitating the real thing. Look them up online. Check the organization's 501(c)(3) status, which indicates not only that your donation will be tax deductible, but also that they're on the up-and-up, according to the IRS.

Make a real-live contact within the organization—which means contacting an executive director or a representative from a fund-raising committee, or development department staffer. Meet with this person at the organization's office.

During the meeting, discuss the organization's mission. Gather informational materials. Ask what percentage of your donation will go to charitable purposes—and, if you'd like, if your money can be directed for a specific purpose such as scientific research, community outreach, or political advocacy. If you decide you'd like to make a contribution, before you do, request an IRS form called a 990, which shows the organization's income and expenditures.

Veronica's $140-a-month contribution garnered her a place on Simon's Rock's board. She says: "That invitation taught me how little money it can take to earn influence and power. Now four times a year I sit in a boardroom and vote on policy. I often think, This looks like a scene out of a sitcom. Imagine the contrast between the other board members (mostly men, mostly white) and me, a black girl with dreadlocks, wearing a BCBG dress and slicking on Nars lip gloss during the breaks."

"Being on the board has taught me that the realm of doing good, and of having influence on institutions that matter, is not relegated to the rich."

How Much to Donate: Is What You Give What You Get?

Only you, your accountant or financial adviser, and your conscience know what you can afford to give. If you're deep in credit card debt, tithing is certainly out of the question. Ditto if it's a matter of paying rent or taxes versus making a contribution.

COMMON SENSE FOR VIRGIN CONTRIBUTORS

Never agree to give money during a first encounter.

Beware of sales pitches that tug on your heartstrings.

If you're honest with yourself, however, you'll probably see a few places where you could make sacrifices. "I gave just $140 a month," says Veronica. "That's how little it can take."

How much of a tax break you get from your contribution all depends on your tax bracket. The more money you make, the more your contribution saves you at tax time. Example: If you're in the 25 percent tax bracket and donate $100, you get out of paying $25 in taxes. If you're in the 10 percent (lowest) tax bracket and donate $100, you get a $10 break today.

Also, if you're planning on contributing more than 20 percent of your adjusted gross income, well, consult with your accountant before going ahead with your plan. Things get complicated around there.

Keep Track of What You Give

Monetary gifts can be hard to track, especially if you're a spread-the-wealth kind of girl. So keep your contributions—in the form of canceled checks, receipts, or any other written records—in one file. The smaller the contribution, the less paperwork you need to prove you donated it. A canceled check, a bank statement with the charity's identification, or a credit card receipt is enough for contributions of less than $250. But if you're giving more than $250, you'll need a written acknowledgment of your contribution—on or before the date you file your tax return.

One last thing, before you go.

Here's a riddle for the ages: How does a girl-writer know when her guide to everything is complete?

The answer, ever-so-kind-to-make-it-to-the-end virgins, is that the possibilities for first times are endless. So don't stop seeking new opportunities to lose your virginity just because you ran out of pages. Need help?

How about trying your first:

Film festival
Pet adoption
Rock climb
Scuba dive
Birdwatching expedition
Karaoke contest
Broadway show
Off-Broadway show

Marathon—or 5k
Minor league baseball game
Fly-fishing trip
White-water rafting excursion
Sail
Garage sale
Coffee tasting
Gelato tasting
State fair
Backyard garden
Spring cleaning
House tour
Slumber party

See what happens when we get started?

See how the end of this book is just the beginning of your adventures?

Please come back to see us when you've forgotten how to eat sushi, require a refresher course in dot-com dating, need help packing—or just to say hi. Better yet, share your firsts—and your first-related questions—with us online, at www.virginsguide.com.

Catch you on the flip side.

ABOUT THE AUTHOR

Ask anyone I know—my mom, my sisters, my imaginary boyfriend, my knitting group, my cat Sally—I spend most of my time telling people what to do and how to do it. I'm not sure where my know-it-all-ness came from. Suspects in the matter include Mrs. Baker, my fourth grade teacher at Jenkintown Elementary, and Pop-pop, my Parliament-wielding, polyester-wearing, half-and-half drinking, and endlessly blabbing self-proclaimed sage of a grandfather.

Although my tendency to do things like offer yoga classmates financial advice and tell roomfuls of strangers that their bras don't fit can be off-putting, this habit paid off when my pal Veronica suggested I write a how-to book—on how to do everything. Everything. Might be a daunting task to some. But not to me. Me, I know it all.

Lauren

FIVE WAYS TO TELL IF YOU'RE A VIRGIN:

1. Your last surf trip began with the letters "www." (You're a surfing virgin.)
2. The day you spent at Epcot is your first and only visit to a foreign country. (You're a travel abroad virgin.)
3. You've never engaged in a tug-of-war over reduced-price cashmere. (You're a sample sale virgin.)
4. You consider a clean sports bra to be your sexiest unmentionable. (You're a lingerie virgin.)
5. A pink ceramic pig contains the sum total of your life's savings. (You're a savings and investments virgin.)